THE WAR AND THE RUSSIAN GOVERNMENT

ECONOMIC AND SOCIAL HISTORY OF THE WORLD WAR

JAMES T. SHOTWELL, LL.D., *General Editor*.

RUSSIAN SERIES

SIR PAUL VINOGRADOFF, F.B.A., *Editor*.
(Died, December 19, 1925.)

MICHAEL T. FLORINSKY, M.A., *Associate Editor*.

THE WAR AND
THE RUSSIAN GOVERNMENT

THE CENTRAL GOVERNMENT

BY PAUL P. GRONSKY

FORMERLY PROFESSOR AT THE POLYTECHNIC INSTITUTE OF PETROGRAD
AND MEMBER OF THE DUMA

THE MUNICIPAL GOVERNMENT
AND
THE ALL-RUSSIAN UNION OF TOWNS

BY NICHOLAS J. ASTROV

FORMERLY MAYOR OF MOSCOW AND CHAIRMAN OF THE CENTRAL
COMMITTEE OF THE ALL-RUSSIAN UNION OF TOWNS

NEW HAVEN : YALE UNIVERSITY PRESS
LONDON : HUMPHREY MILFORD : OXFORD UNIVERSITY PRESS
FOR THE CARNEGIE ENDOWMENT FOR INTERNATIONAL
PEACE : DIVISION OF ECONOMICS AND HISTORY
1929

EDITOR'S PREFACE

In the autumn of 1914, when the scientific study of the effects of war upon modern life passed suddenly from theory to history, the Division of Economics and History of the Carnegie Endowment for International Peace proposed to adjust the program of its researches to the new and altered problems which the War presented. The existing program, which had been prepared as the result of a conference of economists held at Berne in 1911, and which dealt with the facts then at hand, had just begun to show the quality of its contributions; but for many reasons it could no longer be followed out. A plan was therefore drawn up at the request of the Director of the Division, in which it was proposed, by means of an historical survey, to attempt to measure the economic cost of the War and the displacement which it was causing in the processes of civilization. Such an "Economic and Social History of the World War," it was felt, if undertaken by men of judicial temper and adequate training, might ultimately, by reason of its scientific obligations to truth, furnish data for the forming of sound public opinion, and thus contribute fundamentally toward the aims of an institution dedicated to the cause of international peace.

The need for such an analysis, conceived and executed in the spirit of historical research, was increasingly obvious as the War developed, releasing complex forces of national life not only for the vast process of destruction, but also for the stimulation of new capacities for production. This new economic activity, which under normal conditions of peace might have been a gain to society, and the surprising capacity exhibited by the belligerent nations for enduring long and increasing loss—often while presenting the outward semblance of new prosperity—made necessary a reconsideration of the whole field of war economics. A double obligation was therefore placed upon the Division of Economics and History. It was obliged to concentrate its work upon the problem thus presented, and to study it as a whole; in other words, to apply to it the tests and disciplines of history. Just as the War itself was a single event, though penetrating by seemingly unconnected ways to the remotest parts of the world, so the analysis of it must be developed according to a plan at once all embracing and yet adjustable to the practical limits of the available data.

During the actual progress of the War, however, the execution of this plan for a scientific and objective study of war economics proved impossible in any large and authoritative way. Incidental studies and surveys of portions of the field could be made and were made under the direction of the Division, but it was impossible to undertake a general history for obvious reasons. In the first place, an authoritative statement of the resources of belligerents bore directly on the conduct of armies in the field. The result was to remove as far as possible from scrutiny those data of the economic life of the countries at war which would ordinarily, in time of peace, be readily available for investigation. In addition to this difficulty of consulting documents, collaborators competent to deal with them were for the most part called into national service in the belligerent countries and so were unavailable for research. The plan for a war history was therefore postponed until conditions should arise which would make possible not only access to essential documents, but also the coöperation of economists, historians, and men of affairs in the nations chiefly concerned, whose joint work would not be misunderstood either in purpose or in content.

Upon the termination of the War, the Endowment once more took up the original plan, and it was found with but slight modification to be applicable to the situation. Work was begun in the summer and autumn of 1918. In the first place a final conference of the Advisory Board of Economists of the Division of Economics and History was held in Paris, which limited itself to planning a series of short preliminary surveys of special fields. Since, however, the purely preliminary character of such studies was further emphasized by the fact that they were directed more especially toward those problems which were then fronting Europe as questions of urgency, it was considered best not to treat them as part of the general survey, but rather as of contemporary value in the period of war settlement. It was clear that not only could no general program be laid down *a priori* by this conference as a whole, but that a new and more highly specialized research organization than that already existing would be needed to undertake the Economic and Social History of the World War, one based more upon national grounds in the first instance, and less upon purely international coöperation. Until the facts of national history could be ascertained, it would be impossible to proceed with comparative analysis; and the different national histories were themselves of almost baffling intricacy and variety. Consequently the former European Committee of Research was dissolved, and in its place it was decided to erect an Editorial Board in each of the larger countries and to nominate special editors in the smaller ones, who should concentrate, for the present at least, upon their own economic and social war history.

The nomination of these boards by the General Editor was the first step taken in every country where the work has begun. And if any justification were needed for the plan of the Endowment, it at once may be found in the lists of those, distinguished in scholarship or in public affairs, who have accepted the responsibility of editorship. This responsibility is by no means light, involving as it does the adaptation of the general editorial plan to the varying demands of national circumstances or methods of work; and the measure of success attained is due to the generous and earnest coöperation of those in charge in each country.

Once the editorial organization was established, there could be little doubt as to the first step which should be taken in each instance toward the actual preparation of the history. Without documents there can be no history. The essential records of the War, local as well as central, have therefore to be preserved and to be made available for research in so far as is compatible with public interest. But this archival task is a very great one, belonging of right to the Governments and other owners of historical sources and not to the historian or economist who proposes to use them. It is an obligation of ownership; for all such documents are public trust. The collaborators on this section of the war history, therefore, working within their own field as researchers, could only survey the situation as they found it and report their findings in the forms of guides or manuals; and perhaps, by stimulating a comparison of methods, help to further the adoption of those found to be most practical. In every country, therefore, this was the point of departure for actual work; although special monographs have not been written in every instance.

The first stage of the work upon the War History, dealing with little more than the externals of archives, seemed for a while to exhaust the possibilities of research, and had the plan of the history been limited to research based upon official documents, little more could have been done, for once documents have been labeled "secret" few government officials can be found with sufficient courage or initiative to break open the seal. Thus vast masses of source material essential for the historian were effectively placed beyond his reach, although much of it was quite harmless from any point of view. While war conditions thus continued to hamper research, and were likely to do so for many years to come, some alternative had to be found.

Fortunately such an alternative was at hand in the narrative, amply supported by documentary evidence, of those who had played some part in the conduct of affairs during the War, or who, as close observers in privileged positions, were able to record from first- or at least second-hand knowledge the economic history of different phases of the Great War, and of its effect upon society. Thus a series of monographs was planned consisting for the most part of unofficial yet authoritative statements, descriptive or historical, which may best be described as about halfway between memoirs and blue-books. These monographs make up the main body of the work assigned so far. They are not limited to contemporary war-time studies; for the economic history of the War must deal with a longer period than that of the actual fighting. It must cover the years of "deflation" as well, at least sufficiently to secure some fairer measure of the economic displacement than is possible in purely contemporary judgments.

With this phase of the work, the editorial problems assumed a new aspect. The series of monographs had to be planned primarily with regard to the availability of contributors, rather than of source material as in the case of most histories; for the contributors themselves controlled the sources. This in turn involved a new attitude toward those two ideals which historians have sought to emphasize, consistency and objectivity. In order to bring out the chief contribution of each writer it was impossible to keep within narrowly logical outlines; facts would have to be repeated in different settings and seen from different angles, and sections included which do not lie within the strict limits of history; and absolute objectivity could not be obtained in every part. Under the stress of controversy or apology, partial views would here and there find their expression. But these views are in some instances an intrinsic part of the history itself, contemporary measurements of facts as significant as the

facts with which they deal. Moreover, the work as a whole is planned
to furnish its own corrective; and where it does not, others will.

In addition to the monographic treatment of source material, a
number of studies by specialists are already in preparation, dealing
with technical or limited subjects, historical or statistical. These
monographs also partake to some extent of the nature of first-hand
material, registering as they do the data of history close enough to
the source to permit verification in ways impossible later. But they
also belong to that constructive process by which history passes
from analysis to synthesis. The process is a long and difficult one,
however, and work upon it has only just begun. To quote an apt
characterization; in the first stages of a history like this, one is only
"picking cotton." The tangled threads of events have still to be
woven into the pattern of history; and for this creative and constructive work different plans and organizations may be needed.

In a work which is the product of so complex and varied coöperation as this, it is impossible to indicate in any but a most general
way the apportionment of responsibility of editors and authors for
the contents of the different monographs. For the plan of the History as a whole and its effective execution the General Editor is
responsible; but the arrangement of the detailed programs of study
has been largely the work of the different Editorial Boards and
divisional Editors, who have also read the manuscripts prepared
under their direction. The acceptance of a monograph in this series,
however, does not commit the editors to the opinions or conclusions
of the authors. Like other editors, they are asked to vouch for the
scientific merit, the appropriateness and usefulness of the volumes
admitted to the series; but the authors are naturally free to make
their individual contributions in their own way. In like manner the
publication of the monographs does not commit the Endowment to
agreement with any specific conclusions which may be expressed
therein. The responsibility of the Endowment is to History itself—
an obligation not to avoid but to secure and preserve variant narratives and points of view, in so far as they are essential for the understanding of the War as a whole.

*   *   *   *   *

In the case of Russia, civil war and revolution followed so closely
upon the World War that it is almost impossible for history to

measure with any degree of accuracy the effects of the World War itself upon the economic and social life of the country. Those effects were so distorted by the forces let loose in the post-war years and so confused with the disturbances of the revolutionary era that the attempt to isolate the phenomena of the War from the data of civil war and to analyze the former according to the plan followed in the other national series of this collection has been a task of unparalleled difficulty. Over and above the intricacies of the problem and its illusive character, the authors of the Russian monographs have had to work under the most discouraging circumstances and with inadequate implements of research. For those who know the scarcity of the documentary material available, it will be a matter of no little surprise to find, in the pages of this Russian Series, narratives and substantiating data which measure up so well in comparison with those prepared by the collaborators in other countries. The achievement of the Russian Division of the History is, all things considered, the most remarkable section of the entire collection. This is due, in the first place, to the fact that the authors, all of them exiles who live in foreign lands, have not only brought to this task the scientific disciplines of their own special fields but also an expert knowledge drawn from personal experience which in several instances reached to the highest offices of State.

While these volumes in the Russian History constitute so very considerable an achievement, they cannot in the very nature of the case cover with adequate statistical or other specific data many of the problems with which they deal. No one is more conscious of their shortcomings in this regard than the authors themselves. Nevertheless, with inadequate material and under hampering circumstances they have prepared a body of text and a record which, if admittedly incomplete as history, contains at least one element that would otherwise be lost for the future understanding of this great crisis in human affairs, an element which no other generation working from Russian archives could ever supply. We have here the mature comment upon events by contemporaries capable of passing judgment and appraising values, so that over and above the survey of phenomena there is presented a perspective and an organization of material which will be a contribution to history hardly less important than the substance of the monographs.

The Russian Series was in the first instance planned by one of the most distinguished of Russian scholars who had long been a resident of England, Sir Paul Vinogradoff, Corpus Professor of Jurisprudence at the University of Oxford. To the planning of the Series Sir Paul gave much time and thought. His untimely death in December, 1925, prevented him from seeing its fruition or from assuming the editorial responsibility for the texts. Nevertheless, the Series as a whole remains substantially as he had planned it.

J. T. S.

I

THE EFFECTS OF THE WAR UPON THE CENTRAL GOVERNMENT OF RUSSIA

CONTENTS

II

THE EFFECTS OF THE WAR UPON RUSSIAN MUNICIPAL GOVERNMENT AND THE ALL-RUSSIAN UNION OF TOWNS

CONTENTS

Chapter VII—Public Health 198

The arrival of wounded and their evacuation. General scheme of evacuation. Refreshment stations and hospital trains. Organization of clearing stations and hospitals. Number of hospital beds in various towns. Relief of wounded in Petrograd and Moscow. Hospital supplies; drugs, surgical instruments, and medical staff. Special treatment; rest-cures, dental hospitals. Chemical warfare. Cultural and educational work in the hospitals. Relief of disabled men.

Chapter VIII—Work in the Army 220

General conditions of work. Field detachments. Engineering units. Bathing stations. Laundries. Civic relief. Other work at the front.

Chapter IX—Relief of Refugees 231

Flight of the population as a result of the retreat of the army. Suffering of the refugees. Policy of the Union for the relief of refugees. The scheme of the Unions of Towns and Zemstvos. Government measures. The settlement of refugees. Their condition in new places of settlement. Professor Whittemore's memorandum. General conditions of refugees. Sanitation, labor exchanges, care of children.

Chapter X—Combating Epidemic Diseases . . . 242

Epidemic diseases during the War. How epidemic diseases are spread during the War. Sanitary conditions of towns. Measures taken by municipalities for the prevention of epidemic diseases. Measures taken by the Union of Towns. Moscow and Petrograd in the war against epidemics.

Chapter XI—Other War Activities 253

Relief of families of former employees serving with the colors. Relief of members of the reserve force. Supply of munitions and equipment. Presents for the army. Military cemetery in Moscow. Prisoners of war. Organization of legal assistance.

Chapter XII—Regional Organization of the Union of Towns 260

The organization of the Petrograd region. The Union of Towns of Finland. The Caucasus section of the All-Russian Union of Towns.

Chapter XIII—The Reorganizing of Economic Life . . 268

Changes in the economic conditions of the towns and of the country due to the War. The policy of the municipalities. Changes in the population of towns and cities. Organization of supplies. Fixed prices. Municipal purchases. Distribution of municipal stocks. Relations with private trading. The Union of Towns and the control of the economic life of the country. Proposals of the Union of Towns and the scheme of supply drawn up by the Economic Conference of July 1915. The outbreak of the Revolution. The Provisional Government and the food problem in towns.

Chapter XIV—The Union of Towns and the Municipalities during the Revolution 299

Financial crisis. The new Municipal Act. New municipal dumas. The new scheme for the work of the Union. The Revolution of 25th October 1917. The ruin of the municipalities. New institutions of local government.

APPENDICES

BIBLIOGRAPHY

I

THE EFFECTS OF THE WAR
UPON THE CENTRAL GOVERNMENT
OF RUSSIA

BY PAUL P. GRONSKY

THE EFFECTS OF THE WAR UPON THE CENTRAL GOVERNMENT

INTRODUCTION

THE CENTRAL GOVERNMENT OF RUSSIA AT THE OUTBREAK OF THE WAR

OF all the countries that took part in the Great War, Russia was the youngest constitutional State. Only nine years before the outbreak of the War—in 1905—Russia had been transformed from an absolute into a constitutional monarchy. The Manifesto of 17th October 1905[1] granting civic liberties to the citizens of Russia and providing for an obligatory participation of a popular representative body known as the State Duma in the making of the laws, marks the boundary between the absolute and constitutional régimes. The fundamental principles of the new Russian constitutional law were fixed by the first Russian Constitution, *i.e.*, the Fundamental Laws of 23rd April 1906.

The structure of the Russian Government was that of a dualistic constitutional monarchy. At the head of the Empire stood the Emperor, who, until recently, wielded sole and unlimited authority. He still retained under the constitutional régime a number of special rights and privileges. In him was concentrated all executive authority throughout that vast Empire; the appointment of Ministers was entirely a matter of his own will, subject to no outside control; he was endowed with the right of absolute veto on legislation passed by either house of the legislature; to him also belonged the supreme prerogative of pardon and amnesty. The very idea of the political responsibility of Ministers to the popular representative organs, the idea of parliamentarism, was essentially opposed to the Fundamental Laws of Russia. The Ministers were responsible for the general conduct of politics to the Emperor alone. A Minister could be made to render an account to the Duma only if there was an interpellation regarding some illegal act on his part, and the houses of the legislature were powerless to exert any influence upon the conduct of the administration, still less upon the appointment of any Minister. The

---

[1] All dates in this monograph are given in accordance with the Russian calendar.

entire structure of the Russian Government was permeated with the spirit of dualism—the legislative authority was completely separated from, and incapable of exerting any influence over, the executive power.

However, while it is a fact that the Russian Empire was a dualistic monarchy, it was at the same time a constitutional State. The Fundamental Laws of 23rd April 1906 established quite definitely the basic principle of a constitutional order, that is, the principle of limiting the legislative authority of the sovereign by the obligatory participation of legislative representative organs. Prior to the constitutional reform the will of the Emperor was supreme. All those institutions which had to deal with legislative measures, among them the State Council before the reform, were merely consultative organs. The Emperor was not only at liberty to dissent from any decision adopted by the majority of the State Council, but was free even to confirm as a law the minority opinion of that body. He could promulgate laws in the form of Imperial ukases, as well as in the form of resolutions of the Council of Ministers, which would be confirmed by His Majesty. Under the Fundamental Laws of 23rd April, "the Emperor exercises legislative authority conjointly with the State Council and the State Duma."[2] "No new law can be passed without the approval of the State Council and the State Duma, nor become effective without the confirmation of the Emperor."[3] "The law cannot be repealed in any way except by force of law. Therefore so long as the new law has not definitely abrogated the existing law, the latter continues in full force."[4] Under these provisions of the Fundamental Laws the authority of the sovereign was limited by the participation of the legislative chambers, and the Emperor was transformed from an autocratic and absolute sovereign to a constitutional monarch with limited powers.

Thus the Fundamental Laws of 23rd April 1906 set up in Russia a constitutional form of government. But why is the legislative act which gave a constitution to Russia not designated as a constitution? The answer is that the Fundamental Laws of 23rd April represent, in a strictly formal sense, merely the old Fundamental Laws of the Russian Empire, revised and radically amended. The new constitutional wine was simply poured into the old bottles of autocracy. The decrees providing for the limitation of the Emperor's

[2] Article 7.   [3] Article 86.   [4] Article 94.

authority, for his exercise of legislative functions in common with the legislative chambers, for the personal freedom of the citizens, and for the establishment of a popular representative organ, were incorporated with the old Fundamental Laws, and these, including now the radical changes just mentioned, were simply reissued on 23rd April 1906. Such was the origin of the designation of Fundamental Laws applied to the Russian constitution, having been borrowed from the old legislation. We should point out in this connection that the term Fundamental Law, used as a definition of constitutional charters, existed not only in Russia, but also in other constitutional monarchies.

There was a special procedure for the revision of the Fundamental Laws, for they could be revised only on the initiative of the Emperor. Special procedures for the revision of constitutions, designed to render them more stable, existed in many other countries. Russia, however, stood alone in that the stability of its constitution was safeguarded by the grant to the monarch of the exclusive right of initiating a revision. It was the Emperor himself who, under the provisions of the Fundamental Laws, was to safeguard the principles of a dualistic constitutional monarchy.

The Emperor was the head of the Russian Empire. He held the supreme power in the State, and he stood under the special protection of the laws, any attempt upon his person being punishable by exceptionally severe penalties.[5] The Russian imperial throne was passed on hereditarily, in order of primogeniture, in the male line of the reigning Romanov dynasty. Females might ascend the throne only if the male line of the Emperor ceased entirely, in which event the eldest daughter of the last reigning Emperor was to be made Empress. Under the provisions of the laws of succession, the imperial throne could never remain vacant. As soon as an Emperor died his heir ascended the throne, always being designated as heir by special imperial manifesto during the lifetime of the Emperor.

In his capacity as head of the State, the Emperor was endowed with a number of special prerogatives in all spheres of government. Russian constitutional law was permeated with the idea of the supremacy of the sovereign; the reins that guided the work of the legislative chambers and of the entire administration of the Empire were concentrated in the hands of the sovereign; and justice was

[5] "The Emperor's person is sacred and inviolable" (Article 5).

everywhere dispensed in his name. Even more extensive were the prerogatives of the monarch in the administration of the army and navy, and in legislation relating thereto.

With respect to the legislative chambers the Emperor had, above all, the right to convoke and prorogue, adjourn and suspend, the sessions of the State Duma and State Council.

The State Council and State Duma "are convoked every year by the Emperor."[6] It will thus be seen that the Russian Fundamental Laws imposed but one restriction upon the free will of the monarch in the convocation of the legislative bodies; they were to be assembled every year. The usual practice in times of peace was to convoke the chambers in October or November, their sessions lasting, with some intermissions, until the following June.

The recesses, as well as the duration of sessions in the legislative chambers, were prescribed by Imperial ukase. According to Article 99 of the Fundamental Laws, "the duration of the annual sessions of the State Duma and State Council, and the length of recesses, in the course of the year, are prescribed by the ukases of the Emperor." The length of the sessions of the legislative chambers, therefore, depended upon the commands of the Emperor. He could so use his right of adjournment or suspension as to paralyze completely the work of the legislature. But in actual practice the chambers were in session for six or seven months every year, and recesses were taken mostly during the Christmas and Easter holidays.

Lastly, the Emperor had the right to dissolve the Duma entirely, thereby depriving the deputies of their parliamentary powers before the expiration of the term for which they were elected. The only restriction imposed upon the Emperor's right of dissolving the Duma was the provision of Article 105 of the Fundamental Laws requiring that the decree of dissolution should also contain an order for new elections to the Duma and state the time of its convocation. As the sessions of the Duma were to be held every year, the period of time within which new elections should be ordered was by implication laid down; the elections were to be held in such a way as to enable the new Duma to assemble in the following year. The Emperor Nicholas II twice dissolved the Duma before the expiration of its term: the first and second Dumas were dissolved soon after they opened their sessions in 1906 and 1907, respectively, and on both occasions new

[6] Article 98.

elections were ordered to be held within a few months following the dissolution.

The Emperor was in a position to exert his influence, not only on the duration of the sessions, convoking, proroguing, and adjourning the Duma at will, but also on the composition of the upper house, since one-half of the members of the State Council (90) were appointed by Imperial ukase. The remaining members were elected, but the President of the State Council was also appointed every year by Imperial decree.

Lastly, the Emperor took part in the very process of making the laws. Without his approval no bill, even if passed by both houses, could obtain legal force. He had the right of absolute veto on any legislative measure he might consider undesirable, and he could withhold his sanction without having to give his reasons.[7] After a bill had been passed by the Duma and the State Council, the President of the latter submitted it to the Emperor for his approval. In actual practice the Emperor Nicholas II very rarely refused to sanction legislative measures; only twice did he veto such bills, and these were of no great political importance.

In the administrative field the Emperor had absolute power. "The power of administration, in its entirety, belongs to the Emperor throughout the Russian State." The entire administrative machinery of the Empire had the Emperor as its head and was subordinate to him. Although these administrative powers of the sovereign were of an all-embracing and inclusive character, they were subject to law, as all dispositions of the Emperor had to be made in conformity with the law. The principle of this subjection of the supreme administration to law was established by Article 2 of the Fundamental Laws; "The Emperor by virtue of his supreme administrative authority, issues, *in accordance with the laws*, decrees for the establishment and operation of the various branches of the State administration, as well as the orders necessary for the execution of the laws."[8]

[7] "The Emperor confirms the laws, and without his confirmation no law can become effective" (Article 9).

[8] The question of the difference between supreme and subordinate administration has been stated by Russian jurists of the constitutional period. *See* Lazarevsky, *Lektsii po Russkomu Gosudarstvennomu Pravu* (*Lectures on Russian Constitutional Law*), St. Petersburg, 1908, Vol. I, p. 163; Baron B. E. Nolde, *Ocherki Russkago Gosudarstvennago Prava* (*Outlines of Russian Constitutional Law*), St. Petersburg, 1913, p. 53; Kazansky, *Vlast*

The Emperor directed the activities of the entire administration of the country, and all important government posts were filled by Imperial ukases. The President of the Council of Ministers, all the Ministers, and the highest government officials (posts of the first four ranks) were appointed by the Emperor himself.[9] In the hands of the Emperor was also concentrated the power of granting titles and decorations, the conditions and the procedure of such grants being determined by him directly.[10]

To the Emperor also belonged the right of imposing certain restrictions upon the power and civil rights of government officials when this was in the interest of the government service. In this way the whole administrative machinery, all government officials in all branches of the administration, were subject to the absolute will of the Emperor, who determined the procedure of conferring distinctions and could impose restrictions on the exercise of their powers and civil rights. Persons employed in the government service were servants not only of the State, but also of the Emperor.

The conduct of international relations, the direction of the foreign policy of the Empire, the declaration of war and conclusion of peace, and, finally, the conclusion of treaties with foreign Powers, formed the absolute and exclusive prerogative of the sovereign.[11] This exceedingly important and responsible branch of the government administration was in no wise subject to the control and influence of the legislative chambers. Whenever the Minister of Foreign Affairs spoke in the plenary sessions of the Duma or of the State Council on questions of foreign policy (in the Duma this was mostly connected with the discussion of the annual budget of the Ministry of Foreign Affairs), he began his address with the phrase "With the consent of the Emperor." Thus the very communication of reports on foreign policy to the legislative chambers could take place only with the special permission of the sovereign in each case. All the most important decisions respecting international relations were reached

Vserossiskago Gosudarya (Powers of the All-Russian Sovereign), chapter on supreme administration; Kokoshkin, *Lektsii po Russkomu Gosudarstvennomu Pravu (Lectures on Russian Constitutional Law)*, Moscow, 1913, chapter on supreme administration.—In this brief introduction we shall not dwell upon this question, especially as it did not arise in practical form during the War.

[9] Article 17.   [10] Article 19.   [11] Article 13.

solely by the Emperor himself. Of course, in the discussion of these decisions, and in their application, the Minister of Foreign Affairs took an intimate part; but from the legal standpoint the whole realm of foreign policy was within the exclusive jurisdiction of the sovereign.

The proclamation of martial law or of an "extraordinary state" (state of emergency) in any locality was also left by the Fundamental Laws to the jurisdiction of the Emperor.[12] During the period 1905-1914 this prerogative was of far greater importance in Russia than in other countries. Usually, martial law or an "extraordinary state" is proclaimed only in cases of extreme necessity, such as war or national calamity. In Russia, however, the "extraordinary state" became very common at the close of the nineteenth and beginning of the twentieth century. A number of different localities were for many years kept in an "extraordinary state." For some time after the revolution of 1905 in particular, most of the cities and provinces of the Russian Empire were systematically kept in an "extraordinary state." This enabled the administration to issue ordinances which had the full force of law, and to take measures to combat the popular movement.

Among the prerogatives of the Emperor were, furthermore, the right of coinage[13] and the right to remit fines and penalties and to grant special favors.[14]

Most peculiar, however, and characteristic of the régime of a dualistic monarchy was the right of the Emperor to promulgate exceptional decrees that had, temporarily, the force of law. Article 87 of the Fundamental Laws, which introduced this right of exceptional legislation into the government system of Russia, has been studied in minute detail by Russian scholars, who have traced the system of exceptional legislation in all its ramifications and the vast number of acts that have temporarily obtained the force of law under the provisions of this article.[15] The text of Article 87 of the Fundamental Laws reads as follows:

During the recess of the State Duma, if exceptional circumstances

[12] Article 15.   [13] Article 16.   [14] Article 23.

[15] Baron B. E. Nolde, *87 statya Osnovnikh Zakonov (Article 87 of Fundamental Laws)*, in *op. cit.*; Y. M. Magaziner, *Chrezvichainoe zakonodatelstvo po 87 state Osnovnikh Zakonov (Legislation under Article 87 of Fundamental Laws)*, St. Petersburg, 1913; Kazansky, *op. cit.*, also devotes many pages to Article 87.

call for a measure that requires legislative discussion, the Council of Ministers shall report on it to the Emperor direct. This measure shall not, however, introduce any change in the Fundamental Laws of the State, or in the statutes of the State Council or State Duma, or in the provisions concerning elections to the Council or Duma. The operation of such a measure shall cease if the respective Minister or Chief of Department shall not have submitted to the Duma within the two months following the resumption of the session of the Duma a legislative bill corresponding to the adopted measure, or if this bill is not passed by the Duma or the State Council.

In virtue of Article 87 the Emperor, upon the proposal of the Council of Ministers, might promulgate ukases which had temporarily the force of law. To enable such legislation to be passed, two conditions were required: (1) that there should actually exist "exceptional circumstances" demanding such a ukase, and (2) that the Duma should not be sitting.

Thus the old legislative machinery which had existed under the autocratic régime might be restored, conditionally and temporarily, during those periods when the Duma was not in session. The Emperor, approving the proposals of the Council of Ministers, issued a ukase which had the force of law. Although it was necessary, for the promulgation of such ukases, to establish the existence of "exceptional circumstances," this provision of Article 87 was interpreted very broadly, so that numerous ukases were issued under Article 87 in spite of the fact that there were no exceptional conditions warranting their immediate promulgation. It is true that legislation under Article 87 was of a conditional nature. All measures inaugurated by means of exceptional decrees were to be submitted to the Duma within two months of the resumption of its sessions. If the respective Minister during that period should not have submitted the exceptional decrees to the Duma, these decrees were to be considered abrogated. The same fate awaited such measures in the event of their rejection by the Duma or the Council after being submitted.

In the hands of the legislative chambers rested, therefore, the supreme control over the temporary legislative functions of the Emperor and Council of Ministers under Article 87 of the Fundamental Laws. It was, however, difficult to abrogate entirely in the next session of the Duma a large number of exceptional decrees issued under Article 87, since these temporary measures had already introduced changes in the existing law and a complete reversal might have conflicted with the interests of a number of people.

The provisions of the Fundamental Laws, however, the Statutes of the State Council and Duma, and the election laws for the two chambers could not be altered by extraordinary ukases issued in virtue of Article 87. That is why the Imperial ukase of 3rd June 1907, which radically curtailed the franchise of Russian citizens in the election of Duma deputies, was issued without reference to Article 87 of the Fundamental Laws, and constituted a direct violation of the letter of this Article, as well as of a number of other articles of the Fundamental Laws—amounting to something in the nature of a *coup d'état*.

To the Emperor, as head of the State, belonged the supreme command of all the armed forces of the Empire.[16]

Moreover, apart from the rights that belong to every supreme commander-in-chief, the Emperor enjoyed certain special rights in the field of army and navy legislation. This specially privileged position was guaranteed by Article 96 of the Fundamental Laws, which authorized the Emperor to promulgate "orders concerning the combatant, technical, and general supply services, as well as regulations and instructions relating to the organization and officials of the army and navy departments," after these measures had been examined by the Councils of the Army and Navy. The latter, which had also existed during the period of absolute monarchy, were special consultative organs advising the Emperor; it was their function to examine legislative bills dealing with the army and navy. The Duma and State Council, in virtue of Article 96 of the Fundamental Laws, were excluded from participation in the examination of the overwhelming majority of new army and navy bills, and in this domain of legislative work the old order of the absolute monarchy was preserved. A huge branch of legislation of vast importance was thus taken from the normal jurisdiction of the legislative institutions and handed over to the sovereign and to military bureaucratic consultative organs. No doubt, all these army and navy "orders, regulations, and instructions" were not formally regarded as laws, but merely as Imperial ukases, nor could they affect matters of general law and give rise to expenditure of State funds; actual practice, however, put a very broad interpretation upon the provisions of Article 96,

[16] Article 14.

so that almost the entire army and navy legislation was *de facto* the prerogative of the monarch. To legalize this branch of legislative activity it was not even necessary that the legislative chambers should not be sitting, as was the case with measures adopted under Article 87, and army and navy legislation was regularly adopted in a manner that differed in no wise from that prevailing under the absolute monarchy.

If we add to this the fact that, according to Article 119 of the Fundamental Laws, the legislative chambers, in the matter of determining the quotas of new recruits for army and navy, had only the right to object to an increase of the quota, but not the right to reduce it, the reader will derive a clear impression of the almost complete exclusion of the legislative chambers from all influence over the affairs and legislation of the army and navy departments.

Until 1917 there existed in Russia a bicameral system; the lower chamber, entirely elective, known as the State Duma, and the upper chamber, half elective and half appointed by the Emperor, known as the State Council.

Russian franchise law as it existed at the beginning of the War was regulated by the Act of 3rd June 1907, which had radically changed the electoral system established by the Law of 11th December 1905 promulgated while Count Witte presided over the Council of Ministers. The Law of 11th December had enabled various groups of Russian citizens to be represented in the legislative chambers, and the elections to the First and Second Dumas in a considerable degree reflected the public opinion throughout the nation. The Act of 3rd June 1907 changed the basis of the franchise with a view to giving the dominant position in the Duma elections to the large landowners. Promulgated in manifest violation of the Fundamental Laws, and in particular of Article 87, this act completely changed the proportion in the Duma elections between the votes of the owners of large estates and the votes of the electors of other classes (peasants, townsfolk, workers), in favor of the former, giving them in the overwhelming majority of provinces an absolute majority of votes. Leaning upon the system of suffrage established by the Act of 3rd June, the Imperial Government was able to create a submissive organ, a kind of *Chambre Introuvable*, represented by the Third Duma.

The system established by the Act of 3rd June was one of the most complicated suffrage systems that ever existed. This suffrage was *neither universal, nor direct, nor equal,* and only the secrecy of the ballot was preserved.

The members of the Duma were chosen for terms of five years, and if the Emperor dissolved the Duma before the mandate of its members expired, the ukase of dissolution was to indicate the date of the new elections to the Duma, and of its convocation.[17]

The general qualifications required of all voters were the following: to be at least twenty-five years of age, a male, a Russian subject, not to be attending any school and not to be serving in the army or navy. The following were excluded from the right to vote: (a) Any person who had been convicted of a serious crime, or dismissed from office by the verdict of the court, or who was charged with a criminal offense or subject to investigation on such a charge punishable by loss of the franchise; (b) insolvent debtors placed under receivership; (c) unfrocked priests or persons expelled from assemblies of the nobility or other corporations to which they belonged; (d) any person convicted of evading military service; (e) governors, vice-governors, city prefects, and members of the police force within the provinces or cities subject to their authority or within which they held office.

The voters were divided into four large groups or electoral *curiae:* (1) landowners, (2) inhabitants of cities, (3) peasants, (4) industrial workers. The *curia* of the landowners was divided into two subdivisions, large and small owners, while the city curia was divided into two groups of voters of first and second class. Let us review these different groups one by one.

In order to take part in the landowners' convention for the choice of electors, that is to say, of the future participants in the elections of the members of the Duma for a given province, it was necessary to have held for at least one year prior to the election, either as absolute owner, or as tenant for life, land, subject to a zemstvo tax, of an area of 125 to 800 deciatines.[18] The number of deciatines required as a voting qualification varied in the different parts of Russia. In common with the large landowners, proprietors of real estate other than land, valued for purposes of zemstvo taxation at not less than 15,000 rubles, also took part in the convention. Moreover, small landowners and proprietors were likewise entitled to participate in the elections. They could not, however, take part in the

[17] Articles 101 and 105.   [18] One deciatine = 2.7 acres.

landowners' convention directly, but had to do so through delegates previously chosen at special conventions. All owners of landed property subject to zemstvo taxation, whatever its extent or value, might assemble at a preliminary convention and elect as many representatives as they were entitled to on the strength of the combined amount of landed property owned by all the delegates attending the convention. The representatives so chosen took part in the landowners' convention on an equal footing with the big landowners.

There was one other class of voters entitled to choose representatives to attend the landowners' convention. These were the principal clergy of churches and other houses of worship of all creeds, if those churches owned land in the district.

The city voters were divided into two groups, unequal in point of numbers. In the first group voted owners of real property valued, for purposes of zemstvo or municipal taxation, at not less than 1,000 rubles in cities with a population of more than 20,000, and not less than 300 rubles in the other towns; also proprietors of commercial and industrial establishments of a certain importance. In the second group voted all the remaining city voters: (1) owners of real property and commercial and industrial enterprises not belonging to the first group; (2) persons paying rent; (3) persons paying the tax on commerce and industry; (4) persons in the government or zemstvo service, employed by municipal or communal institutions, or by the railways.

The elections from every group were held separately and in the elections of the members of the Duma electors chosen by the first and second class of city voters participated.

The elections by the peasants were carried out by the organs of peasant local government, the communal (*volostnoi*)[19] meetings. Each communal meeting in the district chose two representatives, and all the representatives gathered in a convention at the district town and chose electors to take part in the provincial electoral convention.

The working-men took part in the elections only if the establishment in which they worked employed at least 50 workers. Every establishment having from 50 to 1,000 workers elected one representative, and each additional complete 1,000 chose one additional

[19] *Volost*—a rural administrative unit comprising several villages (from 2 to 60).

representative, so that an establishment employing 3,500 hands would choose three representatives. The chosen representatives then gathered at the chief town of the province and chose electors from the industrial workers to take part in the provincial electoral convention.

All the electors chosen by the different groups of voters gathered at the chief town of the province for the purpose of choosing members for the Duma, and there elected members according to the number provided by law. This number varied from one to thirteen, according to the population of the province. The number of electors chosen by the various groups of voters was far from equal. In nearly all the provinces the electors representing the landowners had an absolute majority and could outvote the other groups of electors.

The elections themselves took place in the following order: first, a deputy would be chosen from among the electors of the peasantry; second, one from among the landowners; third, from the city inhabitants of the first and second class; and finally, in the industrial provinces (St. Petersburg, Moscow, Vladimir, Ekaterinoslav, Kostroma, and Kharkov), one from among the electors of the workingmen. The remaining deputies from the province were chosen from among the total number of electors, irrespective of their belonging to one or another group. The most remarkable provision of the Act of 3rd June 1907 was this system of election from each group of electors by the whole of the electors. Owing to this system the deputies were chosen from all the groups; but since the electoral convention as a whole, and not the electors of the respective group, made the selection, it followed that the landowners' *majority* was enabled to choose from each curia the candidate who, by his political views, was most acceptable to this majority. The members of the Duma chosen from the peasants, industrial workers, and city inhabitants were actually elected by the landowning majority, and this is why the Third and Fourth Dumas represented, in their majorities, not the interests of the entire country but only those of the landowning class.

However, in five big cities, St. Petersburg, Moscow, Kiev, Odessa, and Riga, the members of the Duma were chosen by direct ballot by the voters themselves, in such a manner that the voting was done separately by the first and second class of city voters. The qualification for voters of the first class was somewhat raised; in the two capitals they were required to possess real property valued at 3,000 rubles; and in Kiev, Odessa, and Riga they were required to possess real property valued at 1,500 rubles or to be paying taxes of not less than 50 rubles a year.

We shall not detain the reader by expounding the details of Russian parliamentary electoral procedure, but must call attention to one of the most extraordinary provisions of the election law. The Act of 3rd June 1907 provided that the voters of various groups might be subdivided into several still smaller groups, for which different qualifications were assigned. By an order of the Minister of the Interior the voters might be split up into smaller groups by reason of their residing in different sections of the same district, or according to the kind or extent of their property qualifications, or according to racial groups. This disposition, enabling the Minister of the Interior to create smaller units and electoral districts which would vote separately for their own electors, placed in his hands one of the most powerful means of influencing the results of elections. In this manner the boundaries of the original electoral districts were not fixed by law, but might arbitrarily be shifted by the higher administration of the country for the purpose of obtaining results advantageous and convenient to the Government.

The Government took great advantage of this competence during the elections to the Third and Fourth Dumas, splitting up the voters into smaller groups according to racial groups, territorial and property qualifications. It did this more particularly during the elections of 1912 to the Fourth Duma, when the clergy, being dependent upon the favor of the Government, were set apart as a special group by the church authorities and frequently voted for those government candidates who had been indicated to them.

This complicated electoral system, based on the principle of property and other qualifications, and on a method of indirect voting and curial representation calculated to secure the predominance of the landowning class, assured the victory of the candidates of those parties which supported the Government in the 1907 elections to the Third Duma.

In its internal organization the Duma was autonomous. It chose its own president, vice-presidents, secretary, and assistant secretaries. Under the law all business of the Duma was managed by a conference (*soveshchanie*) composed of the president, vice-presidents, the secretary, and one of the assistant secretaries. As a matter of fact, however, the directing part was played by an institution provided for by no legislation whatsoever, namely, the Council of Elders (*soviet stareishin*). This institution, under the chairmanship of the president of the Duma, was composed of the leaders of all the parties represented in the Duma, and the result was that the Council of Elders came to wield most of the power and authority in that body.[20]

In imperial Russia the State Council formed the upper chamber. The Council consisted of two separate institutions: (1) the State Council proper, forming the upper chamber of the legislature, and (2) the various departments and special committees of the Council.

The State Council in its stricter sense (the upper chamber) was composed of two groups of members equal in number: (1) those chosen by the five different electoral curiae of voters, and (2) those appointed by the Emperor. The elected members of the State Council were chosen by the clergy, the provincial zemstvo assemblies, the nobility, the Academy of Sciences and universities, and by the merchants and manufacturers. In this manner the members were to represent the interests of the two upper classes, the zemstvos, science, trade, and industry. Members of the State Council were elected for terms of nine years, and every third year one-third of the membership of each curia was retired and replaced by new members chosen by that particular curia. The provincial zemstvo assemblies chose members of the State Council for three years only, as these assemblies themselves were chosen for three years.

The elections of members of the State Council from the orthodox clergy were arranged in a most peculiar manner. There were only six of them, three from the monastic clergy and three from the secular clergy. The elections by the monastic clergy were, strictly speaking, no elections at all, as the candidates were simply designated by the authorities of this class of clergy, that is to say, by the bishops. Each bishop was free to propose three candidates and was not bound by the limits of his own diocese. A list of all such candidates was submitted to the Holy Synod (a committee of higher clergy appointed by the Emperor and administering the affairs of the orthodox church), which considered as elected those candidates who received the majority of votes, even if it were only a relative

[20] Cf. P. P. Gronsky, *Soviet Stareishin* (*The Council of Elders*), in *Pravo*, 1909, Nos. 5 and 6.

majority. Members representing the secular clergy were elected directly by the Synod itself from among candidates chosen by the diocesan clergy at the church conventions, one candidate being selected for each convention.

The Holy Synod, therefore, possessed the decisive vote in these elections, and in actual fact it was not at all the clergy as a class which formed the electoral college, but a government committee which ever since the time of Peter the Great had managed the affairs of the orthodox church and controlled its advisers, the bishops, whom it appointed. This system of choosing the clerical members of the State Council expressed most strikingly that subjection to government control which was the lot of the orthodox church under the imperial régime.

Elections of members of the State Council by the zemstvos were organized in such a manner that the members of the Council were chosen only for three years by the provincial zemstvo assemblies, that is, by the highest organs of self-government existing in imperial Russia. For election to the State Council by the zemstvo the property qualification was three times as high as that required for participation in the elections to the Duma, and the length of time for which the qualification must have been held was likewise multiplied by three, that is to say, raised to three years.

The elections by the provincial zemstvo conventions were organized in such a way that only a big landowner could ever be elected to the State Council to represent the zemstvo.

The third class of members of the Council was elected by the nobility. All the provincial body of the nobility chose from their own ranks two electors for each corporation, and these assembled at St. Petersburg and proceeded to choose members of the State Council to the number of 18.

The fourth group, comprising six members of the State Council, was elected by the Academy of Sciences and all the universities of Russia. The Academy and the councils of the universities each elected three electors from among the academicians and professors, and these, assembled at St. Petersburg, chose from among themselves the six members of the State Council.

Lastly, twelve members of the State Council representing trade and industry were chosen by electors elected by the Council and

Committee of Trade and Industry, Trade Exchange committees, and chambers of commerce.

As regards the position of members of the State Council who were nominated by the Emperor, there were invited from among their number every year, to participate in the work of the upper legislative chamber by imperial appointment, as many members as there were seats in the State Council filled by the elections. The practice of the Government in this respect by no means conformed with the law, for in the new lists which used to be published annually on New Year's Day it frequently happened that the names of those members of the State Council who for some reason or other were not considered desirable by the Government were not included at all. Under such a system of excluding from the lists members not to the liking of the Government, the irremovability of the members of the Council, guaranteed by law, was in fact annulled, and the members of the State Council found themselves in absolute dependence on the Government, which had the power to transfer them from the category of active members of the Council to that of non-active members.[21]

If we add to this that the president and vice-president of the State Council likewise were nominated every year by the Emperor from among the appointed members, the reader will readily perceive to what an extent the composition and direction of the State Council were in the hands of the sovereign.

The elected members of the State Council and the members of the Duma enjoyed perfect freedom of discussion and opinion in matters within the competence of the two legislative chambers and were not bound to render any account to their constituencies. During the sessions the members could be deprived of liberty only with the consent of the chambers themselves, with the exception of cases in which the member was detected in *flagrante delicto* and of crimes committed in the exercise of their duties as members of the Duma or the Council. During recesses of the legislative chambers its members could be arrested only by order of the judicial authorities and not by administrative process.

In this way the members of the Duma and the State Council

[21] For details, *see* the verbatim record of the sessions of the Duma of 18th February 1917, containing the speeches of Deputies Godnev and Gronsky on the interpellation as to the illegality of such a practice of excluding members of the State Council from the active list.

chosen by popular vote were very far indeed from enjoying those customary privileges of parliamentary immunity which are granted to members of legislative chambers in modern constitutional States. They could be arrested by order of the judicial authorities in the intervals between sessions and, more important still, there even existed in Russian legal code a class of delinquencies *sui generis*, that is, special parliamentary crimes which might be committed by a member of the Duma or the Council in the "exercise of the duties incumbent upon him by virtue of his official position." It was provided, in this connection, that permission to start prosecution against a member of the Duma or Council should be obtained from the Emperor, after which the case was to be dealt with in the First Department of the State Council; but in the event of the Emperor seeing fit to hand over a deputy or member of the Duma or State Council to the courts, the case was submitted to the Supreme Court. It is impossible, therefore, to say that there was real freedom of opinion for the members of the legislative chambers in Russia prior to 1917, for the Emperor, if he felt so inclined, could always have them tried for malfeasance.

The principal functions of the legislative chambers were: (1) legislation, (2) examination of the budget, and (3) questions and interpellations.

Legislative initiative was very peculiar under Russian law. According to Article 34 of the Statutes of the Duma a bill might be submitted to the Duma by the Minister, the Duma committees, or the State Council; thus individual members of the Duma or the Council did not possess the right to initiate legislation. In order to bring into motion the mechanism of legislative initiative independently of the Ministers and the committees of the legislative chambers, a whole series of obstacles had to be surmounted. If members of the Duma or Council wished either to change an existing law or to pass a new law, the president of the Duma or the Council must receive a special declaration on the subject signed by at least thirty members of the respective chamber and accompanied by a bill embodying the fundamental principles of the new law with an explanatory memorandum. The President would then put it on the calendar of the general session and the date when this declaration was to be discussed would be communicated to the Minister whose department the new bill affected, and then, at least one month before that session was held, a copy of the bill was submitted to the Minister in question. If the general session of the Duma or Council agreed that it was desirable to pass the new law or repeal the old law, a corresponding bill would be drawn up and submitted to the legislative chambers by the Minister concerned. Only if the Minister refused to undertake the drafting of such a bill might a committee be appointed by the Duma or the Council to do it.

Such was the long and tortuous road by which legislation had to be effected by the Duma and the State Council. The most interesting aspect of this procedure was the part played by the Ministers, who were supposed to exercise tutelage over the legislative chambers and to guard their privilege of initiating legislation. The Duma and Council, as it were, acted the part of petitioners before the Ministers in favor of their legislative proposals, while the Ministers were supposed to exercise supervision over the legislative institutions. The small political groups in the Duma that numbered less than thirty members found great difficulty in the very act of initiating legislation, since, in order to collect the thirty signatures required by law, they had to appeal for coöperation to members of other groups. All these obstacles were deliberately created in order to paralyze the legislative initiative of the Duma. Nevertheless, this initiative was frequently displayed, particularly in the First and Second Dumas. As for the initiative in the revision of the Fundamental Laws, that was a right reserved for the Emperor alone.

The further course of a bill in the chambers differed but little from the usual procedure of constitutional legislation. The only thing that is of some interest in this connection was the method of solving conflicts that might arise between the lower and upper chambers concerning a bill. When the Duma or State Council amended a bill submitted to it by the other chamber without rejecting the bill itself, the entire bill might either be sent back amended, or, by the decision of the chamber which had discussed and amended it, it might be turned over for further discussion to a special committee composed of members of the Duma and Council and chosen in equal numbers by both chambers. The members of the committee selected a chairman from among themselves and, after investigating the subject in dispute, reported their decision; after this the bill would be referred back to the Council or the Duma. These conference committees proved a good method of conciliating the two chambers, for when a bill was submitted to the Council or the Duma accompanied by the decision of a committee which included members of both chambers, and this decision was supported by a considerable majority of the committee, the passage of that bill as revised by the committee was, in a great measure, assured.

Legislative bills passed by both chambers were referred to the Emperor for confirmation, and he, if he decided to confirm the bill, affixed to it the words "Let it be so" and his signature.

The budgetary rights of the Russian legislative chambers were very limited. The Duma and the State Council had no right to discuss the budget as a whole, and had jurisdiction only over separate parts of the State budget, while about one-half of all budgetary appropriations could not be reduced by a vote of the chambers.[22]

No revenue or expenditure based upon the laws, statutes, and imperial orders in force at the time the budget was drawn up could be excluded when the budgetary bill was discussed in the Duma and the State Council. To the same category of irreducible and irremovable appropriations also belonged the service of State debts and other State obligations. The expenditure and appropriations of the Ministry of the Imperial Court were entirely exempt from discussion by the legislature so long as these did not exceed the sums appropriated under the Budget of 1906; there might likewise be no discussion of any change in the appropriations made under the provisions of the Statutes of the Imperial Family. Thus the expenditure for the maintenance of the Imperial Court and members of the Imperial Family could not be reduced by the legislature.

Furthermore, the Duma and the Council were deprived of the right to refuse to pass the budget and thus to start a conflict over the financial provision for the year. If the State budget failed to obtain ratification at the beginning of the budgetary term, the last normally sanctioned budget remained in force. Pending publication of a new budget by order of the Council of Ministers, all Ministries were granted monthly appropriations to the extent of one-twelfth part of the apportionment of the previous year.

[22] N. I. Lazarevsky in his *Lektsii po Russkomu Gosudarstvennomu Pravu* (*Lectures on Russian Constitutional Law*), St. Petersburg, 1908, 1st edition, p. 474, calculates this ironclad portion of the State appropriations for the 1908 budget to be 1,160 million gold rubles, out of a total budget of 2,500 million gold rubles.

Lastly, extraordinary appropriations, not provided for in the budget, for the needs of war-time and for special preparations for war were granted to all Ministries by the supreme administrative authority.

From the juxtaposition of the above-mentioned provisions of the Fundamental Laws and the Rules of 8th March 1906 it is clear that the rights of the legislative chambers in budgetary matters, which form the basis of parliamentary privileges, were reduced to a minimum.

The Russian chambers were entitled to address two kinds of inquiries to Ministers: in the form of questions and interpellations. Questions were an easier form of interpellation. The Duma and the Council were entitled to address such questions to the Ministers concerning matters under discussion in the chambers. Ministers had the right to refuse to reply if "considerations of public policy" made it undesirable to publish the information asked for.

Interpellations might be addressed to Ministers, not merely to obtain information, but for the purpose of exercising control over the activity of the State administration. The Duma and the Council might address interpellations to the Ministers "concerning such acts on the part of individuals and institutions within their jurisdiction as are irregular." The right of interpellation did not extend to the Ministry of the Imperial Court, the Department of the Institution of the Empress Marie, all the institutions which formed the Secretariat of the Emperor, and the Chancery of the State Council and the Council of Ministers.

An interpellation had to be addressed to the president of one or the other chamber in written form supported by at least thirty signatures of members of that chamber; the chairman would then submit it to discussion in plenary session.

The rules of the Duma modified the Statutes of the Duma as follows: interpellations which were not declared to be urgent were handed over for examination to the Committee on Inquiries, and this committee submitted its report on the interpellation to the plenary session. If urgency was claimed for the interpellation, the president reported the contents of the interpellation to the Duma, and the Duma, having heard one speech for urgency and another against it, then decided the question whether the interpellation was to be discussed at once or later. If the Duma or the Council decided by a majority vote to pursue the interpellation, it was to be communicated to the Minister concerned who was bound not later than a month after the acceptance of the interpellation by the legislative chamber to offer the necessary explanations to the Duma or the Council, or inform the Duma or the Council of the reasons that prevented him from communicating the required information and explanation.

If, after the Minister had submitted his explanations on the essential part of the question, the Duma or the Council should, by a two-thirds majority, vote the explanation unsatisfactory, it rested with the President of the State Council to bring the matter to the attention of the Emperor.

Such were the regulations concerning the right of interpellation. The system entailed on the Ministers no real responsibility for their actions. They were not obliged to answer questions or interpellations of the legislative chambers, and were always able to evade responsibility; more than that, when the Duma or the Council refused to rest satisfied with the explanations offered, the only consequence involved was that the entire matter might be submitted to the Emperor. This latter provision emphasized the fact that if a Russian Minister was responsible to any one at all it could only be to the Emperor.

At the head of the whole administration of the vast Empire there stood, subject directly to the Emperor, the Council of Ministers established on 19th October 1905 at the suggestion of Count Witte. At the moment when Russia changed from an autocratic to a constitutional régime, two days after the promulgation of the historic Manifesto of 17th October 1905, Russia obtained a cabinet united under the authority of the President of the Council of Ministers (the first President of the Council of Ministers was Count Witte).

The foremost function of the Council of Ministers was to direct and coördinate the work of the individual Ministers in the field both of legislation and of administration.[23] The Council was composed of all the Ministers and heads of departments. All legislative bills drafted in the various Ministries for submission to the chambers were first examined and approved by the Council of Ministers. All administrative measures of great importance and all appointments to the chief offices were likewise considered by the Council.

[23] Imperial ukase of 19th October 1905, on the Measures for Coördinating the Work of the Ministries and Departments, Article 1.

The Council of Ministers, its President, and the individual Ministers were appointed by the Emperor, and dismissed or retired by his ukase.

The Russian Council of Ministers did not represent a mutually dependent, cohesive cabinet, for the Ministers were not responsible for each other even to the Emperor, and if the Prime Minister should leave his post, it was not at all necessary that the other Ministers should follow him. The unity of the Council of Ministers was thus of an exclusively administrative and not political character.

The relations between the legislative chambers and the Ministers were reduced to a very limited right of interpellation which we have explained, and to the participation of the Ministers in the discussion of the budget and legislative bills submitted either by themselves or initiated by the Duma or the Council, in the course of their passage through the different stages of legislative procedure, that is to say, in the committees and plenary sessions. The Ministries and the Duma formed the two principal and fundamental parts of the central government administration, working separately, and politically independent of each other. The system of constitutional dualism was carried through with all possible firmness and thoroughness.

CHAPTER I

THE FIRST YEAR OF THE WAR. THE YEAR OF PUBLIC AID FOR THE WOUNDED AND OTHER WAR SUFFERERS

THE declaration of war by Germany on Russia and the actual beginning of hostilities created conditions that were extremely favorable to the increase of the authority of the executive power and the military command. The struggle in which Russia was involved called for the exertion of the whole force of the country, and this effort was naturally directed toward upholding the authority of the Government that was in power at the time the War broke out.

From the very beginning of the War the problems of nationalities, and especially the Polish question, acquired very great importance. The Russian army on the western frontiers of the country had to carry on the campaign in the midst of a Polish and Lithuanian population, and the Commander-in-Chief, the Grand Duke Nicholas Nicholaevich, issued a manifesto to the Polish people promising them not only in Russian Poland, but also in Austrian Galicia and the Polish provinces of Germany, that the Russian army would not be an army of oppressors, but on the contrary that it would secure to the Polish people national unification, the development of local self-government, the use of the Polish language in local affairs, and the rights of cultural self-determination. To carry out these promises of the Commander-in-Chief's manifesto, and to work out the corresponding practical legislative measures a special committee was afterwards established at Petrograd. This committee, however, began its work rather late, and in 1915 the Russian army, hard pressed by the Germans, retreated from Poland far into Russia and thus all Polish territories found themselves in the possession of Austria and Germany.

The first year of the War brought no serious changes into the organization of the Russian central government institutions. However, as a result of the War and its "extraordinary circumstances," legislation under Article 87 of the Fundamental Laws was intensified, so as to evade the normal legislative method. The legislative bills were examined only by the Council of Ministers and if the Council approved them they were submitted for confirmation to the

Emperor. The extensive application of Article 87 was possible because the legislative chambers were convoked only for exceedingly brief terms, and during the rest of the time the Emperor and his Government remained the sole arbiters of Russia's destinies.

All current legislation made necessary by the War was passed in virtue of Article 87 of the Fundamental Laws. Among such measures were those dealing with questions of State finance and money circulation, military censorship, the care of soldiers' families, changes and amendments of the law of conscription, changes in rates of taxation, and the imposition of new taxes or tariffs, customs duties, regulation of imports and exports, as well as a large number of measures affecting trade and industry, measures of coöperation with the organs of zemstvo and municipal government, the establishment of restrictions on landownership by subjects of countries at war with Russia and by immigrants from such countries, and many other measures which should have been passed in the regular legislative manner.

Such current legislation, with all the special features occasioned by war-time conditions, was promulgated with feverish haste through ukases of the Emperor as fast as the resolutions of the Council of Ministers were submitted to him. There was also a peculiar revival of the autocracy, under which the Emperor, neglecting to convoke the legislative chambers and taking advantage of the legislative procedure provided by the Fundamental Laws for the event of "extraordinary circumstances," legislated personally, with the coöperation of the Council of Ministers.

In the course of the first year of the War the legislative chambers were convoked only for two brief sessions, one, 8th August 1914, which lasted only one day, and the other which lasted from 9th to 11th February 1915. Both parliamentary sessions were important merely as an outward token of the harmony between the Government and the organs of popular representation. As for the result of their legislative efforts, it was insignificant. In the course of the one-day summer session there were passed only two fiscal laws sanctioning the issue of bank notes and an increase in the rates of various taxes. The main significance of this one-day session lay in the fact that all the parties of the Duma with the exception of the small socialist opposition of the extreme Left combined and formed a united front in support of the Government in its difficult and responsible task of prosecuting war against two great powers, Germany and Austria-Hungary, soon to be joined by Turkey. The representatives of the moderate opposition, Deputies Milyukov and Efremov, and the representatives of the national minorities, unanimously declared themselves in favor of supporting the Government during the War.

The three-day session was devoted to a discussion of the budget. It will be understood, of course, that it was impossible in such a brief time to give the matter proper attention, since the representatives of the different groups in the Duma obtained only fifteen minutes each to speak on the subject. It is true, the Budget Committee met a few days previous to the opening of the session and had the opportunity of studying carefully the estimates of expenditure and revenue. In the course of this February session the Minister of War, General Sukhomlinov, spoke at the secret session of the Duma Committee on National Defense, assuring the members of the Committee that the army was adequately provided and had no lack of munitions or food. The united front of all the political parties represented in the Duma, which had made it its object to support the Government in the prosecution of the War, thus remained unshaken, and only the representatives of the Social-Democrats criticized the government policy.

The chief task that was mapped out during the first year of the War, so long as the economic conditions of the country were relatively little affected by military operations, was relief of the wounded and other war sufferers and assistance to the families of men called to the front from the reserves, and to the widows and orphans of soldiers killed in battle. To meet the needs of the work of relieving the wounded, and the families of the mobilized men, new institutions arose among the organs of the central Government, and institutions already existing had their functions extended.

The first institution to respond to the call was the Duma. On the day following the one-day summer session of the Duma, its members met privately under the chairmanship of their President and decided to establish a Provisional Committee of the Duma for the Relief of the Wounded and Sick Soldiers and War Sufferers. The membership of this committee included all the deputies of the Duma present in Petrograd. Its president was the President of the Duma, and the representatives of the Left and Right wings of the Duma, Deputies

Shingarev and Prince Volkonsky, were chosen as vice-presidents. By this choice of the representatives of the two wings of the Duma as vice-presidents the members of the Duma meant to demonstrate the coöperation of all the important political groups in the prosecution of the War. The primary object of the Provisional Committee was the relief of wounded and other war sufferers, and in this direction the Committee did extensive work, creating several medico-sanitary units and establishing hospitals at the front.

Far more interesting, however, was the political significance which the Provisional Committee of the Duma acquired. During a recess of the legislative chambers this Committee was the only organ of the Duma (except the President, secretariat, and chancery), which, though sanctioned by no law and brought into existence *de facto*, remained, as it were, the guardian of the interests of the Duma. The Committee usually met twice a week and whenever matters of importance arose the President could summon the Committee at any moment. Besides the relief of the wounded, the Committee also discussed a number of current problems of general politics and very frequently its meetings were turned into large political assemblies of deputies, in which political questions were discussed and resolutions adopted which it was made incumbent upon the President of the Duma to carry out. At these meetings the reports of those Duma members who were engaged in the relief of the wounded would be heard, and these reports frequently dealt on the general situation at the front and on the shortage of army supplies. It is true, at the beginning of the War the Committee was mainly concerned with questions of relief for the wounded, but already in the spring of 1915 it began to discuss questions of general politics and especially the necessity of calling a session of the Duma for a longer term, that it might share in the work of legislation. The more alarming the news from the front, the greater was the attendance at the meetings of the Committee and the more insistent became the demands of the deputies for the convocation of the Duma. The President of the Duma was urged to use his right of personal report to the Emperor to obtain the immediate resumption of the work of the legislature. Thus the political activities of the Provisional Committee greatly overshadowed its purely humanitarian work.

By this time the Government itself had decided to establish certain central institutions to care for the needs of public welfare, under the presidency of members of the Imperial Family. On 11th August 1914 there was formed, by Imperial ukase, the Supreme Council for the Care of Soldiers' Families, and of Families of the Wounded and Dead. At the head of this Council, in the capacity of president, was placed the Empress Alexandra, who was assisted by her sister, the Grand Duchess Elizabeth, and the eldest daughter of the Emperor, the Grand Duchess Olga, as vice-presidents.

The membership of this Council included a number of the highest officials, the Ministers of the Interior, Finance, Transport, and Agriculture, the President of the Red Cross and the Chief Commissioner of the All-Russian Union of Zemstvos. Besides these members, the Council included also the Presidents of the Duma and the State Council, as well as two members of the Duma and of the Council. The functions of the Council consisted in the general direction of the work of caring for the families of mobilized men and of the wounded and dead. Its proceedings, however, were not very important and were confined chiefly to more or less formal meetings. A singular feature of the membership of this institution was that the representatives of the State Council and Duma were appointed by the Empress. Moreover, the Empress was free to invite whomever she pleased to be a member of the Council, and to bring up for discussion any question she chose.

While the Supreme Council was supposed to take charge of the work of caring for soldiers' families, the Committee of the Grand Duchess Tatiana for the Temporary Relief of War Sufferers, which was established by Imperial ukase of 14th September 1914 was concerned with the grant of relief to the vast numbers of refugees from areas occupied by the enemy. The honorary president of this Committee was the second daughter of the Emperor, the Grand Duchess Tatiana; the president of the Committee, who presided over the meetings, and the vice-presidents and members were appointed by Grand Duchess Tatiana with the sanction of the Empress. The Committee comprised representatives of the Ministries of the Interior, War, Transport, and Finance; in addition to these, the president might invite to the meetings of the committee representatives of other government departments and such persons as might be thought useful.

The refugees included many non-Russian inhabitants of the western provinces of Russia, Poles, Lithuanians, Letts, Jews, as well as

Ruthenians from the sections of Galicia occupied by the Russians. That is why the Committee was composed of representatives of various organizations of racial groups for the relief of refugees of their own race. Unlike the Supreme Council, the Committee of the Grand Duchess Tatiana proved itself an active and energetic institution.

Lastly, we must mention the Romanov Committee, which had been established in 1913 on the occasion of the third centenary of the Romanov dynasty, for the purpose of coöperating with public and private philanthropy. By resolution of the Council of Ministers of 1st September 1914 confirmed by the Emperor, the activities of this Committee were extended to include the children of soldiers called to the colors, as well as orphans and children made homeless by the War.

In this manner all institutions created during the first month of the War were devoted to the relief of the sick, the wounded, and the refugees. The energies of public opinion and the Government were directed toward the task of promoting social welfare, which the War made urgent. The economic organization of the country and measures for the improvement of army supplies became matters of urgency only because of the failures at the front during the spring and summer of 1915; these were caused by the deficiency of munitions, especially as regards the artillery, and by the economic disorganization in the rear due to the shortage of fuel, the deterioration of the means of transport, and certain difficulties in supplying the population with food.

As early as the spring and summer of 1915, the Government, acting under Article 87 of the Fundamental Laws, had adopted a series of legislative measures by which the power of the Ministries of War, Transport, and Commerce and Industry were extended in matters of army supply and economic reorganization. However, it was only at the beginning of the second year of the War that the organization of the supply of the army, the regulation of transport and fuel, and arrangements for feeding the population were effectively completed, in the form of the Laws of 17th August 1915 adopted by the Duma and the Council creating Special Councils on National Defense, Fuel, Food Supply, and Transport. In view of the fact that the measures taken by the Government in the course of the spring of 1915 directly preceded the law creating the Special Councils, we shall review them together in the following chapter.

CHAPTER II

THE SECOND YEAR OF THE WAR. A YEAR OF ECONOMIC DIFFICULTIES

THE War dragged on and the resulting economic difficulties increased. These difficulties first of all made themselves felt in the insufficient supply of fuel for official and private institutions such as factories and other establishments working for the national defense, among them also the railways. The Minister of Transport was given[1] in March 1915 a number of powers with regard to all kinds of enterprises engaged in preparing fuel, designed to facilitate the immediate supply of the army and navy, the railways and enterprises working for the national defense. By the Act of 31st March there was created, to deal with the most important measures and problems connected with the fuel supply, a special committee at the Ministry of Transport composed of representatives of the governmental departments, and of commerce and industry. This committee was the imperfect prototype of the Special Councils which were to be established later, by Law of 17th August 1915.

The next question made urgent by the War was that of the insufficient and irregular supply of the army with food and especially the shortage of forage, which had a serious effect on the condition of the horses. To regulate the food supply, special rights and powers were conferred upon the Minister of Commerce and Industry by a resolution of the Council of Ministers confirmed by the Emperor on 19th May 1915 enabling that Minister to control agriculture and prices of food products, and also to acquire reserves of food and forage for the needs of the army. In order to assist the Minister in carrying out these functions there was also created at the Ministry of Commerce and Industry, as well as at the Ministry of Transport, a committee composed of representatives of the various departments of trade and industry, and Members of the municipalities of the capitals.

Lastly, under the influence of the events at the front, when the Russian Army was compelled to retreat from Galicia owing to the

---

[1] Imperial ukase of 4th March 1915 and the decision of the Council of Ministers confirmed by the Imperial ukase of 31st March 1915.

vast superiority of the enemy in artillery and munitions, and its own almost total lack of munitions, especially shells, the Government, partly in deference to the representations of the President of the Duma, M. Rodzyanko, who was acting at the request of the Provisional Committee of the Duma, decided to take the general management of army supply out of the personal control of the Minister of War and hand it over to a Special Council, so as to coördinate all the measures adopted in this connection. This Special Council was created on 7th June 1915 by a resolution of the Council of Ministers confirmed by the Emperor.

The Special Council of 7th June must be regarded as the immediate predecessor of the Special Councils brought into existence by the Law of 17th August. In its structure this committee differed materially from the Fuel and Food Committees and was already known as a "Special Council" (*Osoboe Soveshchanie*), which designation was retained under the Law of 17th August. The Special Council of 7th June was placed under the presidency of the Minister of War. It included the President of the Duma and, by imperial appointment, four members of the State Council, four members of the Duma, four representatives of trade and industry, representatives of the Ministries of the Navy, Finance, Transport, and Commerce and Industry, a representative of the State Audit Department, and officials of the various war departments appointed by the Minister of War.

The Special Council was included in the category of the highest government institutions of the Empire and was subordinate only to the Emperor himself. The Minister of War, in his capacity of president of the Special Council, was granted various powers enabling him to influence the production of military supplies by prescribing the execution of orders for the army, commandeering establishments, ordering requisitions to be made, and exercising control over factories and other industrial establishments working for the supply of the army. All instructions issued by the Minister of War, in his capacity as president of the Special Council, were to be carried out without delay by the civil and military authorities.

Under the influence of the serious defeats suffered by the Russian army, owing to the failure of the Minister of War to take the necessary measures during the winter of 1914-1915 for the manufacture of indispensable munitions, the Government, on the persistent representations of the President of the Duma, decided to call a session of that body; the Legislature was to examine bills creating a number of Special Councils to deal with the supply of the army, and others designed to combat the consequences of the economic chaos. Throughout the second year of the War the executive branch of the Government continued to exercise absolute control over the legislature. The Special Councils, however, were now admitted to assist the executive in carrying out the army supply program; and in these Councils members of the legislative chambers took part. By this measure the members of the Duma and State Council were given access to the institutions which coöperated with the Government in the supply of the army and in the administration of the economic life of the country.

The Duma was convoked on 19th July 1915 and the Government submitted to it bills for the creation of four Special Councils, to discuss and coördinate measures: (1) on national defense; (2) on supply of fuel for the railways, for government and public institutions, and for industrial undertakings working for the national defense; (3) on food supply; and (4) on the conveyance of fuel, food, and army stores. Within less than one month these bills were examined, amended, and passed by the Duma and State Council, and on 17th August 1915 they were confirmed by the Emperor. All the measures adopted by the Government during the spring of 1915 to deal with the fuel crisis, and with the food and other supply requirements of the army, were replaced by the Law of 17th August, of which those measures were the forerunners.

Two ideas formed the basic principles of the Law of 17th August. One was that of concentrating in the hands of the Special Councils, which were placed above other government institutions, the direction of the defense of the country, the supply of fuel and food, and the regulation of transport. The second was that in these Special Councils members of the Duma and State Council were to sit as fully qualified members, and that not by appointment of the Emperor, as was the case under the Law of 7th June, but by the choice of the Duma and Council, as representatives of the legislative chambers.

To these four Special Councils there was later added, on 30th August 1915, a Special Council for the Relief of Refugees, under the presidency of the Minister of the Interior.

In their essential structure, both as regards organization and powers, all the five Special Councils were formed on the same model, that of the Special Council on National Defense.

The Special Council for the Discussion and Coördination of Measures for the National Defense under the presidency of the Minister of War comprised the following members: (1) the President of the State Council, (2) the President of the Duma, (3) nine members of the State Council and nine members of the Duma elected by the respective chambers, (4) one representative each from the following Ministries: Navy, Finance, Transport, Commerce and Industry, and State Audit, appointed by the several Ministers in agreement with the Minister of War, (5) five representatives from the Ministry of War appointed by the Minister of War, (6) representatives of the All-Russian Unions of Zemstvos and Towns, one from each Union to be chosen by their committees, and (7) four representatives elected by the Central War Industries Committee.

The other Special Councils were similarly constituted, although each of them, and more particularly the Special Council on Refugees, had its own peculiarity. They all possessed certain features in common. Each of them was presided over by a Minister, selected because the work of the conference was closely connected with the work of his own department. In all the Councils the houses of the legislature were represented by the most numerous group, composed of members chosen by the houses themselves. In all the Councils were found representatives of the various departments in different combinations, including groups of officials who were experts in departments closely connected with the work of the several Special Councils. Lastly, there were in all of them representatives of the Unions of Zemstvos and Towns. Thus we see that in the Special Councils legislative institutions and government departments were equally represented.

The Chairmen of the Special Councils were empowered to invite to the meetings of the Special Councils all those persons whose presence they might consider useful.

As regards the powers of the Special Councils, they were extensive and varied. Each Council within its own field,—the supply of the army, supply of fuel, provisions, regulation of transport, and the care of refugees,—was to have the complete administration of the work with which it was charged. The main object in creating the Special Councils was to concentrate as much as possible, in the interest of national defense, the management of army supplies and of the various branches of the national economy. It is only natural, therefore, that the decisions of the Special Councils should be accepted as guiding principles by the government departments and by private concerns working for the national defense. The statutes of the Special Councils on National Defense define the powers of the Councils in the following terms:

Article I. Matters within the jurisdiction of the Special Council are: (1) the supervision of the work of all government factories, arsenals, and workshops, as well as of private factories and other industrial establishments manufacturing munitions and other materials for the army and navy; (2) assistance in the establishment of new factories and other industrial enterprises manufacturing the articles above-mentioned, and assistance in the reorganization, expansion, and proper utilization of existing plants; (3) allotment of army supply orders among Russian and foreign factories and other industrial establishments; and (4) supervision of the execution of orders referred to above.

The other Special Councils likewise exercised general supervision over work on national defense, and allotted their own orders, with the assistance of officials from the various Ministries.

Of a different nature were, of course, the duties of the Special Council for Refugee Relief, which had charge of the work of regulating the movement of the refugees and establishing them in new homes, the valuation of property left behind by the refugees, the payment of compensation for losses caused by the War and by requisitions, the grant of loans, and the care of the educational needs of refugees.[2]

To execute the tasks imposed upon the Special Councils (with the exception of the Special Council on Refugees), the Chairmen of these Councils had at their disposal the following means:

(1) the right to demand from all government institutions and from private individuals assistance in carrying out the tasks imposed upon the Councils;

(2) the right of requiring private as well as public undertakings

---

[2] It is very interesting to note the very broad legal definition of a refugee given in Article 1 of the Statutes of the Special Council on Refugees: "Refugees are those persons who have abandoned localities threatened or already occupied by the enemy, or who have been evacuated by order of the military or civil authority from the zone of military operations; also natives of States hostile to Russia."

to take steps to give precedence to orders and deliveries for the needs of the Special Councils, and of obtaining all necessary information regarding the work of these undertakings;

(3) the right to requisition establishments and entrust their administration to persons appointed by the Chairman of the Special Council;

(4) the right to remove, in case of necessity, members of the administration, directors, and managers, of government and private factories and establishments, and to appoint other persons in their stead;

(5) the right to order requisitions of goods, both general and specific;

(6) the right to inspect, through specially appointed persons, the above establishments, and to examine their accounts and other documents;

(7) the right to demand priority for the transport of food and fuel for the army;

(8) the right of reorganizing the process of manufacture in respect of articles required for the War, and, in case of necessity, the right of granting loans for that purpose;

(9) the right to fix the rate of wages in such undertakings;

(10) to the Special Council on Fuel was granted power to fix the maximum prices of fuel; to alter, by agreement with contractors and purveyors, the terms of contracts already concluded; to fix the precedence and the conditions of the allotments of fuel to consumers; and to manage and dispose of government reserves of fuel;

(11) the Special Council on Food Supply was empowered to overrule decisions of local authorities, affecting the storage and distribution of provisions, the regulation of trade, and the fixing of prices; to take measures to ascertain the quantity of food and forage available throughout the Empire, and issue regulations concerning storage and detention of provisions;

(12) the Special Council on Transport had the right to set up, regardless of existing laws, special provisional rules for the receipt, loading, storage, and unloading of stores; to make exceptions from the usual methods of railway operation, as the exigencies of war-time might require; to grant permission for the construction of branch railways; and to issue regulations for the compulsory use of river shipping.

All these measures might be applied by order of the Chairman of a Special Council, after they had been discussed by the Council; but whenever there was need of their immediate application, the Chairman had the right to adopt them without preliminary discussion at the Council. He was bound, however, to report his action to the following meeting of that body.

The Special Councils held an extraordinary place among the central government institutions. The law designated them "State institutions of the highest order." In their composition they stood somewhere between a joint committee of the legislative chambers and an advisory organ attached to the Ministry, as regards problems of national defense and war-time economic policy; in their jurisdiction they were a peculiar kind of government institution of the highest order with very extensive duties and vast powers; and, as such, they were not subject to any other government institution; lastly, no account could be demanded of them by the executive branch of the Government. All members of the Special Councils, in respect of responsibility for criminal actions committed by them in the discharge of their official duties, were liable in the same manner as the members of the State Council and Duma.

The Special Councils were not included among the administrative institutions, and were placed above them. But their functions were entirely administrative in character, with all the special features that go with the highest administration in time of war, when it is necessary that the management of army supply and the regulation of the economy of the whole country should be concentrated in a few central institutions.

The presence in the Special Councils of members chosen by the State Council and Duma from the ranks of the members of these chambers gave to their decisions a particular authority.

Their chairmen, that is, the respective Ministers, acted as executors of the decisions of the Special Councils. Hence each Special Council had at its disposal the staff of officials serving in the corresponding Ministry, as the immediate subordinates of the Minister. Moreover, all chairmen of the Special Councils had the right to demand assistance in the execution of the decisions of the Special Councils from all government and public institutions and officials, as well as private citizens. Any one failing to comply with these demands and decisions, or to furnish the information required by the

Special Councils, was made liable to imprisonment or confinement in a fortress for a term of not more than three months or to a fine not exceeding 3,000 rubles. Where the crime was of a deliberate character, the penalty might be imprisonment for a term of one year and four months up to two years.

As regards the orders of the Minister of War, in his capacity as Chairman of the Special Council on National Defense, the immediate execution of such orders was enjoined on the military and civil authorities.

The Special Councils on National Defense, Fuel, and Food Supply were empowered to establish their own local organs under their direct control in the persons of authorized representatives appointed by the Chairmen of these Special Councils; these representatives might form in their respective localities councils of representatives of the local administration and self-government. These local councils were obliged to include among their members representatives of the local organization of the All-Russian Unions of Zemstvos and Towns and of the local war industries committees. Moreover, in order to fix the prices of requisitioned fuel, and to fix the prices of cattle, food, and forage for the army, local special committees were formed of a mixed character, composed of representatives of the local administration, local government institutions, and industrial and agricultural organizations.

The Special Councils, as organs of the highest central administration, were subject to the authority of the Emperor; it may be said, nevertheless, that the will of the Emperor did not influence the composition of the Special Conferences. Their entire membership was made up either by election by the legislative chambers and public institutions, or by the appointments of the Ministers. Where there was disagreement between the Minister of War, as Chairman of the Special Council on National Defense, and the Minister of the Navy, on questions belonging to the jurisdiction of this Council, the opinions of the two Ministers would be submitted to the decision of the Emperor, who thus acted as final arbiter in such questions.

The Special Council on National Defense ranked above the other Special Councils, and to its Chairman were granted special rights with respect to the proceedings of the other Special Councils, as follows: The Minister of War, in his capacity as Chairman of the Special Council on National Defense might veto all decisions of the Chairmen of the Special Councils on Fuel, Food Supply, and Transport, and consequently also those decisions which had been adopted by them as a result of discussion by the Special Councils. Orders that had been vetoed were referred for discussion to the Special Council on National Defense, and to this discussion were invited the Chairman and the members of the Special Council concerned. If no agreement could be reached, the matter would at once be submitted for review to the Council of Ministers. Thus the Council of Ministers acted as the final authority in such questions.

The fact that the Special Councils, presided over by the Ministers, were reckoned among the highest organs of the central administration, was especially emphasized by the provision of the Law of 17th August, which granted to the Duma and State Council the right to address interpellations to the Chairmen of the Special Councils in the same manner as to the Ministers. But the control over the proceedings of the Special Councils by the legislative chambers was exercised not only through interpellation; at the conclusion of the War the Chairmen of the Special Councils were to present to the State Council and Duma a detailed report on the measures that they had adopted, submitting at the same time the minutes of the proceedings of the Councils.

The most effective and permanent connection between the various Special Councils and the legislative chambers was provided in the persons of those members of the Councils who were elected by the legislative chambers. Although the law did not oblige them to render account to their respective chambers of the work of the Special Councils, the Duma as well as the State Council were in fact always informed of the state of affairs.

As regards the jurisdiction of the Special Councils, it was of a twofold character. On the one hand the decisions were ordinary administrative orders for the discharge of the duties imposed upon the Councils; orders for various articles and supplies, contracts, supervision of the execution of orders, etc. On the other hand, there were a number of acts and resolutions which had a general importance, setting up entirely new regulations and even changing for the time being the existing provisions of the law. These acts had the character of decrees and the effect of new legislation. Thus, for instance, the Minister of Commerce and Industry issued a series of orders which fixed compulsorily the prices of fuel.[3] The Minister of Agriculture fixed the prices of food and forage.[4] The Minister of Transport issued new rules for the receipt and loading of consignments of goods and the disposal of unclaimed consignments.[5] Under the Special Council on National Defense were established special evacuation commissions whose procedure was laid down by a resolution of the Special Council.[6] This Special Council also issued rules regarding the assistance to be rendered to enable evacuated industrial concerns to resume work.[7] A number of other measures having the character of propaganda were passed by the various Special Councils.

This elaborate and peculiar system was intended to satisfy the demands of public opinion and the desire of the legislative chambers to participate in the organization of the defense of the country and to help in overcoming its economic difficulties.

Unwilling to alter the system of a dualistic constitutional monarchy, the Emperor could not bring himself to form a Government that would rest upon a majority of the lower chamber and prosecute the War and administer domestic affairs in a manner approved by a majority of the Duma. Still, the participation of the legislative chambers in the work of national defense and in the struggle against economic difficulties became absolutely indispensable in the face of the insistent demands of the Duma and public opinion. Moreover, the Government itself, conscious of its heavy responsibility for the unsuccessful conduct of the War, due largely to the faulty organization of army supply, was anxious to transfer at least some share of this responsibility to the shoulders of the representatives of the nation. It was for this reason that the system of Special Councils was adopted. At the same time there was inaugurated, through the medium of the Special Councils, a system of serious and far-reaching interference with the affairs of private citizens and with private busi-

[3] *Sobranie Uzakoneni,* 8th October 1915, No. 278, Art. 2053; *ibid.,* 23rd October 1915, No. 296, Art. 2240.

[4] *Ibid.,* 17th October 1915, No. 288, Art. 2136; *ibid.,* 25th October 1915, No. 300, Art. 2259.

[5] *Ibid.,* 9th October 1915, No. 277, Art. 2049; *ibid.,* 9th October 1915, No. 277, Art. 2050; *ibid.,* 9th October 1915, No. 277, Art. 2051; *ibid.,* 16th October 1915, No. 285, Art. 2111; *ibid.,* 27th November 1915, No. 339, Arts. 2515 and 2516.

[6] *Ibid.,* 17th October 1915, No. 288, Art. 2135.

[7] *Ibid.,* 9th October 1915, No. 277, Art. 2036.

ness, which, while indispensable for the defense of the country, yet constituted an injury to private interests. This system of so-called Military Socialism consisted in sacrificing the interests of private enterprises to the interests of the State as a whole and its defense.

This interference of the Government in private business went so far that the Special Councils were in a position to fix compulsory prices for fuel and provisions and regulate wages. In addition to this the control of industrial establishments lay with the Special Councils, and the agents of these establishments, as well as their administrative staffs, might be dismissed by order of the Chairman of the Special Councils.

In this way the Special Councils, both by the position they held among the central government institutions of Russia and by their exclusive powers of intervention in the industries of the country, constituted an entirely new phenomenon in Russian political life.

CHAPTER III

THE DOWNFALL OF THE MONARCHY AND THE FIRST FIVE DAYS OF THE REVOLUTION

In the course of the summer session of the Duma from 19th June to 3rd September 1915, at a time when the Russian armies were retreating all along the front in Galicia, Poland, and Lithuania, there occurred a profound change in the grouping of political parties within the Duma itself.

The policy of the Government provoked bitter criticism, directed especially against the Ministry of War. It is true that the law establishing the Special Councils, which has been analyzed in the preceding chapter, had afforded the representatives of the Duma the opportunity of participating in the organization of national defense and in the economic measures for the supply of the army and of the industries engaged in war work; at the same time, however, the leadership of the political life of the country remained entirely in the hands of the Emperor and of his Ministers. Only a few changes had been made among the Ministers, but these did not imply any change of government policy.

In the meantime, the original coalition of all parties in the Duma, with the exception of the extreme Left, which had been formed in the interests of national defense, disintegrated. The whole opposition, as well as the central groups, influenced by the reverses at the front, united in a demand for a government that would enjoy the confidence of the nation and conduct the national defense successfully in harmony with the opinion of the public and of the Duma. This coalition of the parliamentary groups was given the name of the Progressive Bloc and included all parties represented in the Duma, except the extreme Left and Right, thus combining more than two-thirds of the entire membership.

The Government, however, refused to meet the wishes of the Duma. On 3rd September 1915 the Duma was prorogued, and from this moment began a protracted struggle between the Government on the one hand and the Duma and the nation on the other, leading finally to the Revolution of February 1917 and the collapse of the monarchy. We shall not attempt to describe the steadily widening breach between the Government and the Duma, as this is a subject properly belonging to the province of a general political history of Russia during the War.[1] In the structure of the central government institutions nothing was changed during this period of one and a half years; the system of Special Councils set up by the Law of 17th August 1915 continued in force until the outbreak of the Revolution of 27th February; and the entire system of mutual relations between the Emperor and his Ministers on the one hand and the legislative chambers on the other, as well as the whole structure of the Government described in the Introduction to the present volume, continued unaltered up to that Revolution.

During the last weeks of 1915, the whole of 1916, and the first two months of 1917 a state of conflict prevailed between the Duma and the Government. The Duma, dominated by the Progressive Bloc, adopted a program of reforms vitally needed by the country, in addition to proclaiming openly the necessity of a Government that should be responsible to the popular representative bodies. The Government, however, was anxious to administer the country without the participation of the representative organs, jealously guarding its privileges and convoking the legislative chambers for brief sessions only.

One of these brief sessions of the Duma, held in February 1917, was interrupted, a few days after its opening, by an Imperial ukase ordering a recess until April. This ukase was issued at a time when the food shortage in Petrograd was giving rise to disorders which culminated in the mutiny of the Petrograd garrison and the Revolution of 27th February.

The ukase of the recess was received by the President of the Duma on the evening of 26th February, and on the following morning occurred the revolt of the Volhynian and Lithuanian Guards. In the course of the 27th and the succeeding two days all the armed forces stationed at Petrograd and its environs joined the rebels.

It is not our task to furnish a detailed account of the events of the February Revolution; we have merely to trace the development of the revolutionary process in so far as it effected changes in the organization of the central government institutions of Russia.

---

[1] This process has been presented in a brilliant manner by P. N. Milyukov in his *Historya Vtoroi Russkoi Revolutsii* (*History of the Second Russian Revolution*), Sofia, 1921, Vol. I, pp. 22-36.

The members of the Duma, arriving at the Tauride Palace on the morning of 27th February, were informed that the Duma had been prorogued and that the Petrograd garrison had revolted against the existing régime. Reports of the spread of the revolutionary movement were arriving in rapid succession, and the deputies assembled in one of the halls of the Tauride Palace for a private conference, under the chairmanship of the President of the Duma, M. Rodzyanko. After a brief but stormy discussion, it was resolved that the Council of Elders[2] should be instructed to select a Provisional Committee of the Duma, and that no member of the Duma should leave Petrograd.

The Committee thus was to adopt a program of action and determine the part which the Duma should play in further events. The Council of Elders met at once and selected a Provisional Committee composed of twelve deputies; this Committee included representatives of all the parties that formed the Progressive Bloc, as well as of the two Socialist groups. As for the party of the Right in the Duma, it remained without representation in the Provisional Committee. Those elected as members of the Committee were: the President of the Duma, M. Rodzyanko, M. Shulgin (Nationalist), M. Lvov (Center), M. Dmitryukov (Octobrist), M. Shidlovsky (Left Octobrist), M. Karaulov (Non-partisan), M. Konovalov (Progressive), M. Rzhevsky (Progressive), M. Milyukov (Constitutional Democrat), M. Nekrasov (Constitutional Democrat), M. Kerensky (Labor Group), and M. Chkheidze (Social Democrat). The object of the Committee was stated to be quite indefinitely and vaguely, "to restore order and to deal with institutions and individuals."

The Provisional Committee of the Duma was the first organ of revolutionary authority and was intended to serve as the agency by which the will and the desires of the Duma itself were to be expressed. It started work at once and chose M. Rodzyanko for President. In this way the President of the Duma came to be the head of the very first institution formed by revolutionary procedure.

M. Chkheidze, the Social Democrat, declined the offer of membership in the Provisional Committee, while Kerensky, as a member of the Labor Group, accepted it with reservations. This attitude of the representatives of the parties of the Left was explained by the fact that, a few hours after the election of the Provisional Committee,

[2] For the functions of this institution *see* the Introduction, p. 17.

there was to be held at the Tauride Palace the first meeting of that other revolutionary organ, formed on the pattern of a similar organ in the revolution of 1905: the Soviet (Council) of Workmen's Deputies. On behalf of the Provisional Executive Committee of the Soviet of Workmen's Deputies, invitations to attend this meeting were extended to all the troops that had gone over to the revolutionary side, and to the workers in the factories of Petrograd. The soldiers were to send one Soviet delegate for each company, while the factories were to have one delegate for each thousand workers.

On the very first day of the Revolution there were thus formed two organs—both of revolutionary origin—which came to be the two sources from which were to develop within the next few days two different systems of revolutionary institutions: The Provisional Committee of the Duma created the Provisional Government, while the Petrograd Soviet of Workmen's and Soldiers' Deputies laid the first foundation stone for the future Soviet régime.

Concerning the creation of the first Soviet institutions we have the following information, furnished by the historian of the Soviets for the year 1917, a participant in all the events of the revolutionary movement, Nicholas Sukhanov-Gimmer. The organizing nucleus, in the form of the Provisional Executive Committee of the Soviet of Workmen's and Soldiers' Deputies, was composed of leaders of the working-men's group in the Central War Industries Committee, Socialist members of the Duma, and other prominent Socialists. This Provisional Executive Committee summoned a meeting of the Soviet of Workmen's and Soldiers' Deputies at seven o'clock in the evening of 27th February. It also appointed a food commission, invited the coöperation of Socialists from the army, and established contact between them and the Duma.[3] About nine in the evening such delegates from the regiments and factories as it had been possible to elect were gathered together; to these were added some of the other Socialists, who were to participate as individuals; and, as a matter of course, the meeting was also attended by the Provisional Executive Committee. Presided over by the member of the Duma, Chkheidze, the first session of the Petrograd Soviet of Workmen's and Soldiers' Deputies was then opened.

Chkheidze, Kerensky, and Skobelev were elected the presiding

---

[3] Sukhanov, *Zapiski o Revolutsii* (*Notes on the Revolution*), Berlin, 1921-1922, Vol. I, p. 86.

committee (*praesidium*), while the secretariat was composed of Sokolov, Gvozdev, Grinevich, and Pankov. At this first meeting of the Soviet, there was chosen an Executive Committee, taking the place of the Provisional Committee of the Soviet. The Executive Committee was constituted on the principle of proportional representation for the various political parties represented in the Soviet. This Committee was to have eight members. In addition, there was included in it the entire presiding committee; and representatives of local and central organizations of the Socialist parties were admitted with a decisive vote.[4] In this manner came into being the first executive organ of the Soviets. From the very first day of the Revolution there became apparent that dualism in the revolutionary institutions which was destined to end in the downfall of the Provisional Government and in the capture of power by the Soviets.

The Provisional Committee of the Duma, which stood at the head of the revolutionary movement, was faced with the exceedingly responsible and difficult task of organizing the new Government. The old Government had fallen almost without a struggle; the Ministers of the Emperor were brought one after another to the Tauride Palace and arrested. The entire administrative machinery, however, remained intact, and the Provisional Committee of the Duma took care, even before the establishment of the Provisional Government, to appoint special commissaries from among the members of the Duma to all the chief government departments, so as to prevent any interruption in their routine. These commissaries of the Provisional Committee constituted the first organs of revolutionary administration. On 28th February and 1st March they went from the Tauride Palace to all the departments, and the entire personnel of the latter, from the higher officials down to the junior clerks and messengers, acknowledged the authority of the Provisional Committee of the Duma; thus the work of the departments was interrupted for only two or three days.

Having placed the revolutionary authority in effective control by the appointment of commissaries to all central government institutions, the Provisional Committee of the Duma proceeded to form the Provisional Government, the first supreme organ of the revolutionary authority.

The composition of this new Government had been contemplated

[4] *Ibid.*, Vol. I, pp. 148-149.

long before, at the time of the great retreat of the army during 1915; and in the Duma, as well as among the public bodies, lists of Ministers of "public confidence" or of a "responsible Ministry," had been circulated. The candidacy of Prince George E. Lvov, President of the All-Russian Union of Zemstvos, for the post of Prime Minister was a popular issue. After the arrival of Lvov from Moscow, on the morning of 1st March, the Provisional Committee of the Duma undertook the formation of the Provisional Government. As regards its party composition, it resembled the Provisional Committee of the Duma, including in its ranks representatives of all sections of the Progressive Bloc; as Ministers of Justice and Labor it was proposed to have the Social-Revolutionist, Kerensky, and the Social Democrat, Chkheidze, respectively. The latter, however, refused to join the Provisional Government; elected President of the Petrograd Soviet of Workmen's and Soldiers' Deputies, Chkheidze was unwilling to exchange the presidency of the Soviet for a ministerial portfolio. As for Kerensky, who was Vice-President of the Petrograd Soviet, he finally accepted the Ministry of Justice, but only after he had obtained the formal sanction of the Soviet.

The first Provisional Government was constituted as follows: Prime Minister and Minister of the Interior, Prince Lvov; Minister of Foreign Affairs, M. Milyukov; Minister of War and the Navy, M. Alexander Guchkov; Minister of Justice, M. Kerensky; Minister of Finance, M. Tereshchenko; Minister of Transport, M. Nekrasov; Minister of Agriculture, M. Shingarev; Minister of Commerce and Industry, M. Konovalov; Procurator of the Holy Synod (Minister of Ecclesiastical Affairs), V. N. Lvov; Minister of Education, M. Manuilov; State Controller, M. Godnev.

The Members of the Provisional Government, as we have already stated, were appointed by the Provisional Committee of the Duma, and neither the Soviet nor its Executive Committee took any part in determining the composition of the new Government, for the Executive Committee had decided that representatives of the Soviet were not to take part in the new Government. That is why Kerensky, on accepting the portfolio of Minister of Justice, obtained from the Soviet a special personal permission to participate in the Government of Prince Lvov; nor did he act as the representative of the Soviet in the Provisional Government.

Nevertheless, the question of the support to be given to the Provisional Government by the Soviet and its Executive Committee was raised at a joint conference of the Provisional Committee of the Duma and of the Executive Committee of the Soviet, and, after an exchange of opinions, a declaration was drawn up setting forth the obligations assumed by the Provisional Government. The following principles were laid down in this first declaration of the new revolutionary Government.

"The Government will be guided by the following principles: (1) complete and immediate amnesty in all political and religious cases, including terrorist attempts, military revolt, agrarian offenses, etc.; (2) freedom of speech, press, association, assembly, and strikes, with the extension of political rights to persons serving in the army, within the limits permitted by military conditions; (3) abolition of all restrictions based on class, creed, and race; (4) immediate preparation for the convocation, upon a basis of universal, direct, equal, and secret suffrage, of a Constituent Assembly, which will establish the form of government and constitution of the country; (5) substitution, in place of the police, of a popular militia, upon an elective basis, subject to the authority of the organs of local government; (6) elections to the organs of local government on a basis of universal, equal, direct, and secret suffrage; (7) that the military units which took part in the revolutionary movement shall not be disarmed or removed from Petrograd; (8) while strict military discipline is to be maintained in the ranks and in the performance of military duty, the soldiers are to be freed from all restrictions in the exercise of those civil rights which are granted to all individual citizens. The Provisional Government deems it its duty to add that it by no means intends, by taking advantage of war-time conditions, to delay in any way the realization of the program stated above."[5]

We thus see that, while the personnel of the Provisional Government was chosen by the Provisional Committee of the Duma alone, the program of that Government was drafted by agreement with the representatives of the Soviet. This compromise did not, however, involve any obligation on the part of the Soviet to support the Provisional Government, and the declaration of the Soviet, issued simultaneously with that of the Provisional Government, pledges it to give only conditional support to the Provisional Government. "The new

[5] N. Avdeev, *Revolutsya 1917 goda* (*The Revolution of 1917*), Moscow-Petrograd, 1923, Vol. I, p. 189.

Government," reads the declaration of the Soviet, ". . . has issued today a statement of the reforms it undertakes to carry through partly in the process of its struggle against the old régime, and partly when this struggle is over. Some of these reforms will be welcomed by our democracy; for instance, amnesty for political offenses, the convocation of a Constituent Assembly, freedom of speech, press, and association, the abolition of racial distinctions. . . . We assume that, to the extent to which the new Government favors the realization of these obligations and carries on a determined struggle against the old régime, the democracy must support it."[6] From the very beginning, therefore, the Provisional Government was thus placed in a position in which conflicts with the Soviet were liable to arise.

Simultaneously with the organization of the Provisional Government, the Provisional Committee of the Duma decided to take measures which would assure the abdication of the Emperor Nicholas II in favor of his son, a minor, under the regency of the Grand Duke Michael, brother of the Emperor. With this object in view, the Provisional Committee of the Duma despatched MM. Guchkov and Shulgin to Pskov, where the Emperor's train was held up. Leaving Petrograd at 3 P.M. on 2nd March, the two delegates of the Provisional Committee were received by the Emperor in his car at about 10 P.M. Here they learned that the Emperor himself, influenced by the advice of the Chief of Staff, General Alexeev, and Generals Brusilov and Ruzsky, had already resolved upon abdication.

The draft of the abdication act,[7] however, which had been prepared at General Headquarters, was altered by the Emperor; instead of abdicating in favor of his son, the Tsarevich Alexis, Nicholas II decided to transfer the rights to the throne to his brother, and to renounce the right to the crown both for himself and his son.[8] At the instance of Shulgin, some alterations were made in the text of the act of abdication as drafted, in the sense that the Grand Duke Michael would be required to declare on oath that he would govern the Empire "in complete agreement with the representatives of the

[6] Piontkovsky, *Khrestomatya Russkoi Revolutsii* (*Textbook on the Russian Revolution*), Moscow-Leningrad, 1926, p. 48.

[7] *See* A. Block, *Poslednie dni Imperatorskoi Vlasti* (*Last Days of the Imperial Régime*), Petrograd, 1921, p. 105.

[8] A juridical analysis of the act of abdication of Nicholas II will be found in P. Gronsky, *La Chute de la Monarchie en Russie,* an article published in the *Revue Politique et Parlementaire,* July 1923.

people." At 11:50 P.M., on the night of 2nd March, Nicholas II signed the abdication, and Michael was to ascend the Russian imperial throne. The abdication of Emperor Nicholas II, on behalf of himself and his heir, was an act of paramount importance in the destinies of the Russian Empire. It was in the form of a communication to the Chief of Staff. Its text ran as follows:

GENERAL HEADQUARTERS
To the Chief of Staff:

In the days of the great struggle with the foreign enemy, who has been striving for almost three years to enslave our native land, the Lord has willed that Russia should be put to another heavy ordeal. The outbreak of domestic turmoil threatens to have a disastrous effect upon the further conduct of the stubbornly contested War. The destiny of Russia, the honor of our heroic army, the happiness of the nation, the entire future of our dear Fatherland, demand the prosecution of the War to a victorious conclusion at all costs. The cruel foe is straining his last resources, and the hour is already near when our gallant army, in common with our glorious Allies, will at last be able to crush the enemy. In these days, so decisive for the life of Russia, we have deemed it to be a duty laid upon our conscience to facilitate for our people the close union and consolidation of all the national forces for the speediest achievement of victory and, in agreement with the State Duma, we consider it best to abdicate the throne of the Russian Empire and to renounce the supreme power. Unwilling to part with our beloved son, we transmit our succession to our brother, the Grand Duke Michael Alexandrovich, and give him our blessing on his accession to the throne of the Russian Empire. We enjoin our brother to administer affairs of state in complete agreement with the representatives of the people in the legislative institutions on such a basis as may be established by them, taking an inviolable oath to this effect. In the name of our dearly beloved native country we call upon all loyal sons of the Fatherland to fulfill their sacred duty to him, by obeying the Emperor at this grave national crisis, and to help him, in common with the representatives of the people, to lead the Russian Empire on the road to victory, prosperity and glory. May the Lord help Russia.

(Signed) NICHOLAS.

City of Pskov,
March 2, 1917, 15 o'clock.

(Countersigned) COUNT FREDERICKS,
Minister of the Imperial Court, Adjutant-General.[9]

[9] *Sobranie Uzakoneni i Rasporyazheni Pravitelstva*, 6th March 1917, No. 54, p. 344.

The date on this official document—2nd March, 15 o'clock—was left just as it had been put there originally at 3 p.m. of 2nd March, prior to the arrival of Guchkov and Shulgin. In spite of the fact that alterations were made in the text of the abdication in the evening of 2nd March, the date remained unchanged in this document, even though, strictly speaking, the final abdication act was signed by Nicholas II at 11.50 p.m. 2nd March.

The act of abdication was handed by the former Emperor to Guchkov and Shulgin, who brought it to Petrograd on the morning of 3rd March, after some difficulties had been met with on the way,[10] and handed it over to the keeping of the Provisional Government.

The Grand Duke Michael was immediately informed that, as a result of the decision of his brother, he was to assume the burdens of the imperial authority. Michael, however, upon receipt of the unexpected news that Nicholas II had abdicated in favor of him, and not of the heir apparent, and learning that he would thus become Emperor instead of mere regent for the sickly boy, Alexis, called a conference to discuss the matter. The conference was held at the house of Prince Putyatin, in Petrograd, and invitations to it were sent to all the members of the Provisional Government and of the Provisional Committee of the Duma.

After a lengthy discussion,[11] and a personal conference with the President of the Duma, Rodzyanko, Michael announced to all those present that he declined the throne of Russia.

The draft of Michael's renunciation of the supreme authority had already been prepared by the Minister of Transport, Nekrasov; but it was not quite satisfactory, and the Grand Duke and the members of the conference decided to invite two prominent jurists, M. Vladimir Nabokov and Baron Nolde, to prepare a proper act of renunciation. The two jurists were joined by M. Shulgin, and the document was drawn up anew. The Grand Duke made only two alterations; he substituted the words "I request" for "I command," and added a

---

[10] *See* Shulgin's memoirs, *Dni,* in *Russkaya Misl,* Prague, Vols. VI-VII, pp. 67-71.

[11] This historical exchange of opinions, resulting in the rejection of the throne by the Grand Duke Michael, since, of all those present at this conference, only Milyukov and Guchkov declared themselves in favor of Michael's assumption of the imperial power, has been described in Milyukov, *op. cit.,* Vol. I, pp. 53-55, and by Rodzyanko, in his memoirs in *Arkhiv Russkoi Revolutsii,* Berlin, Vol. VI, 1922, p. 61.

reference to the Divinity. In its altered form, the act of renunciation was rewritten in Nabokov's own hand and signed by Michael.[12]

The text of this Act[13] was as follows:

A heavy burden has been imposed upon me by the will of my brother, who has transmitted to me the imperial throne of the Russias at a time of an unprecedented war and of popular turmoil. Inspired by the idea shared by all the people, that the welfare of our native land is to be considered above all, I have adopted the firm decision to assume the supreme power only in the event that this should be the will of our great people, who must, by universal ballot, through their representatives in a Constituent Assembly, establish the form of government and the new Fundamental Laws of the Russian State. Therefore, praying for Divine blessing, I request all citizens of Russia to submit to the Provisional Government which has been created on the initiative of the Duma and invested with the fulness of power, until the Constituent Assembly, which is to be convoked within the shortest possible time upon a basis of universal, direct, equal, and secret suffrage, shall, by its decision regarding the form of government, express the will of the people.

(Signed) MICHAEL.

Petrograd,
March 3, 1917.

The act of rejection of the offer of supreme power by the Grand Duke Michael Alexandrovich did not constitute an abdication of an Emperor, since the Grand Duke had not ascended the throne, notwithstanding the fact that Emperor Nicholas II, as may be seen from the telegram he sent to his brother shortly after his abdication[14] regarded him already as Emperor. This rejection, however, was a conditional one, since Michael reserved for himself the right to alter his decision in the event that the Constituent Assembly should declare itself for a monarchy.

At all events, for the moment, Michael transmitted full power to the Provisional Government, which was to become the supreme au-

[12] The story of the writing of the act of renunciation has been told by Nabokov in his memoirs of the epoch of the Provisional Government, in *Arkhiv Russkoi Revolutsii*, Vol. I, pp. 21 *sqq*. *See also* V. D. Nabokov, *V 1917 godu*, in *Arkhiv Russkoi Revolutsii*, Vol. VII, pp. 7-8.

[13] *Sobranie Uzakoneni i Rasporyazheni Pravitelstva*, 6th March 1917, No. 54, p. 345.

[14] For the text of this telegram *see* Gronsky, *La Chute de la Monarchie en Russie*, in *Revue Politique et Parlementaire*, July 1923, pp. 95-105.

thority in the country, and which all citizens of Russia were called upon to acknowledge. Thus all the prerogatives of supremacy were concentrated in the hands of the Provisional Government, and this Government not only ruled the country, but also promulgated a series of legislative measures, basing its authority on the Act of 3rd March.

It must be admitted, however, that the prerogatives of the Provisional Government were established by the very fact of the Revolution and the downfall of the old régime itself,[15] rather than by any lawful act. In fact, the members of the Provisional Government had been selected by the Provisional Committee of the Duma, and its prerogatives were conferred upon it by the Act of 3rd March. But the Duma, and still less its Provisional Committee, had never enjoyed the supreme power in the Empire. The Duma, if we admit that the Provisional Committee chosen by its Council of Elders, was the actual interpreter of its will, constitute but one of three elements of the legislative power, all endowed with the same rights, and did not even possess full legislative authority; it could not, therefore, transmit to the Provisional Government full governmental power nor even the power to make laws. The Grand Duke Michael, of course, could refuse to accept the throne, but he could not bequeath "the fulness" of governmental power to the Provisional Government, for the simple reason that he did not possess it. Had he even been Emperor, he could not, in abdicating the throne, transmit "the fulness of power," because as a constitutional and limited monarch he would have exercised his legislative functions "in agreement with the State Council and the Duma," and without their consent he could not transfer the "fulness of power" to any one.

In one respect, however, the Act of 3rd March 1917 marks a turning point in the development of the Government of Russia; the 3rd March should properly be considered the day of the downfall of the monarchy. For, even though the Grand Duke Michael's renunciation was a conditional one, the fact remains that from 3rd March onward there was no longer an Emperor in Russia. The monarchy had come

---

[15] "The Provisional Government which was brought into existence by the Provisional Committee of the Duma had no other title to the supreme power than the standing of its members which was closely dependent on the work of the majority of the State Duma." Milyukov, *Rossya na perelome* (*Russia at the Crossroads*), Paris, 1927, Vol. I, p. 47.

to an end and was replaced by a transitional form of administration with the Provisional Government at its head, which must, however, be considered as a republican form of government *de facto*. The republic was not yet proclaimed, but the monarchy had fallen.

In this manner the first five days of the Revolution (27th February to 3rd March) saw profound changes effected in the Russian system of Government. There cannot be any doubt whatever that the Russian Revolution of 1917 was in a considerable measure occasioned by the course of events at the front. The defeats of 1915 had dealt a heavy blow to the prestige of monarchical rule and the Government. Since the Emperor and his Government were unwilling to compromise with the demands of the popular representatives and of public opinion, while the army—its officers and the rank and file— sided with the Duma, the profound discord between the Government on the one hand and the army and nation on the other at last gave rise to a popular and military movement directed to bring about the overthrow of that Government.

From its very inception, the Russian Revolution was not only a popular but also a military revolution. The troops took part in it, and it was precisely their participation which assured its success. Not in vain did one of the organs created by the revolutionary movement receive the name of "Petrograd Soviet of Workmen's and *Soldiers'* Deputies." Subsequently, Soviets of Soldiers' Deputies were formed in every unit of the army, both in the rear and at the front, and took a most active part in the revolutionary movement.

CHAPTER IV

THE SUPREME POWER IN THE HANDS OF THE PROVISIONAL GOVERNMENT

ALL the central administrative and legislative organs of the pre-revolutionary period had ceased to exist. The monarchy had voluntarily surrendered its powers by the abdication of Nicholas II and by the refusal of Michael Alexandrovich to accept the throne.

The Duma, which had headed the revolutionary movement and had created, through its Provisional Committee, the Provisional Government, continued to exist, but only in the form of its Provisional Committee, which had been reinforced by new members chosen to fill the places of those who had joined the Provisional Government. These additional selections were made at a private conference of the members of the Duma. The President of the Duma, however, requested the deputies to remain in Petrograd and from time to time he called private meetings; but the Duma never met again as a legislative body. Prorogued by Nicholas II on the eve of the Revolution, it was not reconvoked by the Provisional Government, but eked out a dreary existence, meeting only privately in the Tauride Palace, which was being more and more occupied by various Soviet committees and institutions.

As regards the upper house, the State Council, no one even thought of it. If the Duma, which had enjoyed an enormous prestige throughout the land, even according to the testimony of the members of the Petrograd Soviet of Workmen's and Soldiers' Deputies, was permitted thus to sink into oblivion, the State Council, which had played the part of an effective curb on the liberal legislative projects of the Duma, of course aroused no sympathy anywhere and played no part whatever after the Revolution. The old Council of Ministers, whose members had already been dismissed from their posts by order of Nicholas II at his abdication, when he appointed Prince Lvov as Prime Minister, yielded its place to the Provisional Government.

In this way all the highest organs of the former Government came to an end, and by virtue of the successful Revolution (which was recognized subsequently also by Grand Duke Michael, when he refused the throne), the vast prerogatives of those organs were vested in the Provisional Government. This found itself to be the successor to the power of the Sovereign, to the legislative chambers, and to the Council of Ministers. It acted as head of the State and as the possessor of political sovereignty in relations with foreign Powers. In its capacity of supreme authority within the State, it also acted in matters of domestic policy and addressed to the inhabitants and to the army declarations which took the place of the imperial manifestos. In these declarations were outlined the fundamental problems of administration and legislation confronting the Provisional Government. As an example of such announcements we may cite the very first declaration, issued 6th March 1917:

FROM THE PROVISIONAL GOVERNMENT

Citizens of Russia:

The great task is accomplished! By the mighty assault of the Russian people the old order has been overthrown. A new, free Russia is born. The great Revolution crowns long years of struggle. In the Act of October 17, 1905, under the pressure of the awakened popular forces, Russia was promised constitutional liberties. These promises, however, were not kept. The First Duma, interpreter of the nation's hopes, was dissolved. The Second Duma suffered the same fate, and the Government, powerless to crush the national will, decided, by the Act of June 3, 1907, to deprive the people of a part of those rights of participation in legislative work which had already been granted. In the course of nine long years there were wrested from the people, step by step, all the rights they had won. Once more the country was plunged into an abyss of arbitrary and despotic rule. All attempts to bring the Government to its senses proved futile, and the titanic world struggle into which our country was dragged by the enemy found the Government in a state of moral decay, estranged from the people, indifferent to the fate of our native land, and steeped in the infamy of corruption. Neither the heroic efforts of the army, perishing under the crushing burdens of domestic chaos, nor the appeals of the popular representatives, who had made common cause in the face of the national peril, availed to lead the former Emperor and his Government into the path of coöperation with the people. And when Russia, owing to the arbitrary and fatal actions of her rulers, was threatened with the gravest disasters, the nation was compelled to take the power into its own hands. The revolutionary enthusiasm of the people, who were fully conscious of the gravity of the moment, and the determination of the Duma, have created the Provisional Government, which considers it to be its sacred duty to realize the hopes of the nation and lead the country toward free citizenship. The government trusts that the spirit of patriotism exhibited during the struggle of the people against the old régime will also inspire our gallant soldiers on the field of battle. For its own part, the Government will spare no effort to assure to our army everything that may be indispensable in order to bring the War to a victorious conclusion. The government will faithfully observe the alliances which bind us to other Powers, and it will unswervingly fulfil the agreements entered into by the Allies. While taking measures to defend the country against the foreign enemy, the Government will at the same time consider it to be its primary duty to enable the will of the people in the matter of the form of government to find expression, and it will convoke within the shortest time possible a Constituent Assembly on a basis of universal, direct, equal and secret suffrage, insuring that the gallant defenders of our native land who are now shedding their blood on the fields of battle, shall also participate in the elections. The Constituent Assembly will pass the fundamental laws which will secure to the nation the inalienable rights of justice, equality and liberty. Conscious of the heavy burden of the wrongs which have been oppressing the country and impeding the creative enthusiasm of the people at a time of sore trial, the Provisional Government deems it necessary at once, before the convocation of the Constituent Assembly, to guarantee to the country definite legal provisions for the safeguarding of civic liberty and equality, so as to enable all citizens freely to apply their spiritual resources to creative work for the benefit of our country. The Government will also undertake the enactment of legal provisions to assure to all citizens, on a basis of universal suffrage, a share in local government elections. At this moment of national liberation, the whole country remembers with pious gratitude those who, in the struggle for their political and religious convictions, fell a prey to the vindictiveness of the old régime, and the Provisional Government will regard it as its first duty to bring back from their exile, with full honors, all those who have suffered for the cause of our country. In fulfilling these tasks, the Provisional Government is inspired by the confidence that it will thus execute the will of the people, and that the whole nation will support it in its sincere endeavor to assure the happiness of Russia. This belief inspires it with courage. Only in a loyal coöperation of the entire people with its own efforts, can it see a pledge of the triumph of the new order.

March 6, 1917.[1]

In virtue of its principal mission—the institution of a Constituent Assembly—the Provisional Government was bound to give full scope

[1] *Vestnik Vremennago Pravitelstva*, 7th March 1917.

to its legislative prerogatives. At one of the first meetings of the Provisional Government, the question arose as to the manner in which laws should be passed in this post-revolutionary period. One member of the Government held that the new laws ought to be issued under Article 87 of the Fundamental Laws, as temporary measures which would remain in force only until the convocation of the Constituent Assembly. This suggestion, however, met with little favor among the other members of the Government, who took the view that the Provisional Government enjoyed temporary legislative authority, pending the convocation of the Constituent Assembly. Of these legislative powers, the Provisional Government made extensive use. It promulgated a series of acts to give effect to the pledges of the official declaration of 6th March: a liberal amnesty was granted forthwith, capital punishment was abolished, and then, on 20th March, a decree was issued abolishing all restrictions on personal civic rights based upon race and creed.

The Finnish and Polish problems likewise were settled by the Provisional Government. In the Grand Duchy of Finland all the laws which guaranteed its autonomy[2] were restored, and, moreover, a complete program was adopted for the further development and consolidation of the constitutional rights of Finland, providing at the same time for the preservation of a common sovereign authority and the prerogatives of the Russian State as a whole.

The Polish problem was settled by the recognition of Poland's independence within her ethnographic boundaries, provision also being made for a reunion of the three separate parts of the country into a single independent State. As Poland was then occupied by the troops of the enemy, it was out of the question to embody in the form of a definite law the plan for Polish independence, as was done with respect to the constitutional guarantees of Finland. For this reason, the Provisional Government confined itself to a declaration, in the form of a manifesto addressed to the Poles, in which the idea of independence for Poland was proclaimed quite definitely.

"Liberated from their yoke," the manifesto[3] read, "the Russian people recognize also the absolute right of the brotherly Polish nation to shape its own destiny. Faithful to the agreements concluded with the Allies and loyal to our common task of combating militant Germanism, the Provisional Government regards the creation of an

---

[2] Avdeev, *op. cit.,* Vol. I, p. 63.   [3] *Ibid.,* pp. 98-99.

independent Polish State, formed of all the territories where the majority of the population is Polish, as a reliable pledge of lasting peace in the new Europe. United with Russia by a free military union, the Polish State will serve as a staunch bulwark against the encroachment of the Central Powers upon Slavdom. The liberated and united Polish nation itself shall determine its political constitution, after an expression of its will in a constituent assembly to be convoked in the capital of Poland and chosen by universal ballot. Russia hopes that those nationalities which are linked with Poland by centuries of a common life will at the same time obtain a firm guarantee of their civic and national existence. It will be the task of the Russian Constituent Assembly to ratify conclusively the new union and to give its consent to those changes of the territory of the Russian State which are necessary for the formation of a free Poland."

For the preliminary discussion and solution of a number of problems arising from the creation of an independent Poland, there was created a special Liquidation Commission under the presidency of M. Lednitsky.

Besides giving effect by legislation to a series of very important measures, the Provisional Government also assumed the complicated functions of administration. The commissaries of the Provisional Committee of the Duma handed over the Ministries and other central government departments to the Ministers of the Provisional Government. The entire personnel of the Ministries remained at their posts and only individual officials who were known as outspoken opponents of democratic principles and of the new régime were compelled to resign.

As the highest power in the land, the Provisional Government took care to appoint a new Commander-in-Chief of all the armies in the field. By a telegraphic order dated 2nd April and signed by the Prime Minister, General Alexseev was appointed Commander-in-Chief. Moreover, by agreement between the Commander-in-Chief and the Minister of War, considerable changes were made among the officers filling the higher commands.

To prepare a law on the elections to the Constituent Assembly, the Provisional Government created a Special Council of experts and representatives of the political parties.[4] The statutes of this Special

---

[4] Concerning the organization of this Special Council and its labors, *see* Chapter V.

Council and the draft of the electoral law for the Constituent Assembly were prepared by the committee of jurists attached to the Provisional Government; this was an advisory body appointed to draft legislation, but its chief function was to revise and edit the legislative acts of the Government. This Juridical Committee of which M. Kokoshkin was chairman and Baron Nolde, MM. Maklakov, Adzhemov, Lazarevsky, and the Executive Secretary of the Provisional Government, M. Nabokov, members, played a conspicuous part in the affairs of the Provisional Government. It acted, so to speak, as a collective counsellor and advisor to the Government on legal points, and it proved exceedingly helpful in complicated problems of public law.

As the Provisional Government had been chosen by the Provisional Committee of the Duma, the Ministers would from time to time appear at the Tauride Palace to render an account of their activities to the Provisional Committee. At times, individual Ministers would report also to private meetings of members of the Duma still in Petrograd. But the Duma itself appeared to have withdrawn voluntarily from active political life. Simultaneously with the collapse of the dualistic constitutional monarchy and the *de facto* repeal of the Fundamental Laws of the Empire, the Duma, by the consensus of opinion among the majority of deputies, regarded itself as removed from affairs of State.

The Provisional Government was considered as carrying on the policy and ideals of the Duma itself. That is why both the Provisional Committee of the Duma and private meetings of its members, after hearing the reports of the Ministers, invariably voted them their confidence and never raised the question of a convocation of the Duma. Besides, there was the fact that of the most active deputies, some had joined the ranks of the new administration, and others had left town for other places throughout the country, to act as representatives of the Provisional Government in one capacity or another.

In this manner the Duma relegated itself to the background while its place was gradually occupied by the increasingly aggressive Soviet institutions. The Provisional Government, which had come into being with the indirect participation of the Petrograd Soviet, and had the Associate President of this Soviet, Kerensky, as a member, was forced immediately after its organization to reckon with the endeavor of the Soviet, but especially of the latter's Executive Committee, to exert their influence upon the administrative and legislative activities of the Provisional Government.

Let us now turn to the consideration of what the Soviet institutions represented at the outset of their career. To begin with, the Provisional Government during the initial period of its activity had to deal only with the Petrograd Soviet of Workmen's and Soldiers' Deputies and its Executive Committee. In the previous chapter we have seen that the Soviet, while refusing to take part in the selection of the Provisional Government, nevertheless exerted a certain influence upon the shaping of its program. Gradually, however, the attempt to influence the Government and its policy found more and more supporters in the Petrograd Soviet and its Executive Committee. At the same time, following the example of the Petrograd Soviet, similar organizations of workmen and soldiers were springing up all over the country on the initiative of the Socialist parties and in the wake of the rising revolutionary wave. These provincial Soviets were organized along the same lines and principles as the Petrograd Soviet. They were composed of delegates from the factories and reserve regiments. Also, as was the case in Petrograd, they elected executive committees. Thus the Soviet institutions of Petrograd came to be the pattern on which the Soviets were fashioned throughout the country.

From 29th March till 3rd April there met at Petrograd a congress of deputies from the provincial Soviets. This congress was intended to serve the purpose of forming a closely knit all-Russian Soviet organization and of setting up, in the place of the Executive Committee of the Petrograd Soviet, an All-Russian Soviet Executive Committee. But in view of the comparatively small number of delegates (about 400, representing only 82 cities, besides executive committees of army units) the organizing committee of the congress found it impossible to claim that this gathering had any constituent powers or could function as the First Constituent Soviet Congress; for this reason the assembled delegates of the provincial Soviets declared themselves to be merely a preliminary all-Russian congress.

Nevertheless this conference proceeded to discuss and decide the most important questions of current politics, including that of the mutual relations of the Provisional Government and the Executive Committee of the Petrograd Soviet, and reorganized the latter into an All-Russian Executive Committee. This reorganization of Soviet executives was effected in a very crude manner, by the simple process of adding sixteen members to the ranks of the Petrograd Soviet Executive Committee from among those attending the all-Russian conference, and this enlarged committee the conference decided to recognize as the All-Russian Executive Committee. The election was organized on the basis of proportional representation for the various groups composing the membership of the Conference.[5]

After the Executive Committee of the Soviet of Petrograd had thus been augmented and transformed into an all-Russian organ, and as it began its work, the question of its internal reconstruction was raised. The relatively large amount of business to be attended to required the creation of separate sections or departments to consider and decide the great variety of different problems presented. Such departments were accordingly created and to some extent reconstructed from those departments and committees which had existed under the Petrograd Executive Committee. Their jurisdiction, it is true, was not clearly defined; nevertheless, there could be distinguished within the All-Russian Executive Committee the following departments: foreign relations, food supply, agrarian, economic.

Thus, as a result of the conference, there was formed a central all-Russian Soviet organ known as the All-Russian Executive Committee, and around it grew up institutions which took part, side by side with government departments, in current political affairs. The question was also raised of setting apart all those matters that affected only the city and region of Petrograd, and of forming a special Petrograd Soviet distinct from the All-Russian Executive Committee. Such a separation, however, was effected only at the Soviet congress of June; meanwhile, there was established within the All-Russian Executive Committee a City Department, having charge of the Soviet Administration of Petrograd.

The Soviet institutions kept on growing and consolidating their influence. Relations between the Provisional Government and the Executive Committee of the Petrograd Soviet at the time of the formation of the Government had been established on the basis of a formula: "As far as—just so far." *As far as* the Provisional Government was following a policy agreeable to the Soviets, *just so far* the Soviet organizations were willing to support it. But within a few days after the establishment of the Provisional Government, Steklov

[5] Avdeev, *op. cit.,* Vol. I, p. 173.

came out in the Soviet with the proposal that mere public control on the part of the Soviets was not sufficient and that it was necessary, by a gradually increasing and well-organized pressure, to compel the Provisional Government to pursue a policy agreeable to the Soviet.

The Soviet agreed with Steklov and appointed a special Contact Committee, including among its members, Skobelev, Steklov, Sukhanov-Gimmer, Filipovsky, and Chkheidze. Subsequently, after the reorganization of the Soviet institutions, the place of the Contact Committee was taken by the Bureau of the Executive Committee. The members of the Contact Committee would go to the Marinsky Palace, which was made the seat of the Government, and in one of its halls would be held conferences between them and the members of the Provisional Government.

Some of the proposals of the Committee were accepted by the Government; others were rejected. But no direct pressure upon the Provisional Government, as demanded by Steklov, was exercised. The Government continued to pursue the policy which seemed to it most appropriate, taking into account the desires of the Contact Committee, but refusing to be guided by its demands. The idea of the organizers of the Contact Committee—Steklov and Sukhanov— was that there should be not merely "contact" with the Provisional Government, but pressure upon it and supervision of its activities. The resolution adopted at the meeting of the Soviet of Workmen's and Soldiers' Deputies on 7th March, concerning its attitude toward the Provisional Government, was couched in the following terms:

First, acting in accordance with the decision of the Soviet of Workmen's and Soldiers' Deputies and with the general policy laid down by it, the Executive Committee of the Soviet of Workmen's and Soldiers' Deputies finds it necessary to adopt immediate measures to keep the Soviet informed regarding the intentions of the Government; to keep the latter, in turn, informed regarding the demands of the revolutionary people; *to exert influence upon the Government* for the purpose of satisfying these demands; and to exercise constant supervision over their execution. Second, to carry out this resolution, the Executive Committee of the Soviet of Workmen's and Soldiers' Deputies elects a delegation composed of the following comrades: Skobelev, Steklov, Sukhanov, Filipovsky, and Chkheidze, and it instructs them at once to enter into relations with the Provisional Government, with a view to appropriate negotiations. Third, after the result of these negotiations has become known, to elect a delegation for the establishment of permanent relations with the Council of Ministers, as well as with individual Ministries and government departments, for the purpose of carrying into effect the demands of the revolutionary people.[6]

The Soviet of Workmen's and Soldiers' Deputies also received very favorably the motion of Sukhanov to set up a special Soviet Committee on legislative proposals, which was to draft bills for new revolutionary legislation and transmit these through the Soviet to the Provisional Government, insisting that the Government should publish them as laws. However, even though such a committee was actually formed by the Soviet, the results of its work were quite negligible.

Another proposal of Sukhanov received with favor by the Soviet urged the appointment of delegations, or persons specially authorized by the Soviet, who should constantly watch over the activities of the various Ministries, "penetrate all pores of the Government, and gradually take into their own hands the organic work of the State, or, at least, acquire there the dominant influence," as the author of this proposal himself wrote.[7] To realize this object, Sukhanov proposed to set up a regular system of infiltration of the Soviet delegates into the Ministries. In each Ministry, in the ranks of the ministerial council, there were to be special Soviet delegates who should be fully informed of the affairs of the Department and "advise" the Minister.

All these plans, however, were ahead of the times; they were meant to drive the Soviet from the very outset of the Revolution toward a line of action which it actually took at a later stage. The committee on legislative proposals, as was stated above, although appointed, betrayed practically no sign of life. As for the delegations to the Ministries, they visited the Ministries and were listened to, but not obeyed.

The Contact Committee, likewise, failed to exercise any influence or control, and its work was confined to mere conversations with members of the Government and to the submission of sundry projects, which were by no means always accepted. In the beginning, the usual

[6] *Petrogradski Sovet Rabochikh i Soldatskikh Deputatov* (*The Petrograd Soviet of Workmen's and Soldiers' Deputies*), Minutes of meeting, Moscow, 1925, pp. 26-27.

[7] Sukhanov, *op. cit.*, Vol. II, p. 81.

procedure was for the Provisional Government to appoint several of its members to carry on the conversations with the Soviet committee. Later on, when the most important problems had to be considered, sessions were held also in the evening, and these were usually attended by the entire Government, or, at all events, a majority of the Ministers. Sometimes the members of the Provisional Committee of the Duma would be invited to these joint sessions of the Provisional Government and Contact Committee. These meetings, however, at no time passed resolutions. Responsible decisions were adopted exclusively by the Provisional Government, since it alone possessed full power within the country. The representatives of the Left wing of the Soviet were dissatisfied because the Contact Committee failed to show sufficient initiative. "Matters are altogether in bad shape with this Contact Committee, which is to reflect generally the mutual relations between the Soviet and the Provisional Government," complained Sukhanov in a speech to the All-Russian Executive Committee of the Soviets about the middle of April. "The Contact Committee confers with the Council of Ministers in a tone and form that appear strangely intimate, especially of late. We put questions to the Government and we address requests to it just as any organization or group might do. The Ministers listen to us, they give us the facts, and then, most of the time, they refuse our requests."[8]

It will thus be seen that during the first two months of its existence the Provisional Government concentrated in its own hands all the prerogatives of the supreme power in the land. Chosen by the Provisional Committee of the Duma, it constituted a Russian revolutionary government of popular origin and nation-wide recognition. Its principal and fundamental task was to lead the nation to the Constituent Assembly, and only to the sovereign will of the latter should the Provisional Government be responsible. For this reason, the original revolutionary authority, the Provisional Committee of the Duma, never made the claim that the Provisional Committee, or even assemblies of the members of the Duma, should be entitled to control the activities of the Provisional Government, or, still less, to insist upon any responsibility of the Ministers to the Provisional Committee of the Duma. If the Ministers actually did appear before the Provisional Committee, as well as before private meetings of the members of the Duma, to report to them, it was not meant to signify

[8] Sukhanov, *op. cit.*, Vol. III, p. 208.

any political responsibility of the Ministers to Duma circles, but rather a desire to act in harmony with the original organ of authority created by the Revolution.

The Soviet institutions, on the other hand, were anxious to set up a system of mutual relationship under which the Provisional Government should remain under their constant pressure and control. However, during the first two months of the Revolution, the Soviet institutions proved powerless to establish such domination, and the Provisional Government succeeded in maintaining unimpaired all its prerogatives and independence, leaning upon the general support of the nation and of the army.[9]

On the anniversary of the opening of Russia's First Duma,[10] 27th April, the Provisional Government decided to call a joint session of the deputies of all four Dumas, believing that such an assembly of all the former members of the lower house would prove a better and more perfect mirror of public opinion than would be the Fourth Duma, on the one hand, and the Petrograd Soviet, on the other. The Provisional Government had urgent need of the support of a repre-

[9] Here are a few illustrations of the attitude of the army in the field toward the Provisional Government during the period mentioned, which we quote from Sukhanov, *op. cit.*, Vol. II, p. 296. From Minsk the base of the Russian Western Front, the elected army authorities telegraphed to the Provisional Government: "In unity is strength; in divided authority is perdition. The Duma, invested with the confidence of the nation, created the Provisional Government, to which we have sworn allegiance, and for which we are prepared to work with redoubled vigor in order to achieve victory over the enemy. Soldiers and workers of the Petrograd Soviet, we beg you, do not hinder, but help us by supplying us with munitions and arms. We beg you not to create any divided authority."

Another message came from the firing line at the front, which read as follows: "The Divisional Committee of Officers' and Soldiers' Deputies of the Forty-Second Infantry Division, in expressing its absolute confidence in the Provisional Government, demands that no party, organization, or class shall place obstacles in the way of the fulfilment of its announced program. Convinced that only a victorious conclusion of the War can assure our liberty, we request the Soviet of Workmen's and Soldiers' Deputies to facilitate for the Government the continuation of the War."

[10] The first Duma was convoked and dissolved in 1906; the second, in 1907; the third Duma was convoked in 1907 and dissolved in 1912, upon the expiration of its normal term of five years; and the fourth Duma was convoked in 1912.

sentative body which would reflect the various shades of public opinion. The convocation of the Constituent Assembly was still remote; the Soviets reflected the views of a mere fraction of the population and the Fourth Duma represented chiefly the interests of the landlords.[11] The members of the First and Second Dumas on the other hand had been chosen on the basis of the original election law not yet distorted by Stolypin's *coup d'état* of 3rd June 1907 and had thus been genuine representatives of public opinion in Russia.

The Prime Minister and the other Ministers addressed the joint session of the members of the four Dumas, reporting on the work accomplished, and deputies spoke in turn. This, however, was all; no permanent organ was created which might have acted as the representative of the four Dumas and lent its authoritative support to the Government at critical moments.

The Provisional Government succeeded in maintaining an independent position in its dealings with the Soviet institutions up to the crisis at the close of April. After that, under the influence of the agitation launched by the Soviet leaders in connection with the publication, on 28th April, of the note of the Minister of Foreign Affairs, Milyukov, to the Allied Governments,[12] dealing with the aims of the War and Russia's participation in the common struggle against the Central Powers, there arose the question of a change of government policy in the matter of war aims and relations with the Allies.

In connection with the agitation stirred up among the Soviet leaders and the Executive Committee of the Soviets, after the contents of Milyukov's note had become known, the Provisional Government decided to call a joint meeting of the Provisional Government and the Soviet Executive Committee. To this meeting were also invited the members of the Provisional Committee of the Duma. On the evening of 20th April, after the session had been opened at the Marinsky Palace, the Ministers made their reports to the Assembly on current affairs, while Milyukov acquainted them with the recent developments in foreign policy. This was the first instance of a joint meeting of the Provisional Government and of the Executive

[11] For an analysis of the electoral system under which the Fourth Duma was elected, *see* pp. 12 *sqq.*

[12] For the text of this note, *see* Milyukov, *op. cit.,* Vol. I, p. 92. The political side of the crisis is discussed in *ibid.,* pp. 91-117, and in Sukhanov, *op. cit.,* Vol. III, pp. 254-443.

Committee of the Soviets.[13] This session may be regarded as the fore-runner of the impending coalition.

A similar joint session was held on 4th May, when the participants approved the list of candidates for the new coalition government and listened to the reading of the declaration of the proposed new Government.[14]

Formally, the government crisis began only on 30th April, with the declaration of the Minister of War and Navy, Guchkov, that "in view of the situation in which the Government, and especially the Minister of War and Navy, have been placed, I [Guchkov] can no longer with a clear conscience perform the duties of Minister of War and Navy, and share the responsibility for the heavy sin that is being committed against the country."[15]

Guchkov's resignation broke the deadlock[16] in so far as the question of changing the membership of the Government was concerned. The post of Minister of War and Navy was now vacant, and the question was: By whom should it be filled, and how? The leaders of the Petrograd Soviet, who were in favor of a coalition Government, composed partly of Socialists and partly of non-Socialist Ministers, defended the idea that the Socialist Ministers must first obtain permission from the Soviet to accept their portfolios. The same view was held also by a majority of the Ministers of the Provisional Government. An official proposal to reconstruct the Government upon a coalition basis was even forwarded on 27th April by the Prime Minister, Prince Lvov, to Chkheidze, in his capacity of President of the Soviet, so as to bring the proposal to the notice of the Executive Committee and the parties represented in the Soviet.

The Minister of Foreign Affairs, Milyukov, on the contrary, was unalterably opposed to the idea of a coalition Government; he also defended the theory that there could be no change in the composition of the Provisional Government which had pledged itself by oath to bring the nation to the threshold of a Constituent Assembly. The ideas of Milyukov, however, were supported only by a minority of his colleagues, and the Provisional Government decided to fill up its ranks with Socialist Ministers. To Milyukov, as an opponent of a

[13] Avdeev, *op. cit.,* Vol. II, p. 57.   [14] *Ibid.,* pp. 103 and 106.
[15] *Rech,* 1st May 1917.
[16] Milyukov, *Rossya na perelome,* Vol. I, pp. 68-69.

dilution of the Provisional Government by the inclusion of Socialists, there was left but one alternative—to resign.

The new Government was formed of representatives of the Socialist parties, who joined the ranks of the Government with the sanction of the Soviet[17] and of the original Ministers who remained in the Provisional Government. At the same time, seeing that the Socialist Ministers were selected by the Soviet and therefore responsible to the Soviet institutions, the Ministers belonging to the Constitutional-Democratic Party likewise stipulated as an indispensable condition of their consent to take office that their candidacies be approved by the Central Committee of the Constitutional-Democratic Party. Of the three Constitutional-Democratic Ministers who remained in the Government, one—Nekrasov—resigned his membership in the party, and the other two—Shingarev and Manuilov—together with the new Minister, Prince Shakhovskoy, were authorized by the Central Committee of the Constitutional-Democratic Party to join the new Government.

In this way there was constituted, after the crisis of the close of April and beginning of May, a new Government upon a basis entirely different from that of the first Provisional Government. The original membership of the Provisional Government had been chosen by the Provisional Committee of the Duma. This Government had been homogeneous in its composition; with the exception of the Minister of Justice, all its members supported the political tenets held by the Progressive Bloc of the Duma. It recognized no authority higher than itself, and it was responsible to none but the Constituent Assembly which was to be convoked.

The Second Provisional Government was a coalition, made up of three different groups. The first and fundamental group was composed of those Ministers who remained over from the first Provisional Government and had no organized social or political group behind them. These were Prince Lvov, Prime Minister and Minister of the Interior; Tereshchenko, Minister of Foreign Affairs; Nekrasov, Minister of Transport; Konovalov, Minister of Commerce and Industry; Lvov, Procurator of the Holy Synod; Godnev, State Controller. The second group, small in numbers, comprised the three Constitutional-Democratic Ministers, Shingarev, Manuilov, and Prince Shakhovsky who had joined the Government with the sanction

---

[17] Piontkovsky, *op. cit.,* p. 108.

of the Central Committee of the Constitutional Democratic Party. The third group was made up of the six Ministers, Kerensky, Chernov, Pereverzev, Peshekhonov, Tseretelli, and Skobelev, who entered the Government with the sanction of the Petrograd Soviet of Workmen's and Soldiers' Deputies and with the approval of the All-Russian Peasant Congress.

In circumstances such as these, it is only natural that the Contact Committee should have ceased to meet, the more so as some of its own membership had now entered the ranks of the Provisional Government and the latter itself had been transformed into something like a contact committee in permanent session. The Soviet leaders had at last penetrated to the very core of the government machinery. The principle of the continuity of revolutionary authority was observed in so far as the new Ministers delegated by the Soviet and by the Central Committee of the Constitutional-Democratic Party were appointed to their posts by the Provisional Committee of the Duma. This, however, was an empty formality, for the new Ministers, strictly speaking, were the delegates of the Constitutional-Democratic Party and of the Soviet of Workmen's and Soldiers' Deputies.

CHAPTER V

THE PROBLEMS OF THE WAR AND THE PROVISIONAL GOVERNMENT. PREPARATIONS FOR ELECTIONS TO THE CONSTITUENT ASSEMBLY

THE Provisional Government was confronted, in a more acute form, with the same problems of national defense and of efficient organization with which the Imperial Government had had to deal. The War, having already lasted so long, was engulfing ever increasing masses of the people, and the supply of the immense Russian army with munitions and provisions, coupled with the maintenance of proper transport facilities, presented an extremely arduous problem. It should be borne in mind, moreover, that the Provisional Government was compelled to continue the organization of the national defense under conditions far more difficult than had obtained under the imperial régime. The latter had at its disposal a huge administrative apparatus which had worked for decades under the direction of the Ministers of the autocratic sovereign, and the basis of the political order had been firmly established by the Fundamental Laws. The Provisional Government, on the other hand, was forced to elaborate the basic principles of its program and to reform the administrative machinery in great haste, as it went along.

At the same time the Provisional Government had to attempt to carry into effect a number of measures called for by the exigencies of the Revolution; the improvement of conditions for the working class, the reorganization of industry, the establishment of a Ministry of Labor, the regulation of relations between capital and labor, and so forth. This is how the Minister of Commerce and Industry, M. Konovalov, in an address to the representatives of the press[1] defined the problems of the Provisional Government. He began by saying that the Government "must lean on the support of organizations representing the general public and labor." He then continued, "On the one hand, it must lean on the support of organizations representative of trade and industry in the form of various local institu-

---

[1] This interview with the representatives of the press took place on 29th March 1917. For a report, *see Torgovo-Promishlennaya Gazeta*, No. 65, 1917.

tions, such as trade exchanges, chambers of commerce, and on the organizations representing the laboring masses." As regards the problems facing the Government, he regarded them as being of a threefold character: (1) problems connected with the War; (2) those dealing with the satisfaction of the new demands presented by the Revolution; (3) those connected with the conclusion of peace and the restoration of industry to a peace footing. So long as the third problem had not yet assumed primary importance, the first place should belong to problems of national defense. Among these, the most vital were those of the supply of fuel and metals to the railways and manufacturing establishments working for the defense of the country. The Special Council on Fuel should be reorganized and the entire business of the fuel and metal supply concentrated in the hands of the Ministry of Commerce and Industry, for which purpose there had already been created the new post of a High Commissioner for the supply of the country with metals and fuel.

Among the problems of the second group, the labor problem, Konovalov declared, held the center of his attention; and he outlined to the representatives of the press a complete program of measures to be taken in the field of labor legislation.[2] Three weeks later, on 14th April, speaking to the members of the Moscow Trade Exchange, Konovalov urged upon his hearers the importance of industrial reorganization in the interest of the national defense.[3]

"Under existing conditions," said the Minister, "when the country lacks some of the most essential commodities, when factories and other industrial plants are forced to reduce their output on account of the shortage of raw materials and fuel, when transport is disorganized, and when it is necessary, nevertheless, to satisfy the innumerable demands of the front, no other course is open than a certain amount of governmental intervention in private commercial and industrial relations and the admission of a broad public representation and of the democratic elements to a share in the regulation of our commercial and industrial life. We have already a number of committees, such as the Cotton, Linen, Wool, Leather Committees, whose object it is to supply the factories and mills with the necessary raw materials, to attend to the stores of army supplies, and, in a

[2] It does not fall within the scope of the present work to give an analysis of the labor program of the Minister.

[3] Cf. *Torgovo-Promishlennaya Gazeta,* No. 78, 1917.

certain measure, to see to the distribution of manufactured goods among the inhabitants and the army at the front. I presume that we ought to go farther in this direction. Not only is it necessary to reorganize the existing committees so as to impart to them a more broadly representative public character and enlarge their functions, but we must also create, according to the demands of life and the lessons of experience, new committees for a number of the most important commodities. Among the functions of all these committees, which should be made organs of the Ministry, there should be included, in addition to the business of distribution, the task of fixing prices."

While the Ministry of Commerce and Industry was to attend to a proper organization of work in the factories and mills employed for the national defense, the Ministry of Agriculture was charged with the duty of organizing the supply of provisions for the army and for the larger urban communities. As regards the Ministry of Transport, it was required to maintain proper transport facilities by rail and water; in order to deal more effectively with the difficulties of food supply, the system of fixed prices for grain was continued in force, and this was followed by the establishment of a government grain monopoly.

The Special Councils created by the Law of 17th August 1915 proved incapable, composed as they then were, of satisfying those demands that the Revolution had made urgent. However, the very constitution of these special Councils was such as to offer the Provisional Government an opportunity of altering and enlarging their membership. We will recall that the chairman of each Special Council had the right to delegate a certain number of representatives of his department to the Special Council over which he presided, so that the Ministers of the Provisional Government were in a position at any time to recall such representatives as might prove unsatisfactory, and appoint others in their stead. Besides, each Special Council had representatives from various government departments, and these, likewise, might be recalled and replaced by others. Lastly, the chairmen of the Special Councils were empowered to invite experts whose coöperation might prove useful.

Changes of this nature were now in fact inaugurated by the Ministers who were chairmen of the Special Councils. The only exception was the Special Council on Food Supply. At the very beginning of the Revolution there had been formed, under the direct charge of Shingarev, who had been appointed Minister of Agriculture in the Provisional Government, a special committee on food supply, to take charge of the food supply of Petrograd and its garrison. This committee included members of the Duma and representatives of the Soviet and of various organizations. Subsequently this committee, reformed and enlarged, came to be known as the State Food Committee (*Obshchegosadarstvenni Prodovolstvenni Komitet*), and took the place of the Special Council on Food Supply.[4]

In matters connected with the food supply, the Minister of Agriculture acted in concert with the State Food Committee, and the decisions of the latter were executed by the orders of the Minister of Agriculture. The membership of the State Food Committee consisted of four representatives of the Provisional Committee of the Duma, five representatives of the Soviet of Workmen's and Soldiers' Deputies, five representatives of the Soviet of Peasants' Deputies, four representatives each from the All-Russian Union of Zemstvos and Towns, six representatives of the coöperative associations, three representatives of the war industries committees, three representatives of the Permanent Council of the Congresses of Representatives of Commercial Exchanges and Agriculture, two representatives of the Chamber of Agriculture, and one representative of the Executive Committee of the Congress of Statisticians. As for the representatives of the Ministries, they joined the Committee in a consultative capacity.

Thus the State Food Committee, taking the place of the Special Council on Food Supply, was already a revolutionary governmental organ, in so far as its membership was concerned. The place of the deputies chosen by the Duma itself was now taken by four representatives of the Provisional Committee of the Duma, and the delegates of the State Council were replaced by representatives of the Soviet of Workmen's and Soldiers' Deputies.

The remaining Special Councils, after they had been augmented and reorganized by their chairmen, continued to function for a considerable time under the Law of 17th August 1915. Gradually, however, in the course of the summer of 1917, they, too, were reorganized on the model of the State Food Committee.

Next to the urgent tasks of combating the economic disorganiza-

[4] *Cf. Promishlennost i Torgovlya,* Nos. 8-9, 1917, p. 213.

tion and providing for the defense of the country, the most important duty of the Provisional Government was that of preparing for the election of the All-Russian Constituent Assembly. As early as 25th March 1917 the Provisional Government instructed the Juridical Committee to draft a bill providing for a Special Conference to prepare a law for the elections to the Constituent Assembly.[5] It was decided to invite for this purpose the coöperation of authorities on constitutional law, to be selected by the Government, in addition to representatives of the most important political parties and various public bodies. As chairman of the Conference, the Government appointed Kokoshkin, the Chairman of the Juridical Committee.

The unwieldy and complicated organization of this Special Conference was naturally bound to impede very much the progress of the work. To begin with, there was a delay at the outset because the representatives of the Soviet of Workmen's and Soldiers' Deputies were chosen very late. Another delay was due to the fact that the Provisional Government, as also the Special Conference itself, held the view that the elections to the Constituent Assembly could be properly organized only after the new democratic organs of local municipal and rural government had begun to function, and that to assist these bodies there should be formed township, district, provincial, and city election boards. All these organs of local government were to prepare the lists of voters, and the election boards would manage the elections.

Had the Provisional Government, immediately after its assumption of power, simply appointed the local electoral boards, it would have greatly hastened the convocation of the Constituent Assembly, and it is probable that the Revolution would have taken a different course.

As it was, the final composition of the Special Conference on an Electoral Law for the All-Russian Constituent Assembly was determined only on 25th April. The Chairman and the Vice-Chairman were appointed by the Provisional Government, and the very numerous members of the Conference were in part appointed and in part elected. The Provisional Government appointed experts on constitutional law and on statistics, etc.; the elected members were the representatives of political parties, of the Executive Committee

---

[5] *Torgovo-Promishlennaya Gazeta,* No. 64, 1917; Avdeev, *op. cit.,* Vol. I, p. 121.

of the Soviet of Workmen's and Soldiers' Deputies, of the army in the field, of the Peasants Union, of the coöperative associations, the Unions of Zemstvos and Towns, and other public bodies.

The first session of the Conference, held on 25th May, was opened by the Prime Minister, Prince Lvov, who delivered a short address. This was followed by a speech from the Chairman of the Conference, Kokoshkin. "Upon the heaving sea of our Revolution," said Kokoshkin, "there moves a life-giving and creative spirit. This life-giving and creative spirit consists in the principle of national sovereignty, recognized throughout the land. Toward this principle we must hold our course. This is the lodestar which is alone capable of guiding us out of the difficulties which we now experience. To organize our life, to consolidate our liberty upon lasting foundations—this can be accomplished only by the ideal of national sovereignty."[6]

At the first session the representatives chosen by the political parties and public organizations were confirmed as members of the Conference; at the same time two committees were appointed to draft measures with regard to the right to vote, the right to be elected, and the electoral system. The most disputed and burning questions which came up for discussion were those dealing with the proportional and simple majority systems, the participation of the army in the elections, and age qualifications. Later, when we examine the provisions of the electoral law of the Constituent Assembly[7] we shall deal with the substance of these questions; for the present, we confine ourselves to a few remarks concerning the nature of the work accomplished by the Conference.

General sessions were held as occasion required, usually two or three times a week. The rest of the time was devoted to the work of the committees, other committees being subsequently added to the first two appointed on 25th May. In the course of the summer of 1917, the Conference completed its work, and the several parts of the Statutes on the Elections to the Constituent Assembly were ratified by the Provisional Government and made public as fast as the Conference completed the draft of its proposals.

On 20th July, the Provisional Government ratified the first section of the law, embodying the fundamental principles of the same and the first stages of election procedure; it dealt with the institu-

[6] Cf. *Torgovo-Promishlennaya Gazeta*, No. 108, 1917.
[7] *See below*, Chapter VI.

tions which were to arrange the elections, with the preparation of the lists of voters, and with the lists of the candidates.[8] On 11th September the remaining sections of the law were ratified[9] with the exception of that dealing with the method of elections in the army and navy, which was finally ratified as Section III[10] on 23rd September.

This piecemeal publication of the law was due to the desire of the Conference to organize as soon as possible the institution designed to take charge of the elections; for that reason that part of the Statutes which dealt with the fundamental provisions of the suffrage and with the institution of the electoral boards became effective as early as 20th July.

Another matter of an urgent character was the preparation of materials for agrarian reform and the drafting of a bill for a land law to be submitted to the Constituent Assembly. For this purpose, a resolution was adopted by the Provisional Government on 19th March, declaring the inauguration of agrarian reform to be urgent; and for the purpose of collecting materials, determining the area of available free land, elucidating the conditions and forms of land tenure, and similar purposes, the Provisional Government decided to establish at the Ministry of Agriculture a Central Land Committee.[11] Professor Posnikov, member of the Duma, was appointed chairman. The Central Land Committee acted as a permanent advisory organ of the Provisional Government, and sometimes the plenary sessions of the Committee were attended by representatives of local land committees.

[8] Cf. *Vestnik Vremennago Pravitelstva*, 21st July 1917.
[9] *Ibid.*, 12th September 1917.   [10] *Ibid.*, 24th September 1917.
[11] *Torgovo-Promishlennaya Gazeta*, No. 59, 1917.

CHAPTER VI

THE FIRST SOVIET CONGRESS. THE MOSCOW STATE CONFERENCE. THE LAW OF THE ELECTIONS TO THE CONSTITUENT ASSEMBLY

THE second Provisional Government, as we have seen, was a coalition. The Ministers belonging to the Constitutional-Democratic Party represented the Central Committee of that party. The Socialist Ministers, again, had been delegated by the Executive Committee and the Soviet, and they were held accountable to these two institutions for their actions as Ministers. Soon after their appointment, these Socialist Ministers delivered speeches at the Petrograd Soviet outlining the policy that they would follow as members of the Government. Chernov promised that he and his Socialist colleagues would be the faithful spokesmen of the Soviet and that "in the present situation, it will be practically the Soviet of Workmen's and Soldiers' Deputies that will decide matters of State, while the Ministers will merely execute them."[1]

At the same session Trotsky formulated that slogan for the organization of a revolutionary Government which was to become the rallying cry of Lenin and the Bolsheviks; he criticized the midway position of the coalition as a position of divided authority, and he asserted that a genuine, undivided authority would arise only after the "next step" had been taken, that is, after the transfer of power to the Soviets of Workmen's and Soldiers' Deputies.[2] "After that," said Trotsky, "there will begin a new epoch, an epoch of blood and iron, only no longer a struggle of nation against nation, but of the suffering, oppressed class against the ruling classes."[3] The slogan of a transfer of all power to the Soviets was definitely formulated also in the instructions drawn up for the election of the Soviet deputies, which declared that "all power in the country must belong exclusively to the Soviets of Workmen's and Soldiers' Deputies."[4]

[1] *Cf.* Avdeev, *op. cit.,* Vol. II, pp. 148-150.
[2] L. Trotsky, *Sochinenya (Works),* Vol. III, Part I; Moscow, 1925, pp. 45-46.
[3] Quoted in Milyukov, *Historya vtoroi russkoi revolutsii,* Vol. I, p. 107.
[4] Instruction of 7th May, *Cf.* Sukhanov, *op. cit.,* Vol. IV, p. 39.

The task of consolidating, extending, and developing the Soviet organization was accomplished by the First All-Russian Soviet Congress, which opened on 3rd June 1917 in Petrograd. Strictly speaking, this was not the first congress, as one had already been contemplated and convoked in Petrograd at the close of March and beginning of April, and had been turned into a mere "conference" only because of the insufficient attendance.[5] At this conference a special committee was elected and instructed to call the First Soviet Congress. This Congress was attended by 1,090 delegates representing Soviets of Workmen's and Soldiers' Deputies, the front and rear Soviet institutions of the army, and some peasant organizations. In its composition, therefore, the Congress was a body representing the workers and soldiers, supplemented in a small measure by chance representatives of the peasantry.

With regard to the coalition Government the Congress took the attitude that the principle must be established that the Socialist Ministers were responsible to the All-Russian Central Executive Committee, which was to be elected by the Congress, for the entire domestic and foreign policy.[6]

The Congress resolved to elect as its executive organ the All-Russian Central Executive Committee, to be composed of 300 members. Half of this number were to be chosen by the Congress by ballot; 100 members were to be chosen among local workers in the provinces; and 50 members were to be included in the All-Russian Central Executive Committee from the Petrograd Executive Committee. The provincial members of the All-Russian Central Executive Committee were to return to their homes and carry on the work there, while the remaining 200 members were to form the permanently functioning All-Russian Central Executive Committee with headquarters in Petrograd.

The elections were held on the basis of proportional representation, and in this way there were represented in the All-Russian Central Executive Committee the various political groups in proportion to their numerical strength at the Congress. The All-Russian Central Executive Committee, in turn, appointed from among its own members a Bureau composed of fifty persons to act as a permanent organ, while the general direction of all work was concentrated in the hands of the presiding board, at the head of which was placed

[5] *See supra,* p. 62.　　　　　　　[6] *Rech,* 9th June 1917.

Chkheidze. To discuss matters of prime importance and receive the reports of the Ministers, joint sessions were to be summoned of the All-Russian Central Executive Committee and the Executive Committee of the Congress of Peasant Deputies.

Lunacharsky, addressing the Congress, raised the question of doing away altogether with the Duma. "If the Duma is dead," said Lunacharsky in the course of the debate, "let us bury it, because its decomposition is contaminating the revolutionary atmosphere with its cadaverous smell. We ought to deliver the finishing stroke to this suspicious-looking corpse which shows a tendency to revive."[7] The Congress adopted a resolution that the Duma should be abolished, but nevertheless the latter remained in existence until the autumn.[8] Besides his proposal to do away with the Duma, Lunacharsky outlined before the same Congress a program for transferring all governmental power to the control of the Soviet institutions, and he already foreshadowed, along lines not yet clearly defined, the future demand of the Bolsheviks for the destruction of the Provisional Government and its replacement by the All-Russian Central Executive Committee of the Soviets. These proposals, however, were as yet merely the schemes of the minority at the Congress, while the majority stood for rendering support to the coalition Government.

The coalition Government no longer possessed the full power that had been enjoyed by the original Provisional Government. The Socialist Ministers were responsible to the Soviet institutions, the Constitutional-Democratic Ministers were held accountable to the central committee of their own party, and both the former and the latter were liable at any moment to be recalled from their posts. Thus we see that the Ministers of the coalition Government, instead of being responsible to the future Constituent Assembly, in accordance with the oath of the members of the original Provisional Government, were held responsible to class and party organizations. Nevertheless, the Provisional Government continued, as heretofore, to exercise the rights and powers of head of the State and of legislation and administration; to it alone belonged the supreme leadership of the

[7] Sukhanov, op. cit., Vol. IV, p. 425; cf. also V. Vladimirova, Revolutsya 1917 goda (Revolution of 1917), Moscow-Leningrad, 1924, Vol. III, pp. 265-266.

[8] See also speech delivered by Trotsky on 9th June 1917 (Trotsky, op. cit., Vol. III, Part I, pp. 122-124).

political life of the country. All the numerous State institutions, those inherited from the old régime as well as those created during the Revolution, were subject to the Provisional Government.

With some of the newly created advisory organs of the Provisional Government we are already familiar. Such were the Special Conference on an Electoral Law for the Constituent Assembly[9] and the Central Land Committee.[10] Besides these responsible advisory organs, one of which was to pave the way for the Constituent Assembly, while the other was to prepare material for agrarian reform, a large number of others were brought into existence. Let us consider those of most importance.

In view of the fact that the Provisional Government was greatly overburdened with work, many of the less important matters were turned over to a committee which included among its members the Assistant Ministers, presided over by the Assistant Minister of Education, Professor David Grimm.[11] To this "Little Council of Ministers," as it came to be known, were submitted such matters as were not of importance in principle, but still required immediate settlement.

At the Ministry of the Interior there were at work committees of experts, appointed by the Ministry to prepare and work out in detail the reform of local government institutions. The general direction of the work of reform of local government was entrusted to the Assistant Minister of the Interior, M. Avinov. In these committees were elaborated the plans for the establishment of the *volost*[12] zemstvo, reforms of the rural and municipal statutes; as well as reforms of administrative jurisdiction and local police. All draft enactments framed by these committees were submitted to the Provisional Government for examination, after which they were published.

Some of the Special Councils that had been formed in 1915 under the régime of the Emperor, for the purpose of improving the supply of the army and combating the economic difficulties, continued to exist under the Provisional Government, after certain changes had been made and additional members invited to take part in their work. The Special Council on Fuel retained for the longest period

---

[9] *See supra*, p. 76.   [10] *See supra*, p. 78.

[11] This conference was organized on 19th March 1917, *cf. Torgovo-Promishlennaya Gazeta*, No. 59, 1917.

[12] *See supra*, p. 14, n. 19.

its original personnel, as provided by the Law of 1915. Finally, however, this body too had to give way to a new organ, the Central Fuel Committee, under the decree of 25th August 1917.[13]

To this committee were granted the same rights as the Special Council had possessed, but in composition it differed materially from its predecessor. The Chairman of the Central Fuel Committee was appointed by the Provisional Government on the recommendation of the Economic Committee.[14] The Central Fuel Committee was composed of representatives of merchants and manufacturers, fuel consumers, regional fuel committees, public bodies, and the Executive Committee of the Soviet Congress. It will be seen that not only were there no representatives of the State Council in this committee, but not even members of the Duma. The committee met once in three months, and for the management of current business it might appoint a bureau of six to ten members.

The idea of establishing the Economic Council emanated from Soviet circles. At the very beginning of the Revolution, an economic section had been established in the Petrograd Soviet. Later, about the middle of May, a program of economic policy had been elaborated, according to which the Provisional Government should create special organs to elucidate the economic needs of the country and to carry out an active economic policy, directed to the compulsory regulation of the entire economic life of the country. Influenced by these proposals, the Provisional Government, by resolution of 22nd June,[15] established the Economic Council and its executive organ, the Supreme Economic Committee. The rights and duties of the latter were defined rather vaguely; but it was to have general charge of economic policy.[16] In the hands of this newly created government institution there were to be gathered together all the strands of the economic administration of the country and therewith also the supply of the army.

The first coalition Government lasted less than two months. A new crisis began with the resignation of the Ministers belonging to the Constitutional-Democratic Party; this was precipitated by the

[13] *Torgovo-Promishlennaya Gazeta*, No. 184, 1917.   [14] *See infra*, n. 16.
[15] *Cf. Vestnik Vremennago Pravitelstva*, 26th June 1917.
[16] For details *see* S. O. Zagorsky, *State Control of Industry in Russia during the War* (Yale University Press), 1928, of this Series of the *Economic and Social History of the World War*.

policy of the Provisional Government in regard to the autonomy of the Ukraine. Beginning early in July, the crisis lasted until the end of that month, when a solution was finally reached. After the resignation of the Prime Minister, Prince Lvov, the reorganization of the entire Government was entrusted, with the concurrence of all remaining Ministers, to Kerensky, who was now chosen Prime Minister by his colleagues in the Government. Accordingly, by virtue of the resolution of the Provisional Government of 13th July, Kerensky received the resignations of all the Ministers, who remained at their posts only temporarily, and he was to appoint a new Government, not on the basis of representation for the various political parties and social groups, but on individual merits. However, none of Kerensky's attempts to form a new Government were successful, and the old Ministers, together with the few new ones appointed to fill the vacated posts (Efremov, Bernatzky, Baryshnikov), were obliged temporarily to continue in office, pending the meeting of a conference at the Winter Palace, to which the new Prime Minister had transferred his residence. To this conference were invited representatives of the most important political parties; the Constitutional-Democrats, Radical-Democrats, Populist-Socialists, Socialist-Revolutionists, and Menshevik Social-Democrats.[17] There were also invited to this conference, which was held in the night of 21st-22nd July, the President of the Duma, Rodzyanko, the President of the All-Russian Central Executive Committee of Soviets, Chkheidze, and the President of the Executive Committee of the Congress of Peasant Deputies, Avksentev. The political parties were represented at this

[17] "The Bolsheviks and the Mensheviks form the two wings of the Russian Social-Democratic party. At the London conference of the party in 1903 the fateful division between Bolsheviks and Mensheviks was inaugurated as consequence of disagreement concerning the problem of leadership and discipline. The Bolshevik (meaning 'majority') group carried its proposal by a very narrow majority and captured the Central Council of the party from which they excluded their opponents. The insignificance of the immediate cause of the split was only apparent: in truth the division arose from the fundamental opposition between the democratic orientation of Plekhanov (the Menshevik leader) and the oligarchical spirit of Lenin. The struggle was not suggested by a deep cleavage of principle among the rank and file of the party, but by disputes among its intellectual leaders. Questions of principle arose, however, in the course of the Russo-Japanese War and of the first revolution (1905)." (Sir Paul Vinogradoff, *Encyclopaedia Britannica*, 1922).

gathering by all those members of their central committee who happened to be in town. Strictly speaking, only the Constitutional-Democratic Party, the party of Social-Revolutionists, and the Menshevik Socialist-Democratic Party could be regarded as important; for the others were not strong enough numerically to take a place among the most important parties of Russia during that period.

This conference, which lasted until six in the morning, ended by recognizing Kerensky's authority to form a new cabinet.[18] Kerensky, having just returned from his trip to Finland and heard the report of Nekrasov, who had acted as chairman of the night session, accepted the resignation of all the Ministers and opened negotiations with the representatives of various political and social groups, as well as with separate individuals.[19]

In this way it came about that the second coalition Government, whose constitution was made public on 25th July, was nominally selected by Kerensky himself. Actually, however, both the All-Russian Central Executive Committee of the Soviets and the Congress of the Constitutional-Democratic Party (the latter had just met, first in Moscow and then in Petrograd) took part in forming the new Government. The responsibility of the Ministers to their party and to the Soviet organizations was not formally recognized; *de facto*, however, they did consider themselves responsible to these organizations.

During the government crisis in July, the Ministers, trying to relax the dependence of the Provisional Government upon the Soviet

[18] The political motives which prompted the parties to grant authority to Kerensky to form a new Government were not identical, but the practical conclusions remained the same. *"To Kerensky must be given the power* to form a Provisional Government that will stand upon a nationwide basis, and will be composed of persons who are not to be responsible to any organizations or committees,"* declared the resolution of the representatives of the Constitutional-Democratic Party. And the Socialist-Revolutionists, in common with the Social-Democrats, said: *"We have full confidence in Comrade Kerensky;* let him employ the representatives of all parties which are prepared to work on the basis of the program worked out by the Provisional Government under the chairmanship of Kerensky on July 8." (*Cf.* Milyukov, *op. cit.,* Vol. I, p. 36.)

[19] *See* Kerensky's letter of 22nd July, in V. Vladimirova, *op. cit.,* Vol. III, pp. 341-342.

organizations and political parties, sought to create some representative organ which would have neither a class nor party character, but might serve in the place of a national representative body. This seemed especially desirable because the lack of an exponent of organized national public opinion enabled the extreme political currents to exert pressure on the Government, while the elections to the Constituent Assembly were being delayed. In its resolution of 12th July, the Provisional Committee of the Duma had also pointed out that the Government must lean on the support of "all the vital forces of the country"; and at the session of the Provisional Government on the same date Godnev, the State Controller, had moved that the Government should afford the opportunity to all social groups not represented in the Soviets to submit their views to the Government.

For this purpose Godnev proposed to convoke at Moscow a large conference, to be attended by the All-Russian Central Executive Committee of Soviets, the Duma, and representatives of local government, coöperative societies, trade and industry, trade unions, universities, and others. He was supported in this proposal by Peshekhonov and Kerensky.[20]

Thus originated the idea of calling the Moscow State Conference. It was to be opened on 13th August. To the leading group of Ministers, with Kerensky at their head, it seemed that such a conference should strengthen the power and authority of the Provisional Government. The Moscow State Conference was intended to serve as a counterpoise to the aggressiveness of the Soviets. About 2,000 representatives were to attend it. Invitations were sent out to the members of all the four Dumas;[21] to 100 representatives each of the All-Russian Central Executive Committee of Workmen's and Soldiers' Deputies, the Central Executive Committee of the Congress of Peasant Deputies, and of the army at the front; 400 were to attend as representatives of the new rural and municipal government; 300 were to be delegated by the coöperative societies; 150 by the trade unions; 120 by associations of merchants and manufacturers; 100 each were to be invited from agricultural societies and associations of landowners, as well as from the universities and other institutions of learning; eighty members were to represent the interests of the national minorities, and seventy-five the organizations of the wage-earning intelligentsia.

[20] *Cf.* Milyukov, *op. cit.*, Vol. I, pp. 22-23.   [21] *See* p. 67, n. 10.

The Moscow State Conference was thus intended to represent the most diverse strata and groups of Russian society. It was to represent actually "all vital forces of the country," and although, to be sure, it was far from perfect, since various public and social groupings overlapped, it must be admitted that Russian public opinion was more or less fully reflected at that gathering. The primary object of calling this conference had been to obtain the support of a non-partisan opinion for Kerensky's Government; but as the preparations for the meeting proceeded it became evident that the conference was not going to rest satisfied with the part of a spectator of ministerial performances, but that the representatives of the various groups that had received invitations to attend would be anxious to express their own views on the political program of the Government. To meet these desires of the members of the Moscow State Conference, it was decided that the session should extend over three days.

The Moscow State Conference was not called for any constructive work; it was unsuited to that purpose both by reason of its large membership and of the briefness of its session. In these circumstances, of course, it was idle to suppose that it could undertake any legislation or control of the Government, or any change in its constitution.[22] The Government of the second coalition, therefore, continued in power after the Moscow State Conference, down to the third government crisis (which was to be the last before the Bolshevist *coup d'état*), when Kerensky formed his second Government, the Government of the third coalition.

In the meantime, the Special Conference on an Electoral Law for the Constituent Assembly was completing its labors, and the text of the law as drafted by the conference and gradually ratified by the Provisional Government, was being published section by section.

At the basis of the electoral law for the Constituent Assembly lay the principle of "universal and equal suffrage, without distinction of sex, by means of direct elections and secret ballot, and on the principles of proportional representation."[23] In this manner was introduced in Russia, in lieu of the very imperfect system of elections to

[22] The political history of the three-day session of the Moscow State Conference has been given in detail by Milyukov, *op. cit.*, Vol. I, pp. 112-151, and by Sukhanov, *op. cit.*, Vol. V, pp. 147-175. *See also* Piontkovsky, *op. cit.*, pp. 150-156.

[23] Article 1.

the Duma, a system of suffrage that may be regarded as one of the most democratic of modern times.

One of the thorniest problems presented in the organization of the elections was that of the participation of the soldiers who were on active service. Nearly the whole of the male population of the country between 18 and 43 years of age had been enlisted and mobilized, and was either at the front or in the reserve units in the rear. The denial of the suffrage to all those who were mobilized, whether on active service or in the various reserve formations of the army and navy, would exclude millions of citizens from the ballot. The Special Conference which framed the electoral law was fully aware of the inconvenience and danger attending the participation of soldiers in the elections. Nevertheless, it could not bring itself to deprive them of the opportunity to cast their votes.

Special electoral districts were formed exclusively for the troops at the front (five such districts were the Northern, Western, South-western, Rumanian, and Caucasian fronts), for the Baltic and Black Sea fleets, and two districts comprising the Russian troops in France and the Balkans.[24] As for the reserve troops stationed in the rear, they were to take part in the voting with the civilian inhabitants in the districts where they happened to be quartered.[25] Owing to these provisions, the elections were profoundly influenced in a great number of electoral districts by the large masses of soldiery quartered there. There were cities, and even entire districts, where the number of voters belonging to the local civilian populace proved to be smaller than the number of military voters.

The elections were held in the same manner among the troops at the front as within the country, with the observance of the system of proportional representation. The only differences were that the period of voting was prolonged from three to seven days and the electoral district was not a territorial unit, but an army unit: a sector of the front, a separate army, a regiment. Hence the election boards who supervised the elections among the troops came to be known as frontal, army, and regimental election boards, according as they managed the electoral business along an entire front, within a separate army, or in a single regiment.[26] A further difference was that the elections in the navy and among the Russian troops in

[24] Article 212.   [25] Article 203, annex.   [26] Article 214.

France and in the Balkans were conducted on the system of simple majority, and not on the proportional system. Furthermore, the navy was granted even more time for the holding of the elections than the army, namely, fourteen days. This was done for the convenience of such naval units as might be at sea at the time of the general elections.

The extension of the franchise to women did not meet with any serious opposition in the Special Conference, and in those electoral districts where no troops were quartered the women's votes played a decisive part, for the reason that women flocked to the ballot boxes in large numbers, while the male population between the ages of 18 and 43 had almost to a man been drafted into the army.

The voting age required for the elections to the Constituent Assembly was extremely low—20 years on election day.[27] The qualification as to age had been laid down not without hesitation or heated debates. The principal argument of those favoring the 20-year qualification was that it coincided approximately with the age limit of the younger men called to the colors.

The restrictions on the exercise of the franchise were very few in number. They were confined to the disfranchisement of the insane, deaf and dumb, persons placed under guardianship, fraudulent bankrupts, persons convicted of serious crimes, and those indicted by the courts for crimes involving arrest.[28] However, in addition to these classes of citizens denied the right to vote, two other classes were excluded solely on account of the circumstances of the time at which the elections to the Constituent Assembly were to be held. These two categories of disfranchised citizens comprised army deserters and offenders against army discipline, on the one hand, and members of the House of Romanov, on the other.[29]

The elections to the Constituent Assembly were held, as a general rule, by large electoral districts. The usual district comprised an entire *gubernya* (province). Votes were cast for lists of candidates, so that a voting paper contained the names of more than one candidate. All told, there were 75 electoral districts, of which two were formed by the capitals, Petrograd electing 12 deputies and Moscow electing 10. The remainder were either *gubernya* or regional districts. The total number of deputies to be chosen by the 73 electoral

[27] Article 3.   [28] Articles 4, 5, and 9.   [29] Articles 5, 6, and 9.

districts was 730.[30] To these districts should be added the five districts of the army in the field, two districts composed of the Baltic and Black Sea fleets, and two districts for the Russian troops in foreign countries. As has been stated before, the voting was for lists of candidates, and for the same lists throughout the same electoral district. The lists of candidates had to be submitted to the district election board not later than thirty days prior to the beginning of the election, and each list had to bear the signatures of at least one hundred voters of a given district and contain names of candidates numbering not more than one and a half times the number of candidates to which the given electoral district was entitled. The same candidate could not present himself in more than five electoral districts.[31] This question of standing simultaneously in more than one electoral district had been the subject of lively discussion in the Special Conference. Permission to stand in five districts at the same time was conceded only by way of compromise between two differing attitudes: one, in favor of candidacy in any number of districts; the other, demanding the restriction of a candidacy to a single district. The advocates of manifold candidacy pointed out that the conception of political parties in a country like Russia, with a population as yet poorly prepared for the universal suffrage, is linked with the names of popular party leaders, and that a popular name heading a list would attract votes. The opponents of manifold candidacies, on the other hand, claimed that the voters would be led into error if they were to vote for a list, the first three or four candidates on which might choose to represent some other district in which they had also been elected. The compromise by which a candidate was permitted to stand simultaneously in not more than five electoral districts was finally accepted by both sides.

The elections were carried out secretly by the deposit of printed ballot papers.[32] The law safeguarding the secrecy of the ballot was very carefully drawn. All lists of candidates submitted to the re-

[30] For the list of districts and specification of the number of deputies to be elected *see* the Decree of the Provisional Government of 23rd September 1917.

[31] The rules on candidates' lists will be found in Chapter V, Articles 42-54, of the Statutes on the Elections to the Constituent Assembly.

[32] Article 55; under Article 129 of the Statutes, in several districts the voting might be effected by balls instead of papers.

gional election board would be numbered by the board consecutively as they were presented, printed in vast numbers, and sent to the towns and villages for distribution among the voters. The right was also granted to the groups of voters who put forward these lists to announce a fusion of their lists. This meant that at the counting of the votes and at the apportionment of seats under the proportional system these combined lists would count as one.[33] The elections had to take place at the same time throughout Russia, and to be completed within a period of three days.[34] So long a period was provided because of the vast distances between the polls and the difficulties of communication.

After the voting had been completed and all the local election boards had finished counting the votes, the returns were forwarded to the district election board and the latter then had to determine which of the candidates had been elected. The seats were apportioned among the several lists in accordance with the d'Ondt system.[35]

The number of votes cast within the district for the several lists was divided successively by 1, 2, 3, 4, 5, and so on. The resultant quotients were set down in a descending order, one below the other, as many as were needed to get a descending series of quotients equal to the number of deputies to be elected in the district, and the last quotient was considered as the electoral denominator. On each list, that number of candidates was regarded as elected which equaled the number of times the electoral denominator was contained in the total number of votes cast for that list.[36] If a fusion of one or more lists in the district had been announced, the first apportionment was made as if the fused lists were one, and after this first apportionment a separate apportionment was made among the several lists that had been fused. In this calculation, likewise, the d'Ondt system was employed.

The apportionment of seats in the Constituent Assembly under the system of proportional representation had been approved at the Special Conference by a considerable majority of votes, notwith-

[33] Article 53.

[34] Article 72. In the army and the navy, as we have seen, the period was prolonged.

[35] Articles 89, 90, and 91.

[36] To facilitate the work of computation in the district election boards,

standing the objections registered against the plan by experts on constitutional law, with Professor Hessen at their head. The advocates of the majority system pointed out that great numbers of citizens were going to vote for the first time in their lives and that with the level of education then prevailing the voters would find it hard to grasp the idea of the proportional system and to cast their vote for a party ticket instead of a locally known candidate, for an abstract idea rather than a concrete individual. But the gist of the arguments of the majority in the Special Conference was that the proportional system represents the nation more justly, that it protects the interests of the minority, and that the difficulties of the proportional system are felt by the election board when it comes to the apportionment of the seats, rather than by the average voter.

If a candidate was elected simultaneously in more than one district, the All-Russian Central Election Board inquired of him in what district he preferred to claim his election, and if no reply was received from him it was assumed that he stood elected in that district where he had obtained most votes.[37] If a member of the Constituent Assembly vacated his seat, he was replaced by the candidate standing next to him on the list to which he belonged.[38]

The general supervision of the elections was exercised by the All-Russian Constituent Assembly Election Board, which was composed

arithmetical examples of possible calculations were given. One of these follows:

List No. 1 has a total of 51,000 votes;
List No. 2 has a total of 17,000 votes;
List No. 3 has a total of 88,000 votes;
List No. 4 has a total of 21,000 votes;
List No. 5 has a total of 9,000 votes;

The total votes on each list are divided by 1, 2, 3, 4, etc.:

List No. 1	List No. 2	List No. 3	List No. 4	List No. 5
1—51,000 (II)	17,000	88,000 (I)	21,000	9,000
2—25,500 (V)	8,500	44,000 (III)	10,500	4,500
3—17,000	5,666	29,333 (IV)	7,000	3,000
4—12,750	4,250	22,000 (VI)	5,250	2,250

The number which stands in the sixth place is 22,000. It is contained twice in the total votes on list No. 1 and four times in the total votes on list No. 3. Consequently two candidates on the first list, and four candidates on the third list should be considered as elected.

[37] Article 93.   [38] Article 94.

of a chairman appointed by the Provisional Government and of fifteen members appointed by the Provisional Government on the recommendation of the Special Conference on an Electoral Law for the Constituent Assembly. Locally, the supervision of the elections was entrusted to the regional (*okruzhnoi*), district (*uezdni*), and communal (*uchastkovi*) boards.

These boards were composed of representatives of the judiciary, of local government bodies, and of voters who had filed lists of candidates. Such a composition, of course, was calculated to secure the participation of the public in the management of the elections and to permit the exercise of effective control by the representatives of the voters and, consequently, of the political parties contesting in the elections; it provided likewise for the authoritative legal assistance of the judges.

The lists of voters were drawn up by the municipal, township (*poselok*), and *volost*[39] election boards. The voters were empowered to complain to the county election board and to the administrative department of the District Court of any irregularity admitted in the preparation of lists and in this way a guarantee was provided that the lists were correct. A characteristic feature of the procedure of complaint of such irregularities was that the complaints must be discussed in a public session of the county board.[40]

The electoral law of the Constituent Assembly was framed not only at a time of revolution, but also in the throes of a titanic war. The result was that both the Revolution and the War left their indelible stamp upon the law.

Subsequently, in 1918 and 1919, principles similar to those on which the Russian electoral law was based were introduced into many European electoral laws, with the exception, of course, of those extreme features of the Russian Act which were due to war-time needs. The complete realization of the idea of the universality of the suffrage, its extension to women, a low age qualification, and proportional representation—such were the four corner stones of the Russian electoral law. In their desire to establish guarantees for the participation of each and every qualified citizen in the elections to the Constituent Assembly,—the exponent of the sovereign will of the

[39] *See supra,* p. 14, n. 19.

[40] The procedure of compiling voters' lists is dealt with in Chapter IV of the Statute, Articles 25-41.

nation—the framers of the law strove to provide a democratic suffrage.

It is perfectly natural, of course, that the concession of the vote to soldiers, whether at the front or in the interior of the country, should have been due exclusively to the conditions of war—and, moreover, of the greatest war in history. To the framers of the law all the dangerous consequences of involving the army in politics and of holding elections in the trenches, in the face of the enemy, were quite evident. But to deprive the soldiers of the franchise might prove a still graver peril, as it might provoke an armed attempt to obtain the right to vote. These considerations prompted the Special Conference to extend the franchise to the army. In doing so, however, a grave mistake was made when the reserve troops in the interior were lumped with the civilian voters of the districts where such troops chanced to be stationed. Owing to the participation of the reserve troops who happened to be present, the results of the vote in districts where there were large numbers of such soldiers proved to be far from representative of the political views of the residents of those districts.

CHAPTER VII

THE DIRECTORY. RUSSIA PROCLAIMED A REPUBLIC. THE DEMOCRATIC CONFERENCE

THE last days of August wrought some changes in the central government machinery, in consequence of the uprising of the Commander-in-Chief, General Kornilov.[1] Kerensky, the Prime Minister, who was relying on the support of the Soviet to oppose the troops of Kornilov marching on Petrograd from the front, gratified some of the desires expressed by the Soviet Central Executive Committee in the domain of governmental reconstruction. On the other hand, the Executive Committee met the wish of the Prime Minister for the creation of a Council of Five, better known as the Directory.

During these days, filled with alarm, hesitation, and fear of the rapidly approaching troops of General Kornilov, the Prime Minister conceived the idea of forming a dictatorship of the Government, with a view to a more successful struggle against a military dictatorship. Holding that the Provisional Government was too complex, heavy, and unwieldy an apparatus, because of its size and, especially, because of its coalition character, Kerensky believed that at such a critical moment, when there was need of quick decision and bold action, full governmental power ought to be entrusted to a numerically small organ, to be presided over by the Prime Minister. Not prepared to insist upon his own personal dictatorship, Kerensky felt that a firm policy could be adopted without difficulty or delay if a Directory were formed.

The Soviet Central Executive Committee, during the night of 27th-28th August, for its part, deliberated on the question of reconstructing the Government. A number of speakers urged, against the idea of a Directory, the proposal to create a special representative body of all the groups and organizations that had been represented in the Moscow State Conference, but without the Duma. To

[1] For the history of the Kornilov revolt, cf. Milyukov, op. cit., Vol. I, pp. 152-291; Sukhanov, op. cit., Vol. V, pp. 215-369; Kerensky, Delo Kornilova (The Kornilov Affair), Petrograd, 1917, passim.

this was added the demand for the proclamation of a democratic republic and the dissolution of the Duma.

Kerensky's idea of forming a Directory was not favorably received by the Soviets. But, as a result of lengthy negotiations between Kerensky and the representatives of the Central Executive Committee, the latter finally ceased to oppose the creation of a Council of Five, and Kerensky, for his part, agreed to call a democratic conference of representatives of the "organized democracy and of the democratic organs of local government." He furthermore agreed to the proclamation of a democratic republic and the dissolution of the Duma.

However, while consenting to the formation of a Directory, or Council of Five, representatives of the All-Russian Central Executive Committee insisted, as an absolute condition of their consent, on the temporary nature of the Directory. It was to remain the supreme governmental organ only until the meeting of the democratic conference which was to find a method of reconstructing the Provisional Government.

The Council of Five was chosen at the session of the Provisional Government held during the night of 1st-2nd September. But the session was attended by only a few members of the Government, for many of the ministerial posts were vacant. This was due to the fact that the Ministers belonging to the Constitutional-Democratic Party had resigned at the outset of the Kornilov uprising, thereby causing another ministerial crisis. Soon after, some of the Socialist Ministers also resigned, and the Government remained a mere rump.

The creation of the Directory postponed the settlement of the crisis and the formation of a new Government to the day when the democratic conference should be called. In the hands of the Directory was now concentrated all political power, while the remaining Ministers continued to perform merely the technical functions of the administration of their Ministries. The formation of the Directory was decided at the same time as the proclamation of the republic, on 1st September 1917. The official communication read as follows:

Pending the final formation of a Government, and in view of the extraordinary circumstances of the present moment, the Provisional Government, in its session of September 1, has entrusted the direct management of affairs of State to the Prime Minister, Kerensky, the Minister of Foreign Affairs, Tereshchenko, the Minister of War, Major-General

Verkhovsky, the Minister of the Navy, Rear-Admiral Verderevsky, and the Minister of Posts and Telegraphs, Nikitin.[2]

The Provisional Government formed the Council of Five, from among its own members, for the purpose, as has already been stated, of enabling it to reach decisions more quickly. It was the practice of the Council of Five to report at the next session of the Provisional Government on the steps it had taken, but it often happened that decisions could no longer be revoked *post factum*. Thus it will be seen that the Council of Five was something in the nature of a dictatorship exercised not by a single Minister, but by five, who had charge of the most responsible branches of administration, under the presidency of the Prime Minister.

Concurrently with the establishment of the Directory, and in deference to the demands of the Soviet Central Executive Committee, a republican form of government was proclaimed on 1st September. Here follows the text of this Act, which was signed, not by all the members of the Government, but only by Prime Minister Kerensky and Minister of Justice Zarudny, the latter resigning immediately afterwards.

The mutiny of General Kornilov is suppressed. But it has caused great perturbation in the ranks of the army and throughout the country. Again a great danger threatens the destiny and the liberty of the nation. Deeming it necessary to put an end to the apparent vagueness of our form of government, and recalling the unanimity and enthusiasm with which the republican idea was accepted at the Moscow State Conference, the Provisional Government announces that the form of government of the Russian State is republican and it proclaims the Russian Republic. The urgent necessity for taking immediate and resolute measures for the restoration of order in the State has prompted the Provisional Government to vest the fulness of its administrative power in five of its members, with the Prime Minister at their head. The Provisional Government regards it as its principal task to restore order in the State and the fighting capacity of the army. Convinced that only a concentration of all the vital forces of the country can extricate our native land from the difficult situation in which it finds itself, the Provisional Government will strive to enlarge its personnel by inviting to its ranks representatives of all those elements which place the permanent and common interests of our country above the passing and private interests of

[2] *Cf. Novoe Vremya*, No. 14,867, 9th September 1917. *See also* Piontkovsky, *op. cit.*, p. 168.

parties or classes. The Provisional Government has no doubt but that it will accomplish this task within the next few days.[3]

It has already been shown in the course of the present volume that the form of Government in Russia at this period was *de facto* republican.[4] A final decision regarding the form of government was, however, to be taken by the Constituent Assembly, as the exponent of the will of the entire nation. Influenced by the representation of the Soviet Executive Committee, Kerensky consented to a formal confirmation of the existing state of affairs by an Act expressing the will of the Provisional Government. The Act of 1st September 1917 unquestionably exceeded the rights of the Provisional Government and anticipated the decision of the Constituent Assembly. It is characteristic that the proclamation of the republican form of government was made, as it were, incidentally, in an act which also included the announcement of relatively unimportant measures such as the creation of the Directory and the summons to the Democratic Conference. The reason for this procedure was that all the three elements of this Proclamation—Republic, Directory, Democratic Conference—constituted mutually dependent parts of the program of compromises adopted by Kerensky in agreement with the All-Russian Central Executive Committee of the Soviets.

A further demand of the Soviets was for a dissolution of the Duma and the State Council. It should be noted that the proclamation of the republic naturally implied the dissolution of both Duma and Council, which were legislative bodies of the constitutional monarchy. Having decided to proclaim the republic, Kerensky could not help agreeing at the same time to a dissolution of these two organs of monarchical government. Consequently, at the beginning of September, a decree was drawn up abrogating the powers of the Duma and abolishing the State Council; the publication of this decree, however, was delayed in view of the fact that the five-year term for which the Duma was elected would expire automatically in October.

Lastly, there was one more Soviet demand which was gratified. On 31st August, the All-Russian Executive Committee resolved to summon a Democratic Conference for the purpose of a final settlement of the question of governmental authority. In the meantime, Keren-

---

[3] Piontkovsky, *op. cit.*, p. 168.   [4] *Cf.* Chapter III.

sky, as if in expectation of the decisions of this "democratic parliament," governed the country with the aid of the Directory, confining himself to some regroupings within the ranks of the Ministers who had remained, while the Council of Ministers itself, with its rights greatly curtailed, was made to play merely the part of technical advisor to the Directory, in whose hands was now concentrated the supreme power.

For what purpose, by whom, in what manner, was the Democratic Conference called? The initiators of this Conference, which the Soviet leaders intended to serve as a corrective to the mistakes of the Moscow State Conference, were the Soviet representatives. The invitations were, therefore, sent out in the name of the Central Executive Committee. In summoning the Conference, the Soviet leaders intended to use its vote as a means of exerting constant pressure upon the Government, and to demand that the latter be responsible to the Conference. In fact, however, the most vital problem to be solved by the Democratic Conference was that of the organization of the Government. It was to settle the question whether the tradition of a coalition government should be perpetuated or not. Meanwhile, Kerensky, without waiting for the decision of the Democratic Conference, opened negotiations with the Moscow representatives of the Constitutional-Democratic Party and Moscow business circles. The official program of the Conference as planned by the Central Executive Committee was wide, although rather vague. The telegraphic invitation proposed "to assemble all the forces of the country in order to organize its defense, assist in its internal upbuilding, and speak a decisive word regarding the conditions which will safeguard the existence of a strong revolutionary authority."

As regards the composition of the Conference, it was proposed to summon only the representatives of the democratic elements, that is, of the Left wing of the Moscow State Conference. From the Democratic Conference were to be excluded all the so-called property-owning elements, all non-socialist currents of thought. It was only natural, under conditions such as these, that the Conference should from the outset have been a one-sided exponent of a mere fraction of the nation, instead of its entirety, as the Moscow State Conference had been. The Democratic Conference was doomed to be merely a faint, partial copy, drawn in radical colors, of its none too perfect model—the Moscow State Conference. As the meeting place of the

Democratic Conference, of course, revolutionary Petrograd was chosen.

It so happened, however, that the original plan of confining the membership to the Left wing of the Moscow State Conference could not be carried out quite consistently. Numerous and diverse democratic organizations announced their wish to be present, and the list of invited representatives kept gradually expanding until it reached the impressive total of 1,775 delegates, of whom 1,425 had a vote, while the rest were admitted in a consultative capacity. Among the most important representatives were 230 from the Soviets of Workmen's and Soldiers' Deputies, 300 from the municipalities, 200 from the zemstvos, 201 from the post and telegraph workers, 100 from the trade unions, 158 from the coöperative societies, 83 from army organizations. The other groups delegated a relatively small number of representatives, who spoke for the following elements: Soviet commissaries, Cossacks, peasant-soldiers, army officers, disabled men, combatant soldiers, economic organizations, food supply organizations and committees, the Peasant Union, teachers, medical assistants (*feldsher*), the Union of the Orthodox Clergy and Laymen, the press, the Ukrainian *Rada* (parliament), the Moslem Council, the Council of the National-Socialist party, the Georgian Inter-party Alliance, the Poles, and the Jews.

Thus the nucleus of the Democratic Conference was mainly composed of representatives of the Soviets and the new organs of democratic self-government. Relatively solid were the groups representing the trade unions, coöperative societies, army organizations, and post and telegraph employees. All the other organizations had been picked entirely at random and mostly for no other reason than that their representatives had applied to the All-Russian Central Executive Committee of Soviets for permission to attend the Conference. The representation was organized in a haphazard fashion, without any serious plan, and the sole principle determining the composition of the Conference was the purely negative idea of excluding every one who in one way or another might have anything in common with the property-owning elements.

There was, therefore, a fundamental fault in the very selection of representatives for the Democratic Conference—a deliberate partiality and, at the same time, an entirely unnecessary promiscuity. The critics from the Left, in the ranks of the Bolsheviks, argued that there was absolutely no need for the Conference and that a second congress of Soviets must be summoned as quickly as possible in order to elect a new All-Russian Central Executive Committee and exert pressure upon the Government. The critics from the Right, on the other hand, pointed to the purely artificial composition of the Conference.

The Democratic Conference opened its sessions on 14th September at the Alexandrinsky Theater in Petrograd. In view of the vagueness of its jurisdiction and the uncertainty of its political status, as a result of the attitude of the Government, the Conference found it rather difficult to decide precisely what should be the function of this "authoritative organ of the democracy." The Government, in its resolution of 5th September,[5] had declared that the Conference which was being summoned, unlike the Moscow Conference, which had been called by the Government itself, had no right to claim any official status whatever, that it was a purely private affair, summoned by a mere class organization—the Executive Committee of Soviets of Workmen's and Soldiers' Deputies. Therefore, the participation of the Ministers in the deliberations of this Conference was not regarded as obligatory. The Moscow State Conference had been organized by the Provisional Government, the Prime Minister had acted as its Chairman, and every member of the Government had been present. True, the Prime Minister, as well as the other Ministers,[6] addressed the Democratic Conference; but, conceived as a rival of the Moscow Conference, this assembly was unable to play the part which its sponsors expected from it, or to dictate to the Provisional Government the path it should follow.

The principal questions presented for the consideration of the Democratic Conference were those of a new coalition and of the establishment of some representative organ attached to the Provisional Government which might function permanently and serve as an exponent of public opinion.

After a lengthy discussion of the coalition problem, when the Conference proceeded to vote, it was found, first within the groups representing the various organizations, and afterwards also in the general assembly, that the Democratic Conference, according to the admission of Tseretelli, was incapable of adopting any decision on

[5] *Rech,* 6th September 1917.

[6] With the exception of the Minister of Foreign Affairs, Tereshchenko.

the question of government reconstruction. "The praesidium, having discussed the present situation," announced Tseretelli, "has unanimously decided that there is within the organized democracy no unanimity of will that could be translated into action." The fact is that, when a vote was taken on the question whether the Provisional Government ought to be reconstituted on a coalition basis, there were at first 766 for and 688 votes against, the coalition, with 38 members casting no votes. Subsequently, an amendment was adopted, to the effect that the coalition should be formed without the participation of the Constitutional-Democratic Party, the only important democratic non-Socialist party. This amendment was passed by 595 votes against 493, with 72 members not voting.

Naturally, this amendment resulted in an absurdity, for a coalition government could have no meaning at all unless it included members of the Constitutional-Democratic Party. Small wonder that, when the resolution was put to the vote together with the amendment, that is, for a coalition *without* the Constitutional-Democrats, those in favor of the coalition and also its opponents voted *against* the resolution, and the latter was rejected by 813 votes to 180, with 80 members casting no votes. Thus it came about that the Democratic Conference failed to reach a decision with regard to the most important issue of the moment. Formally, of course, this was explained by the mistake of the Chair, which permitted a vote to be taken on the amendment to the resolution after the latter had already been passed. Essentially, however, this merely served to demonstrate the absolute incapacity of the Democratic Conference for dealing seriously with the problem which confronted it.[7]

After this failure of the Conference to adopt a decision regarding the formation of a government, the Soviet leaders decided to divert its attention to the discussion of a possible organ that might serve as an exponent of public opinion, as a kind of substitute for a parliament.

The Bolsheviks, however, had an answer ready to this proposal. They had captured a number of local Workmen's and Soldiers' Soviets, including that of Petrograd, and, taking advantage of this local support by Soviets, they agitated in favor of granting controlling power to the second Soviet Congress which was due to assemble in October. To the Bolsheviks, it seemed desirable to have the

[7] *See* Milyukov, *Rossya na perelome*, pp. 108-109.

reconstruction of the Government postponed until that Congress, which should organize a government that would depend upon the Soviets. For the time being, they urged the Soviets to mobilize their forces. The resolution of 21st September passed by the Bolshevist Petrograd Soviet read:

The Soviets must at once mobilize all their resources, so as to be prepared for the new wave of counter-revolution and avoid being caught by it unawares. Wherever complete control is already in their hands they must under no circumstances surrender it. The revolutionary committees formed by them during the Kornilov days must have their entire machinery ready. To effect this unification and coördination of the measures of the Soviets in their fight against the approaching peril, and to settle the problems of the organization of the revolutionary authority, a congress of workmen's, soldiers', and peasants' deputies must immediately be convoked.[8]

In the meantime, the leaders of moderate socialism tried to correct the mistakes of the Democratic Conference and to solve the problem of a coalition Government. It was decided to submit the question who should compose the new Government to the Democratic Council which was to be chosen by the Democratic Conference and which was to play the part of a preliminary parliament for the Government. Once more a plenary session of the Democratic Conference was held, and Tseretelli moved the adoption of a resolution to the effect that the Conference should form from among its own members a representative body to be entrusted with the organization of a coalition Government, and that the latter should be responsible to the Democratic Council. Furthermore, the Conference was to appoint five of its members to treat with the Government on the question of government organization, and hear the report on the composition of the Democratic Council. Tseretelli's resolution was adopted by the Conference.

The Democratic Conference held one more session, to elect the members of the Democratic Council, after which it was dissolved. The task of organizing the Government was now turned over to the newly chosen Democratic Council. This Council, meeting during the night of 23rd-24th September, passed a very ambiguously worded resolution in favor of accepting a coalition Government. On the

[8] *Cf.* Sukhanov, *op. cit.*, Vol. VI, pp. 158-159.

24th, the third and last coalition Government, under the premiership of Kerensky, was formed of representatives of the Socialist parties, the Constitutional-Democrats, and the business interests.

The Bolsheviks accorded the third coalition Government a very hostile reception. The Soviet of Petrograd, which had just chosen Trotsky as its President, declared:

To a Government of absolute bourgeois authority and counter-revolutionary domination, we, the workers and garrison of Petrograd, will render no support whatever. We express our firm conviction that the news of the creation of the new Government will meet with only one reply from the revolutionary democracy: "Resign!" And relying upon this unanimous voice of genuine democracy, the All-Russian Congress of Workmen's, Soldiers', and Peasants' Deputies will establish a truly revolutionary Government.[9]

To combat these extremist tendencies and to organize the public opinion of the country, the Government decided to have recourse to the creation of the Preliminary Parliament, a permanent representative body to be composed of the representatives of various political parties and social groups. The history of its inception and construction is dealt with in the following chapter.

The Preliminary Parliament was intended to serve as a public backing for the Government until the meeting of the Constituent Assembly, the elections for which had been fixed for 12th, 13th, and 14th November.

Meanwhile, the Preliminary Parliament having been created, and the five-year term of the Duma having expired, the third coalition Government at last decided to yield to the persistent demand of the Soviets and to dissolve the Fourth Duma, which had played so large and important a part in the beginning of the Revolution.

[9] This resolution is quoted in Milyukov, *op. cit.*, Vol. I, p. 75.

CHAPTER VIII

THE PROVISIONAL COUNCIL OF THE REPUBLIC AND THE *COUP D'ÉTAT* OF 25TH OCTOBER 1917

THE idea of creating an organ which would express the public opinion of the country and thus serve as a basis of support for the Provisional Government was seized upon by the leaders of the Soviet organizations and put forward during the Democratic Conference in connection with the question of the reorganization of the Government. From among the members of the Democratic Conference was formed the Democratic Council, to which was entrusted the solution of the problem of a coalition Government, which had been attempted unsuccessfully by its predecessor. In the event of the Government being formed on a coalition basis, the representative body organized by the Conference was to be augmented by representatives of non-Socialist parties and groups, preserving, however, the preponderance of the representatives of the Democratic Conference. To this organ the Government was to be accountable and responsible. The selection of its members was to be made by the Conference, which would also choose five of its members to assist in the formation of the new Government and in framing the statutes of the representative organ.

Such were the basic principles of the projected Preliminary Parliament, as the contemplated representative body came to be called. Two plans were hastily drawn up: one, by Voitinsky, at the request of the All-Russian Central Executive Committee; the other, by the Government.[1] The Government proposed to limit the membership of the Preliminary Parliament to 231; Voitinsky planned for a membership of 300. Under the government plan, the leading position would belong to the representatives of the zemstvos and municipalities, numbering 110; under Voitinsky's scheme, this class of representatives would be given only 90 seats; and, while the government project allotted only 20 seats to the representatives of the All-Russian Central Executive Committee, Voitinsky gave them 75. As for

[1] *Cf.* comparison of these two drafts in *Novoe Vremya*, No. 14,878.

the representatives of the coöperative societies, they were granted a far larger vote under the government plan than under that of Voitinsky.

The functions of the Preliminary Parliament, under the government project, were to be purely legislative; under the Soviet project, they were not clearly defined and, therefore, not restricted. The government plan did not provide for any definite responsibility of the Government to the Preliminary Parliament; under the Voitinsky plan the Preliminary Parliament would be the source and basis of government authority, and the same organ would determine the responsibility of the Government.

Voitinsky's project was taken as the basis of the discussion of the Preliminary Parliament problem by the Democratic Conference. The Preliminary Parliament was intended to reflect, on a smaller scale, every political and social group in the Democratic Conference. Each group, party, or curia was expected to choose 15 per cent of its own delegation as members of the Preliminary Parliament. All told, 308 delegates were elected.

In the meantime, five members of the Democratic Conference were conducting negotiations with the Provisional Government concerning the organization of the Preliminary Parliament. When it was settled that the Government should be formed upon a coalition basis, it was decided to augment the Preliminary Parliament by representatives of non-Socialist parties and groups, which were to have 120 to 150 representatives in that body. There was, furthermore, worked out a plan of mutual relationships between the Preliminary Parliament and the Government. Thus, the Preliminary Parliament was to have the right to address the Government questions, but not interpellations.[2] It was to have only a consultative voice in legislation, and the proposal to establish the responsibility of the Government to the Preliminary Parliament was rejected practically without debate.[3] Tseretelli, who participated in these negotiations, was instructed to report on the principles of the contemplated Preliminary Parliament to the Democratic Conference, and the Provisional Government was entrusted with the task of issuing the statutes governing the Preliminary Parliament. Lastly, the Juridical Committee was charged with the work of drafting a measure determining its constitution.

[2] See supra, p. 23.   [3] Cf. Novoe Vremya, No. 14,880.

The newly organized Government of the third coalition formulated as follows its relations with the Preliminary Parliament, officially designated as the Provisional Council of the Republic:

In this struggle, as in its general policy, the Provisional Government, as the exponent of the will of the revolutionary nation, will act in the closest coöperation with the organizations of the people, seeing in such coöperation the most effective means of solving the important problems confronting the country. In order to assure to the revolutionary authority close contact with the organized forces of the public, and thereby to impart to this authority the indispensable stability and power, the Provisional Government will within the next few days draw up and publish the statutes governing the Provisional Council of the Republic, which is to function until the meeting of the Constituent Assembly. This Council, in which will be represented all strata of the population, and will include the delegates chosen by the Democratic Conference, will be invested with the right to address questions to the Government and obtain answers to them within a definite period, frame legislative proposals, and discuss all questions that may be submitted to it by the Provisional Government for examination, or that may arise on its own initiative. Leaning upon the support of such a Council, and maintaining inviolably, in accordance with its oath, the integrity and continuity of the governmental authority, the Government created by the Revolution will deem it its duty in all its acts to take into account the vast national importance of this Council, until such time as the Constituent Assembly shall provide a complete and perfect representation of the people of Russia.[4]

Tseretelli reported to the Democratic Council that an agreement had been reached. In spite of the fact that the principles on which it was proposed to organize the Preliminary Parliament differed in many respects from those sponsored by the Democratic Conference, the Democratic Council approved the formation of the Provisional Council of the Republic.[5] It only remained to realize the plan in practice.

The Juridical Committee of the Provisional Government at once

[4] Cf. *Novoe Vremya*, No. 14,882; also Piontkovsky, *op. cit.*, pp. 175-178.

[5] While it is true that the Democratic Council proposed to establish the principle of a "formal responsibility" of the Government to the Preliminary Parliament, Tseretelli explained to the Provisional Government that the establishment of formal responsibility would not be insisted upon at once, and that it was viewed by the Democratic Council merely as a program to be carried out in the Preliminary Parliament.

set to work to draft the statutes of the Preliminary Parliament. Tseretelli was invited to share in this work. He declared that the Government should be responsible to the Preliminary Parliament and that a vote of lack of confidence by the latter body ought to be followed by the usual consequences.[6] Nevertheless the statutes of the Preliminary Parliament were drafted on the basis of Adzhemov's[7] recommendations, and the Government was not made responsible to the Provisional Council of the Republic. The number of members was set down as 550, of whom 394 represented Socialist parties and groups, and 156 the non-Socialists.[8]

The Provisional Council of the Republic was thus made up of

[6] Cf. *Novoe Vremya*, No. 14,884.
[7] For contents of Adzhemov's draft *see Novoe Vremya*, No. 14,883.
[8] The membership was divided in the following manner:

I. *On the Lists of Democratic Organizations.*
(a) Parties.

1. Socialist-Revolutionists	63
2. Mensheviks favoring defensive war	62
3. Bolsheviks	53
4. Internationalists (United Social Democrats)	3
5. Popular Socialists (*Norodnii sotsialisty*)	3
6. Unity Group (Plekhanov's)	1
7. Ukrainian Social Democrats	1
Total	186

(b) Organizations.

1. Executive Council of Peasant Delegates	38
2. Zemstvo Group	37
3. Representatives of the troops at the front	25
4. Coöperative societies	18
5. Workers' coöperatives	5
6. Economic organizations	6
7. Land committees	5
8. Cossack self-government organizations	5
9. Cossacks	3
10. Railwaymen's Union	4
11. Post and Telegraph Workers' Union	2
12. Navy	3
13. Teachers' Union	2
14. Peasants' Union	2
15. Conference Bureau of Lawyers' Councils	1
16. Military District Committees	2
17. Provincial Executive Committees	4
18. Zemstvo workers	1

19. Women's organizations ... 1
20. Disabled soldiers ... 1
21. The democratic clergy ... 1
22. Various small democratic groups ... 15

Total ... 181

II. *On the Lists of the Property-Owning Groups (Non-Socialist Democracy and Bourgeoisie).*

1. Constitutional Democratic Party ... 56
2. Representatives of Trade and Industry ... 34
3. Council of Moscow Conference of Public Leaders ... 15
4. Council of Landowners ... 7
5. Cossacks ... 22
6. Academic Union ... 3
7. Radical Democratic Party ... 2
8. All-Russian Society of Editors ... 2
9. Women's Equal Rights League ... 2
10. Main Committee of the Women's Union ... 1
11. Old Believers ... 2
12. Theological Academy ... 1
13. The All-Russian Council of the Clergy and Laity ... 1
14. All-Russian Council of Teachers in Church Schools ... 1
15. Central War Industries Committee ... 1
16. Central Bureau of All-Russian Council of Engineers ... 1
17. National Minorities ... 5

Total ... 156

III. *Representation of National Minorities (Socialistic).*

1. Jews ... 4
2. Moslems ... 4
3. Ukrainians ... 2
4. White Russians ... 2
5. Poles ... 2
6. Lithuanians ... 2
7. Letts ... 1
8. [blank in the official text] ... 1
9. Esthonians ... 1
10. Armenians ... 2
11. Georgians ... 2
12. Council of Mountain Tribes of Caucasus ... 1
13. Volga nationalities ... 1
14. Buriats ... 1
15. Council of Socialist Parties ... 1

Total ... 27
Grand Total ... 550

representatives of sixty-one social groups. The bulk of its membership was composed of the representatives of political parties, and then followed the representatives of the peasantry, zemstvos, army at the front, coöperative societies, trade and industry, and the Cossacks. However, not all the members of the Council were chosen by the broad masses of voters, nor did they represent any particular territorial units, with the exception of the Cossacks and the national minorities; they acted merely as representatives of various political and social groups. The elections to the Provisional Council of the Republic were organized in such fashion as to be held by the central committees of the political parties and of social or racial organizations. Naturally, therefore, the Council did not represent the public opinion of the country as a whole, but only partial currents of thought independent of one another and often mutually exclusive.

The entire membership of the Council was appointed by the Provisional Government on the recommendation of the various public organizations. No doubt, the members were all *elected;* but formally they were *appointed* to the Council by the Government. The function of the Provisional Council of the Republic may be defined as being advisory to the Government. The Council might be consulted in the discussion of legislative and other measures planned by the Government. The Government might submit to it for consideration any measure it thought necessary. The Council had the right of initiative, provided that thirty of its members brought in a proposal. It opened its sessions on 7th October 1917 and was expected to exercise its functions till within two weeks of the meeting of the Constituent Assembly, at which time its powers were to expire.

Full administrative authority, however, remained in the hands of the Provisional Government, and the relations between the latter and the Council were such as leave to the Council only advisory powers. Still, if it could muster the required thirty signatures of its members, the Council was entitled also to address questions to the Government. Within one week of the presentation of such a question, the Government was obliged to deliver its answer, but it might refuse to reply if this should be necessary in the interest of national safety. A vote of lack of confidence on the part of the Council had no effect on the Provisional Government. Such was the nature of the relations between the Council of the Republic and the Government.

What were the relations between the Council and the All-Russian

Central Executive Committee and the Petrograd Soviet? The question had already been raised at the time when the Council was still in process of formation, when Trotsky brought it up at a meeting of the Central Executive Committee. Trotsky then expressed the fear that the Preliminary Parliament might displace the Central Soviet organ, assume its functions, and even become a source of strength to the Government against the Soviets. The result was that a resolution was adopted at the same session, in which it was affirmed that the entire Soviet organization was to remain intact, and that the All-Russian Central Executive Committee was to be responsible only to the general Congress of the Soviets, which would soon meet and elect a new Central Executive Committee.[9] The fact was, however, that the establishment of the Preliminary Parliament drew the most active representatives of the Executive Committee into the work of the Preliminary Parliament, so that the Executive Committee was no longer able to play the important part it had arrogated to itself during the summer of 1917. The formation of the Preliminary Parliament thus involved a loss of prestige for the principal organ of the Soviet machinery. Nevertheless, the Central Executive Committee supported the Preliminary Parliament.

Entirely different and openly hostile was the attitude of the Petrograd Soviet of Workmen's and Soldiers' Deputies toward the Preliminary Parliament. In the Petrograd Soviet the Bolsheviks were already in the majority, and Trotsky had been chosen as its President. This hostility of the Petrograd Soviet was equally directed against the Provisional Government. Having decided to utilize the Soviets to create a counterpoise to the Provisional Government and to usurp the power of government, the Bolsheviks found their chief support in the Petrograd Soviet. Naturally, the Provisional Council of the Republic formed an obstacle in the path of Bolshevik schemes; this is why the Bolsheviks, having decided to declare war against the Government, were anxious at the same time to annihilate the Provisional Council.

The Bolsheviks attended its opening session for the sole purpose of announcing their withdrawal from the Council. Trotsky was instructed to state the reason for this action, and he concluded his speech in the following manner:

We, the Bolshevik faction of the Social Democrats, declare: With this

[9] *Cf.* Sukhanov, *op. cit.,* Vol. VI, p. 174.

government of national betrayal and with this Council we have nothing in common. We have nothing in common with that work, fatal to the people, which is going on behind official curtains. We do not want to act as a screen for it a single day, either directly or indirectly. In leaving the Provisional Council, we appeal to the watchfulness and courage of the workers, soldiers, and peasants throughout Russia. Petrograd is in danger; the Revolution is in danger; the nation is in danger. The Government aggravates this danger. The ruling parties aggravate it. Only the people themselves can save the country. We say to the people: Long live an immediate, honest, democratic peace! All power to the Soviets! All the land to the people! Long live the Constituent Assembly.[10]

This speech constituted a direct incitement to revolution, and its object was to discredit the Provisional Government as well as the Provisional Council of the Republic in the eyes of the workers. The pivot on which these extremist tendencies turned was the Petrograd Soviet of Workmen's and Soldiers' Deputies, which approved Trotsky's speech. The Bolsheviks merely awaited the meeting of the second Soviet Congress, before proceeding to overthrow the authority of the Provisional Government. They felt certain that the majority of that congress would side with them.

During the latter part of the summer and in the course of the autumn of 1917 the Bolsheviks actually succeeded, step by step, in consolidating their influence in the local Soviets in all parts of Russia, and at the close of October they found themselves in a majority in the Soviets of both Petrograd and Moscow, as well as in numerous other industrial centers. All over Russia, in every more or less important urban community, there could now be found, side by side, soviet institutions and organs of the Government, contending for power. Especially after Kerensky had succeeded in putting down the Kornilov uprising with the assistance of the Soviets, the leaders of the soviet organizations became most aggressive and began openly to prepare for the overthrow of the Provisional Government.

The Revolutionary War Committee had its inception during the Kornilov rising, after which it was not dissolved by the Soviets, but left, as it were, in reserve, to be ready for the revolutionary warfare likely to arise in the future. The Bolsheviks of the Petrograd Soviet, engaged in preparations for the revolt, were, of course, bound to

[10] Sukhanov, *op. cit.*, Vol. VI, p. 251; Trotsky, *op. cit.*, Vol. III, pp. 321-323.

turn their attention to the organization of the Revolutionary War Committee, as an organ that would be charged with the task of leading the rebellion. Consequently, at the secret meeting of the Petrograd Soviet Executive Committee of 12th October, the following resolution was adopted:

The Revolutionary War Committee is organized by the Petrograd Executive Committee and constitutes its organ. It includes as members: the presiding board of the plenary membership and the soldiers' section of the Soviet, representatives of *Centroflot* (an elective committee of sailors), of the Finland Regional Committee, the Railwaymen's Union, Post and Telegraph Workers' Union, factory committees, trade unions, party organizations in the army, the Union of the Socialist People's Army, the military section of the Central Executive Committee, the workers' militia, as well as persons whose presence may be found necessary. The immediate objects of the Revolutionary War Committee are to determine what armed forces and auxiliary means are necessary for the defense of the capital and are therefore not to be removed hence; to register the personnel of the garrison of Petrograd and environs; to take stock of munitions and provisions; to elaborate a plan for the defense of the city and measures for its protection from riots and for the prevention of desertions; to maintain revolutionary discipline among the laboring masses and soldiers. Within the Revolutionary War Council there is organized a garrison conference attended by representatives of army units from every branch of the service. The garrison conference will serve as an organ assisting the Revolutionary War Committee in the inauguration of its measures, keeping it informed of conditions in the different localities, and maintaining close contact between the Committee and the army units.[11]

Ostensibly, the principal object of the Petrograd Revolutionary War Committee was to be the defense of the capital against a possible repetition of the Kornilov attempt. But the Committee had no relations whatever with the organs of the Provisional Government and it represented an entirely independent and self-appointed power which now had at its disposal the garrison of Petrograd, thanks to the aid of the garrison conference. Actually, it was not at all an organization for the defense of the capital, but the general staff of the contemplated revolt of soldiers and workers against the authority of the Provisional Government.

[11] Sukhanov, *op. cit.*, Vol. VII, pp. 40-41.

In organizing the Petrograd Soviet and the garrison of the capital for their own purposes, the Bolsheviks did not neglect the consolidation of their influence among the garrisons and workers of the towns in the vicinity of Petrograd. At the beginning of October was held at Kronstadt, a stronghold of the Revolution, the Petrograd Provincial Conference of Soviets, attended chiefly by representatives of garrisons from the various towns of the province of Petrograd. The garrisons of Tsarskoe Selo, Gatchina, Krasnoe Selo, Peterhof, Oranienbaum, were charged by this conference with the duty of resisting a possible offensive against the capital from the south. In this conference, too, the Bolsheviks played the leading part.

About the middle of October the Finland Regional Soviet summoned a Northern Regional Congress of Soviets. This was something in the nature of a rehearsal for the coming All-Russian Soviet Congress. The Bolshevik program demanding the transfer of all governmental power to the Soviets, immediate peace, and the distribution of all the land among the peasants was received with full approval by the Regional Congress.

Encouraged by the success of the Kronstadt Conference and Northern Regional Congress, the Bolsheviks began active preparations for the revolt. On 21st October they convened at the Smolny Institute the representatives of the Petrograd troops, that is to say, the spokesmen of the regimental and company committees, who were addressed by Trotsky, after which the following plan of action was decided upon. As soon as the second Soviet Congress assembles, it must take the government into its own hands, in order to give the people land, peace, and bread. The garrison, through its spokesmen, solemnly promises to place at the disposal of the Soviet Congress all its resources, down to the last man, and it promises, furthermore, to render obedience to all orders of the Revolutionary War Committee.

We thus see that almost on the very eve of the *coup d'état* the representatives of the Petrograd garrison voluntarily acknowledged the authority of the Revolutionary War Committee and of the Soviets. The military power was, therefore, in the hands of the Bolsheviks.

The relations between the Provisional Government and the Petrograd Soviet of Workmen's and Soldiers' Deputies were now frankly hostile, and the Bolsheviks, deriving their support from the majority of the Petrograd Soviet, launched an open campaign against the Provisional Government. The sole support of the Government in

Soviet spheres was now the Central Executive Committee, where moderate Socialist views still prevailed. But the Central Executive Committee had been elected as far back as June by the first Soviet Congress, while the sentiment among soldiers and workers had greatly changed during the four months that had since elapsed; judging by the membership of the newly chosen local Soviets in various sections of the country, there was reason to believe that the second Congress of Soviets, to be held 20th October, would be dominated by the Bolsheviks and that the All-Russian Central Executive Committee which was to be elected anew by this Congress would no longer support the Provisional Government. From this it will be clear that the support afforded to the Government by the Central Executive Committee elected by the June Congress no longer could be taken as an expression of the true sentiments animating Soviet circles, not to mention the fact that the Central Executive Committee itself was doomed politically, since the coming Congress would never reëlect its present members. Obviously, the Provisional Government had lost the support of the Soviet organizations.

Notwithstanding the attempts of the existing All-Russian Central Executive Committee to postpone as long as possible the calling of the second Soviet Congress, it was found necessary to summon it to meet on 25th October at Petrograd. The Bolsheviks had planned the armed rebellion of the Petrograd garrison against the Provisional Government for the same day. Already on the evening of 21st October a telephone message had been sent out in the name of the Petrograd Soviet to all the units of the garrison, couched in incendiary terms, as follows:

Soldiers of Petrograd! The protection of revolutionary order from counter-revolutionary attacks is incumbent upon you, under the direction of the Revolutionary War Committee. Orders to the garrison which are not signed by the Revolutionary War Committee are not valid. Every soldier of the garrison is charged with the obligation to maintain watchfulness, coolness, and unswerving discipline. The Revolution is in danger. Long live the revolutionary garrison.[12]

On the evening of 24th October, the first steps were taken to place such troops as were subject to the authority of the Revolutionary War Committee on a war footing, and on the morning of the 25th

[12] Sukhanov, *op. cit.,* Vol. VII, p. 101.

they proceeded systematically and methodically to occupy the most important strategic points of the capital, dispersing the Provisional Council of the Republic, and investing the Winter Palace, where the Provisional Government was in session. During the night of the 25th the mob and the soldiers broke into the palace, and placed the entire Provisional Government, with the exception of Kerensky and Proko-povich, who happened to be absent, under arrest; accompanied by the threats and shouts of the mob, the arrested Ministers were taken to the fortress of Peter and Paul. The rule of the Provisional Government was overthrown, the Ministers were in prison, and the real power in the capital was now in the hands of the Revolutionary War Committee.[13]

Meanwhile, late on the evening of 25th October the second Congress of Soviets was opened at the Smolny Institute amid discharges of firearms. About eleven o'clock that evening, M. Dan, in his capacity as representative of the outgoing All-Russian Central Executive Committee, declared the Second Congress of Soviets opened. The Congress chose for its President one of the leading Bolsheviks, Kamenev, and the majority of those present were plainly in favor of Bolshevism. Moreover, the Congress stood face to face with a revolutionary fact about to be consummated at that very moment, if not accomplished already,—the fact that the garrison of Petrograd, under the direction of the leaders of the Petrograd Soviet of Workmen's and Soldiers' Deputies, was sealing the doom of the Provisional Government. The reports of the capture of the Winter Palace and arrest of the Ministers were read by the President of the Congress and received by the delegates with enthusiasm. At six o'clock in the morning Lunacharsky read a draft of the proclamation to the workers, soldiers, and peasants, and his draft was accepted with only two dissenting voices and twelve members not voting, for all those delegates who belonged to the moderate Socialist parties had withdrawn from the meeting as a protest against the *coup d'état* planned and carried out by the Bolsheviks. This proclamation, serving at the same time as a formal resolution, gave expression to the views of the Congress on the armed revolt accomplished by the Bolsheviks,

[13] For the history of the Bolshevik *coup d'état, see* L. Trotsky, *Uroki Ok-tyabrya* (*The Lesson of October*) in *Sochinenya,* Moscow, 1925, Vol. III, pp. 36-37; I. Stalin, *Trotskism i Leninizm,* in the volume *Na puti k Oktyabryu* (*On the Road to October*), Leningrad, 1924, pp. 71-76, 83-87.

stamped the revolt with its approval, and announced the transfer of power to the Congress of Soviets:

Resting upon the will of the immense majority of workers, soldiers and peasants, and upon the victorious uprising of the workers and the garrison in Petrograd, the Congress takes the Government into its own hands. The Provisional Government is overthrown. The powers of the opportunist Central Executive Committee have expired. . . . The Congress resolves: All power is transferred to the Soviets of Workmen's, Soldiers' and Peasants' Deputies, which are to secure a genuine revolutionary administration of affairs.

On the following day the Congress elected the Council of People's Commissaries, with Lenin at its head, and a new All-Russian Central Executive Committee. In the one as well as the other organ the overwhelming majority of members belonged to the Bolshevik Party. The rule by the Soviets now began.

CONCLUSION

In the course of her participation in the World War, Russia passed through three different systems of government. She entered the War under a constitutional dualistic monarchy; after the Revolution of 27th February 1917, she passed through the transitional régime of the Provisional Government; lastly, the *coup d'état* of 25th October of the same year transferred the power to the Executive Committee of the Soviets of Workmen's and Soldiers' Deputies, and to the Council of People's Commissaries, with the result that a dictatorship of the proletariat was established under the leadership of the Bolsheviks. The end of the War and the possibility of gauging its effects upon Russia coincided with the moment of the most acute civil strife, and the disastrous consequences of the World War were now aggravated by the fixed policy of the communist régime, which had made it its object to annihilate the bourgeois economic system and substitute a communist economy.

We have surveyed in the present monograph the changes brought about under the influence of the World War in the Russian organization of government down to 25th October 1917, when the power was seized by the Bolsheviks. The history of these changes falls into two periods distinctly and definitely separated by the events of the March Revolution. This Revolution marks one of the outstanding epochs in the history of Russia. It caused the downfall of the Romanov dynasty, which had occupied the throne for more than 300 years, and it led to the abolition of the monarchical form of government.

When Russia entered the War, in the summer of 1914, her political organization rested upon what then appeared to be the strong foundation of hereditary monarchy. At the head of the State was the Emperor, who, by virtue of his own hereditary right and "by the Grace of God," was "Emperor and Autocrat of All the Russias, Tsar of Poland, Grand Duke of Finland, etc., etc." He was vested with wide authority in his capacity as head of State, both in the domain of executive and, in a considerable measure, of legislative power. The order of the succession to the throne was safeguarded by the strict provisions of the Fundamental Laws. The binding force of the Fundamental Laws even for the reigning Emperor was confirmed by his solemn oath at his coronation. The prerogatives of the legislative chambers were extremely limited; the chambers were precluded from exerting any influence upon the general trend of imperial policy; even within the province of those legislative powers with which they had been vested, they were kept dependent upon the Emperor and his Government, who enjoyed the right of priority in initiating legislation, and the right to promulgate ukases that had the validity of laws, under Article 87 of the Fundamental Laws.

Lastly, the Council of Ministers, as well as the individual Ministers were appointed and dismissed by the ukases of the Emperor and were not subject to the influence of the legislative organs. A Russian Minister was a Minister of the Emperor, and of no one else.

This system of dualistic constitutional monarchy guaranteed to the Emperor the supreme power in the land, imposed upon him an enormous political responsibility, and enabled him to direct the entire political life of his immense Empire.

It was only natural that the outbreak of hostilities in 1914 and the needs of war should tend to enhance still further the authority of the Russian Emperor. The normal course of work in the legislative chambers was interrupted, the position of the Emperor as leader of the Russian army and navy gave him the opportunity to exert his influence upon the progress of military operations, and, finally, after the dismissal of the Commander-in-Chief, the Grand Duke Nicholas Nicholaevich, in the autumn of 1915, Nicholas II assumed the functions of Commander-in-Chief, thus combining in his own person the duties of both head of the State and chief of all the armed forces of the Empire.

Within this period falls the beginning of the opposite political process, designed to enlist in the cause of national defense the representatives of the public at large, but especially the representatives of the legislative chambers, independently of the military bureaucracy and the Government.

The inadequate supply of munitions to the army, the economic disorganization within the country, and the military disasters of the summer of 1915, compelled the Government at last to grant some of the demands of public opinion and the Duma. The Council of Ministers was reformed by the dismissal of two of its particularly reactionary members, Maklakov and Shcheglovitov, and by the appointment of others in their stead who, in the opinion of the Emperor, ought to be acceptable to the Duma. At the same time the representatives of the legislative chambers were admitted to a share in the work of supplying the army and coping with the economic difficulties in the interior. Through the establishment of a peculiar system of Special Councils, which included a considerable number of representatives of the Duma and the State Council, parliamentary circles were admitted to the discussion and solution of matters of current military and economic administration. Thanks to the activity of the Special Councils, the supply of the army was improved[1] and considerable progress was made in the struggle with the economic difficulties, especially as regards the food and fuel supplies for the front and the cities. In their efforts to improve transport, on the other hand, the Special Councils were unable to make much headway, in view of the rapidly increasing disorganization of the railways.

The creation of the Special Councils tended to check the further extension of the Emperor's powers, which had been enhanced by the state of war and most strikingly demonstrated by the concentration in his hands of the functions of head of the State and supreme Commander-in-Chief. The structure and the mixed character of the Special Councils, however, which included representatives from different Ministries, no longer satisfied the public and the Duma. The technical assistance and relief afforded to the army and in the organization of the country by the Special Councils were great accomplishments. Politically, however, this form of relationship between the Government and the legislative chambers failed to satisfy public opinion and the Duma. The political sentiments of the country, which were influenced by the Progressive Bloc of the Duma organized during the summer session of 1915, were no longer content with mere technical coöperation with the Government in the Special Councils; they had already brought to the fore the question of a Cabinet of public confidence, that is, a Government enjoying the confidence of the nation and the Duma, and not composed of men who had discredited themselves by the unsuccessful prosecution of the War and their failure to organize the national resources, or who were generally known as enemies of constitutional government and as advocates of a return to absolutism.

Instead of seeking a compromise with the Duma and public senti-

[1] The President of the Duma, Rodzyanko, played a particularly active part in the work of the Special Council on National Defense.

ment, however, the Emperor suspended the Duma and dismissed those of his Ministers who advocated coöperation with the Progressive Bloc. The vacant ministerial posts were filled with persons well known to be opponents of the Duma and capable of going to very great lengths in suppressing symptoms of public discontent.

It was during these autumn months of 1915 that the fate of the throne was practically sealed. Nicholas II failed to take advantage of his last opportunity to compromise with the demands of the Duma and the public, and the ruling bureaucracy lost irretrievably all public sympathy. The Government had condemned itself to complete isolation from all the vital forces of the nation; withdrawing into its own shell, it jealously guarded its exclusive political prerogatives and treated as a violation of the sacred rights of imperial authority every attempt to turn the Emperor into the true path. The dying remnants of absolutism impeded the peaceful progress of national life and prevented the normal evolution of Russia toward parliamentary government.

During the last year and a half of the monarchy there were signs of a widening breach between the people and the Government. Having resolved upon resisting the Duma and ignoring public sentiment, Nicholas II drifted farther and farther away from the political reality, selfishly directing his policy to the sole object of protecting his throne from any encroachments, and refusing to admit the urgent and imperative necessity of resting his Government upon the support of the Duma and nation, if the unprecedented war was to be prosecuted effectively.

The breach between Government and people inevitably led to the only consequence possible under the circumstances—the forcible abolition of the former. But, along with the Emperor who had so obstinately resisted the political evolution of the country, all the other institutions of the Empire fell under the onslaught of the first five days of the Revolution. The downfall of Nicholas II entailed also the downfall of his dynasty, for the Grand Duke Michael refused to ascend the throne and merely reserved for himself the possibility of doing so if the Constituent Assembly should vote for a monarchy. This conditional refusal of the Grand Duke resulted, in fact, in the actual abolition of the monarchy and the transfer of the supreme power to the Provisional Government.

Following the abolition of the imperial throne, the legislative

institutions of the Empire likewise became inoperative. Though the
Duma and the State Council were not actually done away with, but
continued to exist nominally, yet they no longer functioned, and the
Provisional Government made no effort to call any meetings of either
the Duma or the Council. It is true that at the private meeting of
27th February, the Duma vested its powers in the Council of Elders,
which subsequently chose the Provisional Committee of the Duma to
organize a government; but after the Provisional Committee had
elected the first Provisional Government, this Committee voluntarily
withdrew, leaving full powers in the hands of the Provisional Government.

The Provisional Government became the sole possessor of supreme
authority in Russia. In its hands were concentrated all the threads
of the administration of the vast country and also the legislative
power. All the new legal acts of the Revolution, all new decrees, were
now issued in the form of decisions and resolutions of the Provisional
Government. All the legislative measures which were drafted by its
numerous advisory bodies were submitted to the Provisional Government and the latter could alter, amend, or reject them entirely. Only
after ratification by the Provisional Government did these acts obtain legal force, after which it was customary to publish them in
Vestnik Vremennago Pravitelstva, and in the *Sobranie Uzakoneni i
Rasporyazheni Vremennago Pravitelstva.*

The Provisional Government, endowed with the fulness of power,
had the general support of the nation; the public opinion of Russia
treated this revolutionary authority with unlimited confidence, and
as at first composed, the Provisional Government was actually that
Ministry of public confidence which the entire country had been
clamoring for and which the overthrown Emperor had so persistently refused. The new Government enjoyed, furthermore, the confidence of the army, of organized public opinion, and of the democratized organs of local government. Even the Petrograd Soviet of
Workmen's and Soldiers' Deputies supported it, although, to be
sure, only within the limits of its grudging formula "As far as—just
so far."[2] Still, it declared itself in favor of the Provisional Government, which had been formed, to a certain extent, with the participation of Soviet representatives.

[2] *See supra,* p. 63.

In April, however, began a conflict between the Soviets and the Provisional Government. The Soviet leaders launched a campaign against the Government, and, taking advantage of the support of a certain portion of the Petrograd garrison, forced the reorganization of the Provisional Government on a coalition basis, so that it now included a group of Socialist Ministers delegated by the Soviet and responsible to the Central Executive Committee of the Soviets. This introduction of Socialist Ministers into the Government represented a triumph of the Soviets over the idea of the Provisional Government, which had taken an oath to bring the nation to the threshold of the Constituent Assembly and to introduce the most indispensable democratic reforms. The function of any provisional government, and its fundamental idea, consists in taking over the supreme power of a country after a revolution, for the chief and express purpose of creating such conditions as will permit the speediest possible convocation of an authoritative representative body reflecting the public opinion of the whole country; that is, a Constituent Assembly.

The authority of a provisional government is in the very nature of things of a temporary and transitory character, and it is obvious that any crisis through which such provisional authority passes tends to undermine its prestige and reduce its influence in the country, particularly during the troubled times of war.

But the Petrograd Soviet of Workmen's and Soldiers' Deputies, or, to be more exact, its leaders, who belonged to the various Socialist parties, had different views on the subject. To them, the main concern was to intensify still further the process of the Revolution. So persistent were the efforts of the Soviet leaders to meddle in the work of the Government, to direct and correct it, that, when the so-called Contact Committee, which had been formed to deal with the Government, failed to exert upon the latter the pressure that the Soviet considered to be indispensable, they did not shrink before more drastic steps. There was a determined opposition to the clear-cut and firm policy of the Provisional Government within the Government itself, on the part of the Minister of Justice, Kerensky, who was at the same time Vice-President of the Petrograd Soviet. Nor did the Soviet leaders hesitate to call out the troops of the Petrograd garrison into the streets to support their demands by force of arms.

The aggressive policy of the Soviets caused the first ministerial crisis, resulting in the resignation of Guchkov and Milyukov. Representatives of Soviet Socialism were now introduced into the personnel of the Provisional Government, and the latter was reorganized upon a coalition basis. The Socialist Ministers of the first coalition Government were responsible to the Executive Committee of the Soviets of Workmen's and Soldiers' Deputies; the Ministers who were members of the Constitutional-Democratic Party were delegated to their posts by the Central Committee of that party; lastly, the group of Ministers remaining in the Government from the first Provisional Government who did not belong to the Constitutional-Democratic Party, were accountable to no organization. There was thus created a situation fundamentally unsound, since different groups of Ministers were responsible to different public bodies, and a government crisis might easily be precipitated by a mere decision of any one of these groups to recall its representatives. No wonder, therefore, that the second government crisis was caused by the mere recall of the Constitutional Democratic Ministers by their party committee, as a protest against the policy of the majority in the Government in its relations with the Ukraine.

By the middle of the summer of 1917 Soviets of Workmen's and Soldiers' Deputies had been organized in every important city of Russia, as well as in every army unit. In June, the first Congress of the Soviets met at Petrograd and elected the Central Executive Committee. Although the Soviets operated as a professional and class organization, and while it is true that the workers' deputies actually did represent the working class, the deputies of the soldiers, on the other hand, acting as representatives of the army, which included in its ranks nearly one-half of the entire adult male population of the country, could consider themselves not only as the spokesmen of the army but of nearly every male citizen between the ages of 18 and 43. This circumstance naturally added, especially in the eyes of the rank and file of the army, considerable weight to the Soviet organization and increased the importance of the Soviets throughout the country.

Meanwhile the work of drafting a law on the election of a genuine representative body—the Constituent Assembly—was proceeding slowly. The author believes that, if the Constituent Assembly had been elected in the spring of 1917, the Soviet organization could never have gained such influence in the country, and that during those first months of the Revolution all political parties and tendencies would have bowed before the authority of the Constituent

Assembly, with the possible exception of the extreme Bolsheviks. Against the latter, a Government resting upon the prestige of a nationally chosen Constituent Assembly might have been able to fight very successfully. It will be recalled that in France, in 1848, the National Assembly was summoned two months after the Revolution and successfully combated its excesses.

The reason why the Soviets arrogated to themselves the claim to be the sole representatives of the interests of the popular masses was precisely this lack of a genuine representative organ of the nation. The Provisional Government, of course, felt clearly the need of leaning upon the support of an organized public opinion, and, in order to offer some counterpoise to the influence of the Soviets, attempted to create substitutes for a national representation. On 27th April, a joint meeting of deputies of all the four Dumas was held at the Tauride Palace; during several days, in August, the State Conference was held at Moscow; lastly, in October, the Provisional Council of the Republic (Preliminary Parliament) was created, intended to serve uninterruptedly as an exponent of the public opinion of the country.

All these attempts, however, to lean upon the support of organized public opinion, in order to counteract the steadily growing influence of the Soviets, ended in failure. In the first place, the one-day joint session of the four Dumas, the three-day meeting of the Moscow State Conference, and the Preliminary Parliament, which managed to exist for a period of eighteen days, were, at best, only makeshift substitutes for a national representative body. The composition of these bodies was very far from perfect, not to mention the fact that the sessions of the first two were of very brief duration. The Government, but especially its Left Socialist wing, could not make up its mind to lean, as a counterpoise to the Soviet Executive Committee, upon the Provisional Committee of the Duma, or to create an organ, to be chosen either by the four Dumas or the Moscow State Conference, which would be in permanent session. The Soviet organization, on the other hand, had at its disposal the Executive Committee, which was continuously in session, and directed the line of action both of the Soviets and the Socialist Ministers of the Provisional Government. The Preliminary Parliament was formed only in the autumn, when the Soviets were already under the domination of the Bolsheviks, who had turned a number of provincial Soviets, with the

Petrograd Soviet at their head, into bases of operation for the armed struggle against the Provisional Government. The Constituent Assembly, so long awaited and so carefully prepared for, was elected when the Bolsheviks were already in power, and it met on 5th January 1918, only to be dispersed by the Bolsheviks with armed force.

The weakness of the Provisional Government, its downfall, and the seizure of power by the Bolsheviks were the consequences of profound differences between the representatives of the non-Socialist and the Socialist democracy, in respect of their tactics and political program. While the non-Socialists endeavored to consolidate the political conquests of the Revolution and to draft measures of further political and social reform to be submitted to the Constituent Assembly, the Socialists devoted themselves to a systematic, persistent intensification, or, as they termed it, "deepening" of the destructive revolutionary process, clamoring for immediate social reforms without waiting for the meeting of the Constituent Assembly.

To these profound social and political differences within the process of the Revolution itself there should unquestionably be added, as contributory causes, the shortcomings inherent in the structure of the Provisional Government. This Government was suspended in the air, as it were, without the support of any popular representative organ that would carry the weight of authority in the public eye. The first few weeks of its existence were irretrievably lost, so far as the most important and imperative task of summoning the Constituent Assembly was concerned. The Special Conference on an Electoral Law for the Constituent Assembly commenced its labors only on 25th May 1917. But if the electoral law had been ready during the first days of the Revolution and the election boards had been appointed by the Provisional Government, it would have been possible by that date to summon the Constituent Assembly, and the latter could have played the part of an authoritative exponent of the public opinion of the entire country. The fact that the country lacked a properly constituted national representative body permitted the Soviet organizations, which strove persistently for influence and participation in the Government, to develop, organize, and consolidate themselves.

In the autumn of 1917, when the extreme Socialist parties—Bolsheviks and Left Socialist Revolutionists—obtained control of the Soviets and launched their revolt against the Provisional Government, the latter had no means of seeking support in the will of the people as expressed in any representative assembly. In these circumstances no strenuous efforts were required on the part of the Petrograd garrison to enable it to declare the Provisional Government deposed and to proclaim the transfer of power to the Second Soviet Congress.

The Provisional Government, having passed through a number of crises which radically transformed its personnel (of the Ministers of the original cabinet only Kerensky, Konovalov, and Tereshchenko now remained), lost the halo of authority with which the first enthusiastic days of the Revolution had invested it, and was unable to provide itself with a solid foundation, in the form of an authoritative body that might serve as a faithful exponent of public sentiment throughout the country. The vacuum thus created was filled by the Soviet organizations. The Soviets simply stole a march on the Constituent Assembly and usurped its place. In the very nature of their class character, they had to be and were opposed to the idea of a national Constituent Assembly elected, not on the basis of class franchise, but of universal suffrage. Hence, with the triumph of the Soviets over the Provisional Government; the Constituent Assembly likewise was doomed.

The *coup d'état* of 25th October 1917 transferred the power to the Soviets. The All-Russian Soviet Congress was proclaimed the supreme ruling authority of the country, while the Central Executive Committee of Soviets was made the regular and supreme governing organ in permanent operation, combining under its control both the legislative and executive powers. For the administration of the country, the Central Executive Committee, in turn, appointed from among its own members the Council of People's Commissaries, responsible to the Central Executive Committee.

The Provisional Government based upon coalition was displaced by a homogeneous Council of People's Commissaries, and thus began the dictatorship of the proletariat in Russia.

II

THE EFFECTS OF THE WAR UPON RUSSIAN MUNICIPAL GOVERNMENT AND THE ALL-RUSSIAN UNION OF TOWNS

BY NICHOLAS J. ASTROV

THE EFFECTS OF THE WAR UPON RUSSIAN MUNICIPAL GOVERNMENT AND THE ALL-RUSSIAN UNION OF TOWNS

CHAPTER I

OUTLINE OF HISTORY OF RUSSIAN MUNICIPAL GOVERNMENT

"A RUSSIAN town of the seventeenth century consisted of a fortified enclosure surrounded by suburbs; in the centre of the enclosure were the house of the governor (*voyevoda*), administrative offices, the cathedral and the prison; then came a few thatched buildings, wooden cottages and houses, and further on began the fields."

This picture of a Russian town as given by one of the greatest authorities on Russian municipal history,[1] still held good throughout the nineteenth century and even in the beginning of the twentieth. This was especially the case in northern Russia. A statistical survey made in 1870 enumerated some 595 towns; but in only one-sixth of them were the inhabitants engaged in occupations of the urban sort. Those of one-third divided their time between various trades and industries and farm work. And the remainder, about one-half of the total urban population, supported themselves wholly by agriculture and by such winter work as they could find in other parts of the country.[2]

In striking contrast to the dull and humble background of most Russian towns are the two capitals—St. Petersburg and Moscow—and the other large cities; in the latter, economic and social conditions resembled those of western Europe, except for their backwardness in the introduction of modern conveniences. In the vast territory of the Russian Empire with its infinitely differing degrees and forms of civilization—from primitive savagery to the refined culture of the West—the towns, varying so much in size and in the

[1] M. Dityatin, *Ustroistvo i Upravlenie Gorodov Rossii* (*The Municipal Government of Russia*), St. Petersburg, 1875.

[2] *Ekonomicheskoe sostoyanie gorodskikh poseleni Evropeiskoi Rossii v 1861-1862 gg.* (*Economic Conditions of the Towns of European Russia in 1861-1862*), Part II, St. Petersburg, 1863.

number and character of their inhabitants, were bound to reflect the various stages of municipal development. These extraordinary differences between Russian towns had been preserved throughout their entire history and were as marked as ever at the outbreak of the War.

In order to understand what was accomplished by Russian municipalities during the Great War, and to trace the effect of the Revolution that followed upon the conditions of municipal life, it is necessary to make at least a very brief survey of the legal status of Russian municipalities and their financial position. And a survey of this kind is made particularly desirable by the fact that their legal status differs in many important features from that of the municipalities of western Europe and America.

The story of municipal government in Russia is a brief one. Its rights and privileges were formally acknowledged in the reign of Catherine II, when in 1758 a Charter "for the defense of the rights and interests of towns" accorded them the standing and privileges of individuals before the law. Civil rights could then be vested in them, and they became the pioneers of local government.[3] Under this Charter almost the entire population of a town was entitled to take an active part in the conduct of its affairs. But such liberal legislation was notably out of keeping with the whole social structure of that time, and particularly with the complex mass of relationships resulting from serfdom and the class organization which formed the real foundations of the old Russian State. The attempt to bring about the collaboration of the various estates of the realm, the privileged members of which were slave-owners, was doomed to failure. Only after the abolition of serfdom and the emancipation of the peasants was the reorganization of local government again included in the general program of reforms. An Imperial ukase of 20th March 1862 called upon the responsible authorities "to take immediate measures for the improvement of municipal government in all the towns of the Empire." The Municipal Act, which brought into being a new kind of municipal organization, was sanctioned by Alexander II on 16th June 1870. The actual development of community life on the basis of self-government—although a very limited one—dates from the passing of that Act.

[3] Dityatin, op. cit., Vol. I.

The Municipal Act of 1870 by no means created an ideal municipal organization. It was, however, better than previous legislation, and better than that which followed it; and its fundamental principles were preserved, though with important modifications, in the Municipal Act of 1892, which was still in force during the War. Under the Act of 1870 the right of municipal suffrage depended on the payment of local taxes. All citizens who paid such taxes and local rates were entitled to a vote in municipal elections, and were eligible to serve on local government boards. The municipal franchise was fashioned on the Prussian model. The members of the municipal dumas, or councils, were elected by indirect suffrage, the electors being divided into three classes. Municipal government was supreme and independent within its jurisdiction, which included "municipal management and welfare." The functions of control were vested in the governor of the province, who was assisted by a special board (*gubernskoe po gorodskim delam prisutstvie*). But when municipalities came to decisions or enacted local statutes, the governor was not allowed to interfere with them on the grounds of expediency or public policy.

The relatively favorable conditions brought about by the Act of 1870 and the general awakening in Russia at the time produced their effect in the rapid development of the municipalities. These spent their surplus revenue in the promotion of education. This is one of the most important features of Russian municipal government, and the fine tradition which it created was preserved until the very end, surviving even through the years of the War. A Committee appointed by the Senate[4] to inquire into the conditions of certain municipalities in 1880, recorded that the greatest achievement of local government lay in the "promotion of education" and the development of charitable institutions. The Committee pointed out, on the other hand, the lack of any great improvement in other municipal services, particularly in that of public health. The greatest drawback of the Act of 1870 was, in the opinion of the Committee, the preponderating influence in municipal Dumas of the commercial class, and especially of small traders, who greatly outnumbered all other social groups. The system of indirect suffrage, contrary to expectation, did not lead to the creation of local governments which represented all sections of the community. In fact the electors of all

[4] The Supreme Court of Justice.

three classes belonged to the same commercial and industrial group. The heavy burden of "obligatory expenditure"[5] imposed upon municipal budgets was mentioned by the Committee as another flaw in the Act of 1870.

No steps were taken to remedy the defects in the organization of municipal government to which the Committee had drawn attention. Great changes took place in the whole internal policy of the country, and a new Municipal Act was promulgated on 11th June 1892. This Act maintained the existing framework of municipal government and preserved its competence; but it introduced a number of alterations that proved exceedingly harmful to the development of municipal work. All such changes were designed with the same purpose, to weaken the municipalities and deprive them of their independence, to convert them from self-governing bodies into integral parts of the central administration, and to submit them to the control of the bureaucracy. In order to achieve this purpose the old franchise, which depended on the payment of taxes, was replaced by a new one based on the ownership of real property. The right of municipal suffrage was restricted to the owners of real property of not less than a specified value,—on the payment of a rather high fee—to corporations entitled to conduct commercial and industrial undertakings. The introduction of new qualifications for municipal electors led to a reduction of the electorate. And the purpose of this legislation was fully achieved in so much as all small taxpayers were thus deprived of their votes, every elector of the late "third class" and a portion of those of the "second" being struck off the register. In Moscow the number of voters, once 20,000, dropped to less than 8,000. In Odessa, out of a population of 500,000, only 1,850 were now entitled to vote, that is, less than one-half of 1 per cent. In the urban population of all Russia, the ratio averaged less than 1 per cent and of those who still possessed the franchise, not one-half exercised it.

The Act of 1892 also altered the very nature of the municipal executives. The municipal boards (*uprava*)—the real executives of municipal government—were converted into semi-bureaucratic institutions. The names of the members of the municipal board had to be submitted for approval to the representatives of the Ministry of the Interior. The mayors and members of municipal boards were held

[5] *See infra,* p. 154.

to be civil servants, and as such were subject to ordinary legal proceedings and also were under the jurisdiction of the Civil Service Disciplinary Courts. Another most important change was the establishment of government control over the public work and by-laws of municipalities. All by-laws of municipal Dumas were divided into two categories: some of them became operative only after they had been approved by the governor of the province or by the Minister of the Interior; others could be suspended by the governor and laid before a special board (*gubernskoe po gorodskim delam prisut-stvie*). The governor of the province was given power to suspend any by-law or decision of the Duma which, in his opinion, constituted a breach of the laws, or went beyond its competence, or was passed without complying with the established procedure, or was contrary to the policy and requirements of the State as a whole. The Municipal Act of 1892, therefore, submitted to the control of the Ministry of the Interior not only the conduct of municipal affairs from the point of view of their legality, but also the contents of by-laws from the point of view of public policy and expediency. Taking them all together, these provisions were a heavy blow to the independence of local government.

Again the Municipal Act of 1892 not only failed to remove the defects of the Act of 1870 but it added others. The electorate still remained one-sided; it consisted chiefly of owners of real property and representatives of trade and industry, who also owned the bulk of urban real estate. The great masses of the population were disfranchised. The educated were represented—almost always as a small minority—but only in the municipal Dumas of the capitals and of the larger cities. In Moscow this intellectual element was particularly strong and numerous. The municipalities of Russia were now living under the heavy yoke of administrative tutelage. Often it obstructed their work; and at times made it impossible.

The three Acts above mentioned are characteristic landmarks in the history of Russian municipal government. The Act of Catherine II, the most liberal of the three, called almost the whole population to participation in municipal affairs; it proved, however, absolutely unworkable under the prevailing social and political conditions. The Act of 1870 was a great step forward in the development of local government, but it entrusted the management of local affairs almost exclusively to the commercial class. Finally the Act of 1892, which was still in force during the War, further narrowed the already one-sided constitution of municipal Dumas (councils), deprived local government of its independence, brought it under the strict control of the Ministry of the Interior and of its local representatives, and took away its freedom of action and initiative.

The shortcomings of the Municipal Act of 1892 and its failure to provide for the growth of the political instinct and the new economic conditions of Russia were fully realized in municipal circles and were repeatedly acknowledged by the ruling bureaucracy. The publication of the Act was followed almost immediately by suggestions for its revision. The Imperial ukase of 12th December 1904 recognized the necessity of "self-government for the zemstvos and the towns, and of the need for the participation in their work of everyone interested in local affairs, without any distinction whatever." This declaration was a result of the unhappy story of the Japanese War, and of the revolutionary outbursts throughout the country, at its end. But a new wave of reaction swept away these promises and declarations. Promises of a reform of local government were renewed from time to time by the representatives of the Government in the State Duma. But no steps were taken for their realization, and the municipalities concerned continued to live without a definite status and with financial resources that were wholly inadequate. The pressure of the central government and its hostility usually increased in equal measure with the development of municipal activities. Continuous obstruction by the Ministry of the Interior and by its local representatives led unavoidably to hostility even on the part of the very moderate elements. When the municipalities, ending their inactivity, took up their work again, they found themselves obliged to defend their rights against infringement. This led to a stubborn and incessant struggle. Public organizations sought to extend their labors and their duties, and wished to work in security. The bureaucracy considered itself as the only source of justice and claimed absolute obedience. Public-minded Russians saw a cure for the country's precarious condition in the introduction of a constitutional régime. The Government was absolutely opposed to this. The Mayor of Moscow, B. N. Chicherin, who in an address delivered during the celebration of the coronation of Alexander III (1882) brought up the need of crowning the structure of the Empire with a representative chamber, was forced to resign. The resolutions of the municipalities did not go further than the request that the law should be superior over all persons and offices, and the constitutional safeguards should be introduced. This spirit was also embodied in a resolution passed by the Duma of Moscow on 30th November 1904 and supported by a number of provincial Dumas, and in the resolution of the Conference of Municipalities held in Moscow on 16th June 1905. Municipal circles insisted on more independence, on wider financial powers, and on the extension of the franchise. These demands were deemed dangerous by the Government. From 1900 to 1914 the elections of 217 mayors and members of municipal boards in 318 towns were quashed by the Ministry of the Interior, in spite of the fact that these officials were appointed by the very moderate and distinctly "bourgeois" Dumas elected under the restricted franchise. The appointments of doctors, engineers, and other officers made by the municipal boards were systematically canceled. Decisions of a purely business nature made by the Dumas were objected to and canceled. The refusal to confirm the appointment of municipal officers and the voiding of the decisions of the Dumas continued even through the years of the War. The struggle was based on the incompatibility of two points of view, of two ideas. The policy of the Government was inspired by the firmly established principle that the very principle of local government is in flagrant opposition to the unlimited power of the central Government, to the absolute power of the Tsar, to autocracy. On the other hand, after a long period of inaction, interest in public affairs had at last and gradually begun to grow. Russians were becoming conscious of their own strength and resources, and were looking for a wider sphere of activity. Here, indeed, lies the explanation of the attitude of mistrust displayed by the central Government. And it treated them with the same hostility with which it would have regarded foreign elements in the country. The central Government claimed the strict fulfilment of rigidly defined duties; the municipalities desired to learn the real needs of the people, and to provide means for their satisfaction. Every attempt to reconcile these two antagonistic viewpoints and to find a working compromise proved a failure, not only in peace-time but even when all were face to face with the deadly menace of the Great War.

As long as the central Government persisted in this attitude toward public organizations it would have been utterly idle to raise such questions as the democratization of municipalities and the ex-

tension of the municipal franchise. Against the arbitrary infringements of the central administration, municipalities had to fight in
defense of even the most elementary rights.

During the War the position of municipalities became exceedingly
difficult. Treated with suspicion by the Government, they felt, at the
same time, a barrier between themselves and the people at large,
whose conditions, opinions, and interests they did not represent. It
was essential to widen the circle of those on whom the municipal governments could rely, and to enroll new municipal workers; and this
was done by the creation of the Union of Towns. But the relations
between the central Government and local authorities remained unaltered. It is true that immediately after the outbreak of hostilities the
old antagonism between the bureaucracy and public organizations
seemed about to be brought to an end. The municipalities and the
zemstvos gave undoubted proofs of their sincere desire to forget past
offenses, mistrust, and hostility, and to coöperate with the Government in furthering the supreme interests of the country. But no
corresponding feelings were displayed by the Government. It showed
itself ready to treat the work of municipalities and public organizations as some form of dangerous competition rather than of helpful
collaboration. Its old mistrusts and suspicions soon revived, led to
evil misunderstandings; and they were a great hindrance to the work
of these institutions of the people.

In order to understand the condition of Russian towns during the
War it is important to remember that the Act of 1892, which restricted the powers of the municipalities, was introduced at a moment when, under the influence of the general revival of economic
and intellectual life, Russian towns were rapidly developing and
their trade and commerce were beginning to acquire considerable
prominence. The economic progress of Russia was accompanied by
the raising of the educational standard of the trading class that
formed a majority in the municipal Dumas. A new order of well-
educated, enlightened *bourgeoisie* was springing up and was fully
conscious of its social responsibility. At the same time representatives
of the professional and other of the better educated classes in large
cities began to show a certain amount of interest in municipal work
and sought election to the Dumas. The coöperation of bourgeoisie
with intellectuals, and the very high standard of the permanent staff
of the municipalities, which came to be known by the peculiar name

of the "third element," to distinguish it from government officials and from the elected members of the Dumas, weakened the unfavorable effects of the limited franchise, and to a certain extent made up for the lack of a truly representative system. A combination of business men and the representatives of the educated and progressive elements became the outstanding characteristic of many municipalities. For instance, almost without a break from the 'sixties of the last century, the office of Mayor of Moscow had been filled alternately by representatives of commerce and trade, and by the spokesmen of the intellectual and professional classes. This tradition was maintained until the very end, that is, until 1917, when municipal elections in Moscow were held under the new Municipal Act, which introduced universal suffrage. In the municipalities of Moscow, Petrograd, Kiev, Kharkov, Odessa, Riga, Rostov-on-Don, Saratov, Samara, Kazan, etc., an important part was played by the representatives of the well-educated section of the community; and the latter took a lively interest in local government, and made a sincere endeavor both to improve municipal work and extend its scope.

The combination of such forces resulted in the quite distinctive character of the municipal Dumas and their executives. The Dumas were, for instance, rather slow in reaching a decision, but most efficient in the execution of any measure they agreed upon. The development of municipal enterprises on a large scale and the refusal to adopt the system of letting contracts to private interests, are striking proofs of the confidence of these municipalities in their own strength, and their desire to do their work themselves. The very special attention paid by municipalities to the promotion of education is typical of their methods of dealing with social problems. The towns as well as the zemstvos were representative of the best ideals of Russian public life, and they laid down its fundamental principles. They created a fine tradition which was passed from one duma to another. The vast amount of work they did for the promotion of social welfare went on uninterruptedly. The splendid vitality of local government may be seen in every department—the educational, charitable, and economic. Indeed these great towns became cultural centers which promoted the spirit of initiative and raised the standard of living; and the smaller provincial towns followed the lead of the large ones. The general standard of municipal work was improving and though such progress was not, of course, universal, Russian municipalities were entering, obviously, upon a new stage in their development. It was brought to a sudden standstill by the War, and the whole energy of the municipalities was diverted to new aims and to a struggle with new difficulties and obstacles.

The Municipal Act of 1892 remained operative until the Revolution of 1917. After the downfall of the old régime the Decree of 9th June 1917, enacted by the Provisional Government, introduced a dramatic change in the system of municipal government by creating true local government on a broad democratic basis guaranteed by universal suffrage. The new municipalities were now included in the system of national institutions.

The towns of Russia, however, had little time to enjoy the fruits of self-government, democracy, and independence. Five months after the publication of the Decree of the Provisional Government the Bolsheviks seized power, and local government was swept wholly away.

CHAPTER II

MUNICIPAL BUDGETS AND REVENUES

UNDER the Municipal Act of 1892, the financial resources of Russian towns and cities were as limited as their powers. The Act imposed upon them numerous obligations, but it gave them little opportunity to levy local rates and taxes and it strictly limited their powers of assessment. The system of local taxation suffered, indeed, from a lack of elasticity. During the whole period of operation of this Act no substantial changes were introduced into the financial position of municipalities, in spite of the repeated and continuous demands made by them, and by Conferences of Municipalities held in Odessa in 1910 and in Kiev in 1913. The municipal governments of large and small towns alike were continually hard pressed for funds, and the inadequacy of their financial resources for the constantly growing requirements of their communities became a universal and constant characteristic of municipal life. The needs of the population, calling for relief, became every day more obvious and more pressing; they grew and accumulated, but the most urgent measures had always to be postponed for lack of funds.

At the beginning of the War, the financial resources of municipalities consisted of local rates, of tolls and other taxes, of municipal property and enterprises, of government subsidies and private donations. Among local taxes the most important were the tax on real property, the business premises tax, and special taxes such as licenses to keep saloons, to peddle, to maintain public cabs and the like. The relative importance of the sources of revenue named above varied from time to time; until the end it was by no means uniform, and depended on the development of each particular town. For instance, local taxes, and especially the tax on real property, were the chief sources of revenue as long as local life remained stationary. They maintained their position in the majority of such towns as were unable to find new sources of revenue or develop the existing ones. But in the case of capitals and other great centers—large provincial and district towns situated on railway lines and waterways which achieved prosperity through the development of trade and industry —the relative importance of local taxation, in spite of the increase of its net receipts, tended to grow less. It fell below the revenue from municipal undertakings, which had formerly been a negligible item in the budget.

At first the growth of municipal revenue was exceedingly slow. From 1863 to 1887—a period of 24 years—the revenue of Moscow increased only by 3,008,237 rubles or by an average of 125,098 rubles per year. But as early as the end of the last century the rapid development of municipal life became clearly manifest in the growth of municipal revenues. During a period of fourteen years (1888-1901) the revenue of Moscow rose by 10,260,993 rubles, *i.e.*, by a yearly average of 732,928 rubles.[1]

The budgets of Russian municipalities before the War, with the exception of those of the capitals and of the large cities, were very small. In 1913,[2] of the total number of 693 towns, 35 had a budget of over 1,000,000 rubles; 50, of 500,000 to 1,000,000 rubles; 178, of 100,000 to 500,000 rubles; 146, of 50,000 to 100,000 rubles; 182, of 25,000 to 50,000 rubles; 198, of 10,000 to 25,000 rubles; 100, of 5,000 to 10,000 rubles; 74, of less than 5,000 rubles.

The budgets of the municipalities grew steadily. The grand total budget in 1904 was 153,000,000 rubles. It rose to 215,270,000 rubles in 1910. And in 1913 it reached 297,000,000 rubles (*c.* £32,-100,000).[3] The budgets of the capitals and of the large cities of the Volga Region, of Siberia, and of Cis-Caucasia increased with especial rapidity.

[1] Article *Finansi goroda Moskwi* (*The Finances of the City of Moscow*), in the volume *Sovremennoe khozyaistvo goroda Moskwi* (*The Municipal Government of the City of Moscow*), Moscow, 1913, p. 243.

[2] V. Tverdokhlebov, *Mestnie finansi* (*Local Finance*), Odessa, 1919, p. 45.

[3] The rate of exchange of the ruble before and during the War was as follows:

	Rubles for £10
Pre-war	94.57
1st July-31st December 1914	111.4
1st January-30th June 1915	116.7
1st July-31st December 1915	139.9
1st January-30th June 1916	155.7
1st July-31st December 1916	155.3
1st January-30th June 1917	170.9
1st July-16th October 1917	255.2

The revenue of the two capitals is illustrated by the following table:

	Petrograd (in rubles)		Moscow (in rubles)
1873	4,856,000	1863	1,704,000
1883	5,873,000	1887	4,712,000
1893	10,492,000	1905	22,308,000
1903	24,577,000	1909	31,354,000
1913	46,515,000	1913	48,958,000
1915	59,300,000	1915	57,800,000
1916	68,545,000	1916	70,037,000

An idea of the relative amounts of the budgets of the chief capitals of Europe may be gathered from the following table:[4]

Budgets of European Capitals.

Year	Petrograd 1916	Moscow 1916	London 1914	Paris 1912	Berlin 1912	Vienna 1911
Population	2,317,000	2,050,000	4,521,000	2,828,000	2,059,000	2,031,000
			(in millions of rubles)			
Budget	68	70	243	177	141	108

The growth of municipal budgets is mainly due to the increase of revenue from municipal enterprises. At the end of the nineteenth century the tax receipts of Petrograd amounted to about 60 per cent of the total revenue. But subsequent to 1903 the first place was held by receipts from municipal enterprises. In 1916 this represented 58.9 per cent of the total revenue, while rates and taxes yielded only 25.8 per cent. Similar changes took place in the budget of Moscow. From 1904 on, it too was most largely determined by the development of municipal enterprises. The value of the property and of such enterprises owned by the City of Moscow rose from 117,000,-000 rubles in 1908, to 233,000,000 rubles in 1915. The value of municipal enterprises alone increased during the same period by some 84,000,000 rubles, and the value of municipal property by 32,000,000 rubles. In 1901 the gross revenue from all municipal enterprises in Moscow was 4,000,000 rubles or 27.4 per cent of the total revenue. In 1911 it had risen to 21,500,000 rubles or 54 per cent; and in 1916, to 39,000,000 rubles or 55 per cent. Similar changes in the make-up of municipal budgets may be seen in other

[4] The growth of the budgets of 157 Russian towns and the effects of the War upon them are illustrated in Appendices I and II.

large cities and towns with a developed system of municipal enterprises. In the budget of all Russian municipalities for 1912 the revenue from municipal enterprises amounted to 85,500,000 rubles, or about one-third of the total municipal revenue. If we deduct from this figure the revenue from municipal enterprises realized in 1912 by Petrograd and Moscow, which amounted to some 50,500,000 rubles, the residue for the remaining towns of Russia will be 35,-000,000 rubles, or slightly more than one-third of the total sum. The relative importance of the revenue from municipal enterprises increases proportionately with the size of the city or town. It is 45 per cent in Kharkov, 41.4 per cent in Ekaterinoslav, 36.8 per cent in Odessa. In towns with a population running from 400,000 and 1,000,000 it represents 28.8 per cent. Where the population is between 100,000 to 200,000, it averages 24.6 per cent. In populations between 10,000 and 25,000, it is 9 per cent; and in populations from 5,000 to 10,000, 5.7 per cent. These figures include the revenue derived by the municipalities from enterprises under lease to private individuals and corporations.[5]

It was only in the second half of the nineteenth century that Russian towns began to manage their own public utilities. Till then they had been taken from them and put into the hands of contractors by the lack of municipal funds and credit, and by an absence of initiative. The building of street-car lines, and often the construction of water- and gas-works, were almost as a matter of course given over to the contractors; as a rule, too, on terms very unprofitable for the municipality. From the end of the last century the desirability of having municipal utilities constructed and managed by the officials of the municipality made itself increasingly felt in the ruling circles of both capitals. It was a conception that did not become popular at once; but the experimental construction of certain street-car lines and the buying-out of the builders and owners of similar services in Petrograd and Moscow gave brilliant results, and made clear the advantage of the municipalization of such public utilities. The substitution of municipalization for the old leasing system had two general aims: the more complete satisfaction of local needs, and the preservation for the towns themselves of the profits hitherto derived by contractors from the exploitation of these utilities. The financial

[5] Tverdokhlebov, *op. cit.*, p. 244.

difficulties under which all municipalities were laboring kept them from trying to give such service at cost. They were compelled to look upon them as sources of revenue, to be used to meet the general expenses of the community. But, as a rule, these public utilities did not seek to make large profits. Their charges were not high. It was only during the War, in 1915, and especially during the financial crisis that followed the outbreak of the Revolution, that street-car railway fares and the cost of gas, water, and abattoir services were raised. Municipalities used this form of indirect taxation with great caution, though they believed it to be only fair that the whole community should share the cost of the services that contributed to their comfort and enjoyment.

The total revenue of 971 towns in 1912 is given by the Statistical Section of the Department of Apportioned Taxes (*Departament Okladnikh Sborov*) as[6] 275,680,000 rubles. More than half of this sum was derived from municipal services (31 per cent), and from subsidies and repayments of expenses incurred by the municipalities (23.7 per cent) ; only 45.3 per cent was derived from other sources; municipal property contributed 17.8 per cent; and rates and taxes only 27.5 per cent. The revenue from municipal property in 1912 had the following sources: the leasing of municipal property and miscellaneous provided 1,500,000 rubles or 0.6 per cent of the total revenue; interest on capital, 2,200,000 rubles or 0.8 per cent; municipal buildings and markets, 15,000,000 rubles or 6 per cent. Of rates and taxes, the largest revenue was derived from the tax on the value of real property. In 1912 it produced 32,670,000 rubles or 13.2 per cent of the total revenue, in the cities and towns where the Municipal Act of 1892 was in operation, and 6,340,000 rubles or 22.5 per cent in those to which the operation of the Act did not extend (for instance Warsaw, etc.). The law provided that taxation of real property should not exceed 10 per cent of the revenue from the property, or 1 per cent of its value. In the majority of towns (529) taxation of real property had reached its limit even before the War, but the basis of the valuation needed revision and the possibilities for the exploitation of this source of revenue were not really exhausted. The tendency to underrate the actual value of real property in towns was due not only to the "property owning" character of

[6] Tverdokhlebov, *op. cit.*, p. 133.

municipal dumas, but also to the fact that this property was subject to a State tax and a zemstvo tax in addition, and these were assessed on the basis of municipal valuations. It was not until after 1910 that real property in towns began to be assessed for purposes of State taxation on the basis of valuations made by officers of the Treasury. Not only was the rate of municipal taxation limited by law, but it could not be levied on property owned by the Crown, on church property, including monasteries, or on property owned by railways. In Petrograd these exemptions reduced the receipts from the tax on real property by one-half. The power to impose local taxes on trade and industry was also strictly limited. In 1912 these taxes produced only 4,000,000 rubles; the license fees paid by drinking places and restaurants brought in only 6,370,000 rubles; and the receipts from other sources, such as the tax on cabs, private vehicles, on horses, dogs, etc., were altogether insignificant. The total revenue from all these sources in 1912 was only about 9,000,000 rubles.

The sources of municipal revenue provided by the Municipal Act of 1892 are all mentioned above. The inadequacy of the system of municipal taxation in Russia may be seen in the fact that in 1910 the burden of municipal taxation per capita in Moscow was 6 rubles 73 copecks, while it was 21 rubles in Berlin, and 25 rubles in Paris. Yet Moscow had fairly exhausted all resources to which it had access by law. Only a few years before the War—in 1910—some of the towns were authorized, on a special application, to levy a duty on goods that arrived at and left the town by rail. The duty was levied on the weight of the goods; it was imposed for a term not exceeding ten years, and was levied for a special purpose, the construction of sidings. One hundred and fifteen towns exercised this power in 1915; but it was denied to Moscow as a result of the opposition of commercial circles. In the years immediately preceding the War, municipalities were relieved from a part of the "obligatory expenditure"[7] (Act of 5th December 1912). One-sixth of the State tax on real property was allotted to the municipalities in 1913; since 1903, Petrograd alone has enjoyed the privilege of levying a tax on dwelling-houses.

Municipalities insisted on a reform of local finance. In voting the budget for 1911 the municipal Duma of Moscow adopted the follow-

[7] See infra, p. 154.

ing characteristic resolution: "Under the conditions created by the Municipal Act the estimates of revenue and expenditure cannot cover even the most pressing requirements of municipal life; all endeavors to establish a more satisfactory system of city finance are doomed to failure so long as the new sources of revenue repeatedly demanded by the municipalities are not granted, so long as local government is saddled with the burden of State duties, the scope of which still remains most vague, so long as the petitions of municipalities are ignored, and the powers of local government are not extended by a revision of the Municipal Act." The Duma of Petrograd came to a similar conclusion. Analyzing the financial conditions of the municipality of Petrograd in 1916, the Chairman of the Financial Committee pointed out "that the capital of the Russian Empire is kept at the expense of its inhabitants alone and that the Government not only does not help local authorities in their task of maintaining municipal services, but even weakens their financial position by appropriating some of the sources of municipal revenue, and even actual money receipts, for State purposes. The municipality is obliged to make large outlays, the total of which before the War had already exceeded 500,000,000 rubles. Unless the municipality of Petrograd is provided with new sources of revenue all work directed to the relief of even the most pressing needs will have to be abandoned."

Similar appeals to the Government were made by other large cities, and by small towns. Their demands for help became particularly pressing during the War; but even then they were denied those new sources of revenue needed to stop up the gaps in their normal budgets. Their revenue was actually cut down by the abolition of the spirit monopoly in August 1914. This caused a decline in the receipts from licensed houses and restaurants. To repeat,—the municipality had exploited the old sources of revenue to the utmost extent, all their possibilities were exhausted. Real property in towns was revalued almost everywhere and the revenue that had formerly been allowed to escape in that way was now seized upon. To meet new war expenditures, the Government made large subsidies, but the actual outlay considerably exceeded them. The lack of funds was met by short-term loans issued under conditions very disadvantageous and guaranteed by the debentures of the authorized but not yet covered municipal loans, and by other securities forming special capital assets. This policy led to a piling up of deficits which disorganized

the work of the municipalities, brought them financial embarrass-
ment and culminated in their bankruptcy.

A survey of the financial resources of Russian municipalities cannot be complete unless we mention the problem of municipal credit.

The ordinary revenue of the municipality could not suffice for the
carrying out of costly municipal enterprises, above all enterprises requiring considerable initial expenditures. The Dumas sought to
draw in private capital both by the sale of franchises and by means
of municipal loans. All municipalities tried the franchise system, and
when the term of the franchise expired they usually found on their
hands worn-out machinery, and equipment which required a complete overhauling and reconstruction. The execution of works of
public utility, the organization of new municipal enterprises, before
the buying-out of such as were already in existence, the repair and
refitting of those that were handed over to the municipality after
the expiration of the term of the contract—all this could be done
only by means of loans. The development of municipal credit became
imperative. The issue of municipal debentures is a comparatively
new thing. It was first used by Petrograd in 1875. Moscow issued its
first municipal debentures in 1886, to obtain the funds required for
the building of slaughterhouses. The system of long-term credit was
not generally adopted by Russian municipalities until much later.
The solution of the problem of raising the funds required was left
entirely to the mayor. This phase of the work of the municipality had
no proper organization. The Government gave little or no support
to local institutions in such cases, and private commercial banks did
not assist them in obtaining credit abroad. The lack of credit, in
fact, made many difficulties for municipalities. The position of small
towns, which occasionally had to borrow money from private individuals at the highest rates, was particularly hard. The permission
to issue municipal loans could be obtained only by means of a clumsy
procedure, every individual case calling for the consent of the Emperor. Much time occasionally elapsed before this could be secured.
In some cases there was a delay of several years; and in the meantime
all the estimates on which the demand for the loan was based had
become entirely out of date. From the beginning of this century
municipal debentures had usually been taken up by foreign interests, only about 10 per cent of the total amount being subscribed at

home. Most of the municipal loans were floated in France, and, shortly before the War, in England. Moscow issues for 8,000,000 rubles in 1902 and for 6,000,000 rubles in 1903 were floated in Germany.

On 1st January 1913, the total issue of unredeemed municipal debentures in Russia amounted to 444,591,053 rubles. This represented the debt of 65 towns, which issued debentures to the nominal value of 471,182,756 rubles.[8] During the last three years before the War towns and cities were authorized to issue debentures to the value of 250,000,000 rubles.[9]

The indebtedness of separate cities and towns may be illustrated by the following figures: In 1916 the indebtedness of Moscow was 147,253,103 rubles;[10] Petrograd, 124,949,828 rubles; Warsaw, 46,228,400 rubles; Baku, 27,000,000 rubles; Odessa, 20,661,000 rubles; Riga, 18,694,500 rubles; Kiev, 11,539,938 rubles; Kharkov, 10,271,075 rubles; more than 6,000,000 rubles: Astrakhan, Ekaterinoslav, Nikolaev; more than 5,000,000 rubles: Poti, Saratov, Tsaritsyn; Vilna, 4,892,262 rubles; more than 2,000,000 rubles: Kishinev, Tiflis, Yalta; more than 1,000,000 rubles: Kazan, Minsk, Nizhni-Novgorod, Orel, Perm, Poltava, Sebastopol, Tomsk. The indebtedness of 39 towns was less than one million rubles; the smallest issue of debentures was made by the town of Buzuluk: it amounted to 55,100 rubles and was raised for the construction of waterworks.

The indebtedness of Russian cities, including the largest was far below that of the capitals of western Europe and the United States.

City	Year	Issue of debentures (million rubles)	Per head (rubles)
Petrograd	1916	124	56
Moscow	1916	147	81
Berlin	1910	201	97
Vienna	1911	285	140
London	1912	1,079	252
Paris	1912	1,090	377
New York	1912	1,285	255

[8] *Spravochnaya knizhka dlya derzhateley obligatsi russkikh gorodskikh zaimov (Manual for the Use of the Holders of Russian Municipal Debentures)*, published by *Kassi Gorodskogo i Zemskago Kredita*, St. Petersburg, 1913.

[9] *Vestnik Finansov, Promishlennosti i Torgovli*, No. 42, 1917.

[10] In February 1914 the municipality of Moscow was allowed to issue debentures for 36,920,000 rubles, but the declaration of war prevented the floating of this loan.

The rate of interest on municipal loans varied from 4 per cent to 6 per cent, but in certain instances went down to 3.5 per cent (Baku, 1895), or rose to 7 per cent (Kozlov, 1909). The drawings for the repayment of municipal debentures took place once or twice a year. Occasionally the municipalities used their right to redeem debentures before they fell due, or to buy them in. The duration of municipal loans varied from 17 to 73 years, from 40 to 50 years being the usual term.

The average debt of a Russian town amounted to almost twice as much as its annual budget.

Loans were issued for various purposes. Thirty-six towns used the capital raised by loans for the construction of waterworks, for buying out the owners of public utilities, and for improvements and extensions; fourteen, for the construction of sewers; nine, for the redemption or construction of street-railway lines; fourteen, for the rebuilding of slaughterhouses and the erection of cold-storage rooms; sixteen, for electric power stations; five, for market-halls; three, for gas-works; two, for telephone exchanges; four, for the extension and improvement of harbors; thirteen, for the raising of capital and the building of premises for municipal pawnbroking establishments (*gorodskoi lombard*); four, for the purchase of land, laying it out, and adapting it to the needs of the public. Thirty-six towns employed the funds obtained by long-term loans for meeting their short-term obligations, their arrears to the Treasury, various deficits, expenditures exceeding the estimates, etc. Next came loans for the improvement of municipal services in the stricter sense of the word. Under this head, in the case of twenty-five towns, are included road-work and paving, the building of harbors, the maintenance of parks and open spaces, etc. In eight towns funds raised by loans were devoted to the organization and extension of hospitals; in nineteen, to the building of schools; in three, to the building of theaters; in ten, to the building of municipal offices; in fourteen, to the building of military and police barracks. And one town employed the money raised by a loan to establish a special fund to provide pensions for its municipal employees.

All pre-war municipal loans were not used for productive purposes, though most of them were so employed. In 1912, the productive loans of Moscow amounted to 98.4 per cent; in 1915 to 92 per cent. In Petrograd, these loans amounted, in 1910, to 75.8 per cent;

in 1916, to 61 per cent. In Warsaw, they amounted to 80.3 per cent. For all the towns that issued debentures, loans for productive purposes constituted about 60 per cent of the total amount. Municipal loans provided excellent security. The property, entirely free from obligations that was owned by the municipality of Moscow, was valued at 102,197,677 rubles. The actual value of municipal property free from obligations was considerably above the figures that appeared in the balance sheets. The debentures of Petrograd were guaranteed by the revenue from municipal enterprises and property, and this revenue was twice as great as the sum required.

The issue of debentures was not the only form of municipal credit. Four hundred and ninety-two towns borrowed money from private individuals and corporations at a rate of interest varying from 4.8 to 10 per cent. In 1912 this debt reached 31,000,000 rubles. Three hundred and twenty-one towns borrowed 48,200,000 rubles from private and other banks, on which they paid 8 to 10 per cent interest; 389 towns borrowed 18,000,000 rubles from their "special" funds (Petrograd, 2,270,000 rubles; Warsaw, 2,200,000 rubles; Odessa, 1,500,000 rubles). Finally, 249 towns owed 12,000,000 rubles to the Treasury.

With the outbreak of the War the towns were deprived of the usual facilities for floating loans abroad. The policy of long-term loans had to be almost entirely abandoned. Municipalities postponed the issue of debentures already authorized, and did not apply for permission to make fresh issues, in the hope that after the War this practice might be resumed, on possibly more advantageous terms. Private credit within the country was almost the only source left open to them, and to meet the deficits of municipal budgets, it was widely used.

The Government did not begin to finance municipalities until the years immediately preceding the War. June 1912 saw the establishing of the Municipal and Zemstvos Bank, with a capital of 10,000,-000 rubles and a reserve capital of the same amount. The long-term loans of the new bank had a life of from 10 to 66½ years; short-term loans, from six months to six years. Loans were made for the purchase and administration of real property, the organization of large undertakings, and the redemption of debts. The credit allowed by the Bank was very limited; during the War it could not advance more than 1,000,000 rubles a month. The size of short-term loans

was eventually raised to 300,000 rubles. The rate of interest charged
was 7 per cent in the case of loans for building purposes, and 6 per
cent in other cases. The part played by the Bank in the financial life
of the municipalities was insignificant, its clients being almost entirely small towns. It was not a permanent source of credit which
could be relied upon for the execution of large schemes; but it could
be used for small amounts required to meet unexpected and pressing
needs. On 1st December 1916, the total indebtedness of all municipalities to the Bank was 31,418,286 rubles; of this sum, 25,037,545
rubles represented long-term loans, and 6,380,741 rubles short-term
loans.

The capitals and large cities usually found by one method or another the long-term credit needed for the execution of their schemes,
but to small towns, such opportunities were almost entirely denied.
The sources of organized credit for small towns were the municipal
banks (*gorodskie obshchestvenie banki*), the establishment of which
dates back to 1788. The number of municipal banks in 1909 was
276; in January 1911, it rose to 286, of which 47 were opened in
provincial towns, and 239 in district towns. In 1915 the number of
municipal banks was 337. They were designed to meet the financial
requirements of small district towns and were of little importance
for the large cities. In 1909, the capital and deposits of municipal
banks amounted to 181,490,000 rubles; in 1915, to 309,160,000 rubles. The capital employed was 47,800,000 rubles, and the reserve
capital 13,500,000 rubles. The chief operations of these banks consisted in discounting bills of exchange, mortgages, and loans on
goods, securities, and financial paper of various kinds. They could
also advance money to municipalities and often assisted them in
floating their loans and in obtaining credit at a reasonable rate of
interest.

These municipal banks also helped to meet the need of adequate
mortgage loans which is so essential for facilitating the building of
houses by the owners of small properties. For instance, in Samara
in January 1914, 190 properties were mortgaged to commercial
banks for 5,455,538 rubles, *i.e.*, an average of 28,070 rubles each,
while the number of properties mortgaged to the municipal banks on
short-term loans was 635, for 1,980,042 rubles, that is, an average
of 3,110 rubles each.

The policy of mortgage-loans was never adequately developed in Russia, and this may be seen in the character of its town-building. Mortgage of town property was almost entirely monopolized by municipal credit associations. The right of land banks to mortgage urban property was subject to a number of restrictions. As early as 1909 Prof. P. B. Struve defined the most urgent problem of Russian town-building as follows: "It is necessary," he said, "to facilitate the use of unoccupied city land as building sites—both for their owners and for the commercial builder—by giving them free recourse to a system of mortgages. The utilization of building sites and housing are the key problems for the development of the towns of Russia." Municipal credit associations, however, existed only in Petrograd, Moscow, and 34 other cities; the scope of their work was limited to their own city. On 1st January 1914, the debentures issued by the municipal credit associations amounted to 1,215,160,-600 rubles. The reserve capital of the 36 associations was 53,347,200 rubles. Their total assets were 1,447,207,000 rubles.[11] The Municipal Credit Association of Petrograd held the first place among institutions of this type; it issued debentures to the value of 394,444,700 rubles. Moscow came next with an issue of 266,670,800 rubles. The issue of debentures of other associations was considerably smaller.

[11] The assets of these associations amounted to 1,524,989,000 rubles in 1915; 1,543,075,000 rubles in 1916; 1,529,347,000 rubles in 1917.

CHAPTER III

MUNICIPAL EXPENDITURES

THE purpose of municipal government has been defined by Russian law, as the "satisfaction of local needs and interests." Sec. 2 of the Municipal Act gives a more detailed list of the duties of local government. It includes the relief of the poor, the prevention of begging, the advancement of education, measures for the promotion of public health, supervision of the service of food supply, the improvement of public utilities, assistance to local trade and industry, and, finally, the carrying out of the various obligations imposed by the central Government.

Local government bodies, therefore, in addition to their direct functions, had also to meet the requirements of the State. These even had to be satisfied first, and this service was known as "obligatory" expenditure. It included "participation in the maintenance of government offices," in the maintenance of the police, and in the billeting of troops. The "obligatory" expenditure in 1912 amounted to 10.9 per cent of the total budget of all municipalities. The maintenance of police forces, which, however, were not subject to municipal control, was a heavy burden, particularly for small towns. The State subsidy for this purpose, some 3,000,000 rubles, was less than one-fifth of the actual cost. In 1912, the 971 towns spent for the maintenance of their police some 16,300,000 rubles. The "obligatory" expenditure of Petrograd, in 1903, amounted to 2,862,000 rubles; in 1916 to 4,403,000 rubles. In Moscow, it amounted in 1901 to 1,983,400 rubles; in 1916 to 4,213,000 rubles. The municipalities could dispose of their revenue only after "obligatory" expenditure had been duly met.

The maintenance of municipal buildings and services (14.3 per cent) and the administration of other real property (8.5 per cent) were heavy items in the expenditure of local government bodies. The indebtedness of municipalities grew in proportion to the development of municipal enterprises; in the years immediately before the War the payment of interest and provisions for sinking loans became the largest items of expenditure and rose to 41,900,000 rubles, or 15.2 per cent of the total. Wages and other like expenses called for only

7.4 per cent or 20,400,000 rubles. Little more than one-third of the whole municipal revenue was left for meeting all other popular needs —even the most pressing.

Following a tradition deeply rooted in the history of Russian local government, municipalities devoted particular care to the advancement of education. This policy was clearly stated in a resolution passed by the Duma of Moscow as long ago as in 1863. It declared that "no other need could be compared with the demand for popular elementary education. All other demands might be provisionally postponed because of the unsatisfactory condition of municipal finance, but the settlement of the problem of elementary education could not be deferred."[1] Elementary education was made the main consideration in the majority of towns. The expenditure on education in most cases exceeded that on public health, and, as a general rule, was considerably larger than the outlay for the improvement of public utilities. Education in the capitals absorbed 8.7 per cent of their total expenditure; in small towns, 20 per cent of it. This difference is explained by the fact that in the larger cities 29 per cent was required for the maintenance of municipal services, whereas this item was almost wholly absent from the estimates of small towns. In 1913, in 472 towns of European and Asiatic Russia the expenditure for education reached 35,000,000 rubles, which gives an average of 72,000 rubles per town. In 1915 the expenditure on education in 226 towns was 31,622,000 rubles, giving an average of 140,000 rubles per town. The estimates for educational purposes increased by 12.7 per cent in the course of two years, including 18 months of the War.[2]

The ratio of expenditure on elementary education, on municipal services (excluding municipal concerns), and on public health may be seen from the estimates of 56 provincial towns for 1914 (see Appendix III). Of these, in 36 towns the expenditure on education held the first place; in 10, various public utilities, and in the remain-

---

[1] M. Shchepkin, *Obshchestvennoe khozyaistvo goroda Moskwi* (*Government of the City of Moscow*), Vol. IV, Part I, quoted in *Sovremennoe khozyaistvo goroda Moskwi* (*The Municipal Government of the City of Moscow*), Moscow, 1913, p. 26.

[2] *Obshche-gorodskoe soveshchanie po narodnomu obrazovanyu* (*Conference of the Municipalities on Questions of Public Education*), 16th-18th July 1917, published in *Izvestya Soyuza Gorodov,* Nos. 45-46, p. 11.

ing 10, public health. The improvement of municipal utilities and public health took the first place in the expenditure of the towns of the Caucasus.

The growth of expenditure for educational purposes is particularly noticeable in the budgets of the capitals. The estimates and actual expenditure of Petrograd on education in 1903 amounted to 1,677,000 rubles, or 11.5 per cent; in 1913 to 4,350,000 rubles, or 15.6 per cent; and in 1916 to 6,958,000 rubles, or 20.3 per cent. The expenditure of Moscow for the same purpose was 1,308,000 rubles in 1901, 5,495,000 rubles in 1913, and 7,573,000 rubles in 1916, but it was the development of elementary education which was the chief reason for these increased expenditures. At the close of the academic year 1901-1902 Moscow had 176 municipal schools with 22,823 pupils; and at the end of 1910-1911, 299 schools with 51,099 pupils. In the course of ten years the number of pupils increased by 124 per cent. This growth in the number of pupils was the result of the new education policy adopted by the duma of Moscow in 1901, which called for an elementary education accessible to all. In 1909 the duma of Moscow decided to introduce a scheme for free and general elementary education, and extended the course of elementary schools from three to four years.

The steady increase of expenditure on education lifted the school organization of Petrograd, Moscow, and some other cities to a standard which enabled it to meet every demand of the people. Government subsidies, granted under provisions of the Acts of 1908 and 1913, aided the municipalities in solving the problem. Special government grants facilitated the introduction of general education in 13 towns in 1909, in 59 towns in 1912, in 156 towns in 1913, in 286 towns in 1915, and in 293 towns in 1916. Such subsidies were small, from 1,000 rubles to 10,000. Only 25 towns received a sum over 20,000, and three—Moscow, Odessa, and Kiev—over 100,000. The total government subsidies in 1916 amounted to 2,873,000 rubles.

The expenditure on education, as is clear from the statements made above, was not reduced during the War. The plans for the introduction of "education for all" were not dropped. Only in isolated cases and in order to balance their budgets, did municipal dumas reduce their expenditures on education.

Another important item in the budgets of the capitals was their expenditure for public health and sanitation. In Petrograd it reached 3,304,000 rubles in 1903, 7,796,000 rubles in 1913, and 10,503,000 rubles in 1916. For the same purpose Moscow spent 2,646,000 rubles in 1901, 6,374,000 rubles in 1913, and 7,973,000 rubles in 1916.

The sum spent on public utilities was considerably smaller. After the exclusion of the provision for the upkeep of municipal enterprises it amounted in Petrograd to 2,013,000 rubles in 1903, to 3,971,000 rubles in 1913, and to 3,051,000 rubles in 1916. The figures for Moscow are 1,795,000 rubles in 1901, 3,150,000 rubles in 1913, and 3,666,000 rubles in 1916. This item of municipal outlay did not increase during the War, and in Petrograd, it was reduced.

Expenditures for the relief of the poor, and on charitable institutions,—in Petrograd, amounted—in 1903—to 755,000 rubles; to 1,904,000 rubles in 1913, and to 2,446,000 rubles in 1916. In Moscow the items are 704,000 rubles in 1903, 1,069,000 rubles in 1913, and 1,223,000 rubles in 1916.

In the combined budgets of 971 towns for 1912 the expenditure for education accounts for 12.1 per cent of the total, public health for 12.5 per cent, and public utilities for 9.5 per cent.

The district towns of Russia have for long been in a class of their own. The majority of such towns, especially those of central and northern Russia, could only be described as settlements, with a few stone-built houses and one or two paved streets. Most of the houses were built of wood, and the streets were often not even leveled. This type of district town still exists unchanged. The facts available in the data for the valuation of real estate[3] show that, in the case of the towns in the province of Chernigov 94.5 per cent of all buildings were of wood, 26.3 per cent had iron roofs, 32 per cent wooden roofs, and the majority—41.5 per cent—thatched roofs. Seven-eighths of the area of these towns was used for agricultural purposes.

The city life of Russia, with the exception of the capitals, largest centers, and seaports, was monotonous and lacked the brighter features of life in European cities. In nearly all district towns existence

[3] *Materiali po otsenke nedvizhimikh imushchestv, gubernski svod (Data for the Valuation of Land and Real Property)*, 1912, quoted in Tverdokhlebov, *op. cit.*, p. 40.

was particularly dull and colorless. The lack of money and the character of the population rendered existence in them uneventful, and likewise made impossible any rapid change of habits. The majority of such Russian towns were simply small townships; and some general idea of the effects of the War upon their municipal life may be learned from the data to follow.

We can, first, reconstruct the general condition of provincial towns on the eve of the War, by studying the results of an inquiry held by the Electoral Committee of the Province of Moscow into the financial development of district towns within their jurisdiction for the years 1909-1916.

The combined budget of the provincial towns and townships (*possadi*)—15 in all—in the province of Moscow was 973,000 rubles in 1909. It rose to 1,714,000 rubles in 1916, an increase of 76.2 per cent. The growth of these budgets was steady, with a slight interruption in 1912. The increase was particularly marked in 1916, when it grew by 26.3 per cent. The average war-time budget exceeded the pre-war budget by 31.5 per cent.

The chief source of revenue of district towns came from government subsidies and the reimbursement for expenses incurred by the municipalities. The revenue from public utilities and town property was insignificant, the number of municipal enterprises being very small. All 15 towns under investigation had municipal slaughterhouses, six possessed waterworks, and two had electric power stations. Only about 30 per cent of the total revenue was produced by direct taxation.

The small revenues of such towns were utterly inadequate for the requirements of the people. Their municipal organization was most rudimentary; and only in towns where trade and industry had developed could it rise above the primitive forms found in the village community. For the period above, expenditures on municipal services fluctuated between 0.36 and 1.85 rubles per capita. They included the building and repair of roads, the planting of trees, lighting, water supply, the collection of garbage, the repair of bridges, and the like.

The expenditure on education varied from 3.66 to 0.8 rubles per capita; this expenditure was one of the municipal items in the budgets of provincial towns. But even so, the school problem had been met only in part. In Podolsk only about one-half the children attended school, and 50.7 per cent in Koloma. As for the schools of the large industrial town of Serpukhov, they could accommodate 89.3 per cent of its children of school age. Expenditures on public health and sanitation disclose a still more deplorable state of affairs. It fluctuated between 1.21 and 0.07 rubles per head.

On the municipal debts of provincial towns, light is thrown by the following figures. In January 1917, such debts stood, in Voloko-lamsk, at 23.86 rubles per head; in Serpukhov, at 16.34 rubles; in Podolsk, at 12.35 rubles; in Zvenigorod, at 10.96 rubles; and in Bronnits, at 1.92 rubles.

During the War the budgets of provincial towns increased as a result of the general increase in the cost of living. A marked growth of revenue appears under the heading "Subsidies from the Govern-ment" in connection with the mobilization. Municipalities were obliged to increase the tax on real estate. The rise of expenditure was the result of the general economic depression, and had nothing to do with the improvement of public utilities.

The general tendencies in municipal services in the provincial towns of Russia may be gathered from the following data,—the estimates of 210 district towns for 1914 being classified in accord-ance with the three main purposes of such services,—education, im-provement of public utilities and public health. In 155 towns the first place is held by education, in 50 by the improvement of public utilities, in five by the promotion of public health. The expenditure on the improvement of public utilities exceeded that on education mainly in seaside towns and health resorts. In the great majority of cases, the municipal authorities still made education their first con-cern.

Even before the War, lack of money resources, their inadequacy to growing demands and the unsatisfactory organization of munici-pal credits, were, in the case of Russian towns and cities, a kind of chronic disease. After the outbreak of hostilities it was a disease which threw local government into a hopeless position. In normal times it was always possible to postpone the carrying out of some measure for the public good "because of the lack of means." But dur-ing the War the municipalities had to deal with problems the solu-tion of which could not possibly be postponed without endangering the most vital interests of both towns and people; and at the same time even the carrying out of their normal pre-war functions was accompanied by a heavy increase of expenditure. It became necessary, therefore, either to maintain at least an apparent balance of municipal revenue and expenditure by means of a drastic cutting down of the former, or to enter upon the dangerous path of exhausting every possible source of revenue. The former course was a method of self-defense in an emergency; the latter involved the municipalities in all the complication of new conditions, and made them active participants in the struggle in which the whole country was engaged. Both courses were given a trial by Russian municipalities, but neither could avert a complete and final breakdown.

The Ministry of the Interior, as early as the first year of the War, demanded strict economy and the reduction of normal expenditures. Almost all Dumas suspended the execution of various plans for improvements and discontinued the works of building and repair already under way. But a rigid adherence to the principles of economy and self-denial was impossible under the prevailing conditions of economic confusion, and the attempt to cut down normal expenditures gave no tangible results, for they had been already reduced to a minimum. On the other hand, the necessity of meeting the new demands without a definite financial program and in the absence of reliable sources of new revenue, prepared the way for an absolute financial collapse.

The disorganization of municipal work and finances was not due solely to the new problems brought forward by the War, such as the relief of the wounded, caring for refugees, combating epidemic diseases, organizing supplies of foodstuffs, fuel, etc. It was the unavoidable result of the general disorganization of the economic life of the country, and of the breaking down of its administrative and economic machinery. The depreciation of the currency, the universal rise in the price of raw materials and of the necessaries of life, the continual demands for increase of wages made by city officials and employees—demands which could not be met by the financial resources of the municipalities—all these conditions both undermined the work of municipalities and led to a general vitiation of their finances. The crisis was, again, due to the breakdown of the economic system of the State, and not to any careless handling of municipal affairs. It reached its climax during the Revolution that took place as the result of Russia's failure in the War. It could not be prevented, or even relieved, by that reform of municipal finances for which Russian towns had been waiting for years. The Municipal Finance Act published by the Provisional Government on 29th September 1917 came too late. Russian towns had no time to avail themselves of the rights, privileges, and advantages it conferred upon them. A month after the publication of this Act the advent of the Bolsheviks annihilated all municipal institutions, both new and old.

The abnormal and unhealthy growth of municipal budgets during the War may be seen in the following data. The combined budget of all Russian towns in 1913 was 297,000,000 rubles. The preliminary estimates for 1917 amounted to 400,000,000 rubles. The approximate total of municipal expenditures for 1918 was estimated at some 1,000,000,000 rubles.[4] The Bolshevik Revolution makes it impossible to check these estimates. But the figure given need not be considered exaggerated, for as early as 1917 the actual expenditures of the city of Moscow rose to 200,000,000 rubles. A similar increase of expenditures took place in Petrograd, where, by the autumn of 1917, it had risen from 60,000,000 rubles to 180,000,000 rubles, and was rapidly nearing 200,000,000 rubles. The estimated expenditures of Odessa for 1917 increased by 18,000,000 rubles over those for 1916, and reached 32,660,000 rubles. Similar changes took place in the expenditures of Kharkov, Kiev, Saratov, and other cities, but these huge increases of expenditure were in no case due to the development or extension of municipal services. On the contrary, such services—the administration of hospitals, orphanages, and other like institutions, as also other public utilities—were still conducted on a pre-war scale, and were even in certain cases reduced. The additional expenditure was called for by the steady rise in the price of materials, foodstuffs, and fuel; and, finally, as indicated above, by the increased wages which the high cost of living also demanded. In the absence of new sources of revenue the growth of expenditure led to the accumulation of enormous deficits.[5]

[4] Report (*Otchet*) of the Financial Committee of the Union of Towns, 15th October 1917, published in *Izvestya Soyuza Gorodov*, 1917, No. 49, p. 144.

[5] Appendices I and II contain examples of municipal budgets of various types. Appendix I deals with 99 towns which, in spite of the reduction of certain of their normal expenditures, were compelled to increase their liabilities by the addition of new items to their budgets. Such were the large cities along the main lines of communication, through which passed the wounded

The results of an inquiry held in 1915[6] may give an idea of the view taken by administrative circles of the effects of the War upon municipal finances.

The majority of towns (176 in number) that replied to the questions complain of an acute shortage of money and credit. The issue of debentures became impossible, and such towns had to obtain private credit on hard terms. Twenty-nine towns made it clear that they were unable to float loans already authorized. Almost all towns spoke of the compulsory cutting down of expenditures, this being—in the case of 42 towns—effected by a reduction of the provisions made for the improvement of municipal services. In many towns all building and repairs were suspended. The demand for economy was met in certain cases by reducing the expenditure on the maintenance of public enterprises, on education, public health, and sanitation. Azov, Alexandrovsk, Blagoveshchensk, Ekaterinburg, Ivanovo-Voznesensk, Kupyansk, Pavlovsk, and Kherson, halted the building of new schools. Some municipalities were compelled to discontinue the payment of their contribution toward the maintenance of the zemstvos (*zemsky sbor*) and their sinking funds. A number of towns increased street-railway fares and the rates charges for water, gas, electricity, the services of the abattoirs, the collection of refuse, etc.

Almost all towns complained of the rapid deterioration of their finances. To account for this, the following causes are given by the municipalities themselves: the increase of expenditures due to the War, the higher cost of maintaining municipal enterprises, the decline of the revenue from the lease of municipal property, and increased payments on loans. In certain cases—for instance in Riga—the crisis was due to the withdrawal of commerce and industry, and to the sudden decrease in the population (by 500,000) consequent on the advance of the enemy.

All work for the general good was checked by the War. As stated

and the refugees, that is, those cities directly affected by the War. Appendix II gives instances of the cutting down of expenditure during the War. This policy was generally followed by the district towns. The provincial towns included in this class, such as Tiflis, Samara, Astrakhan, Archangel, etc., did not escape the common fate, and in the years which followed could not balance their budgets.

[6] *Kalendar-Spravochnik Gorodskogo Deyatelya na 1916 god* (*Municipal Almanac for 1916*), Petrograd.

above, the municipal life of Russia had been entering upon a period of rapid development after protracted depression. Even small towns were embarking upon various undertakings which were certain to bring revolutionary changes into their hitherto humble existence. Even if we leave the capitals and the large cities out of count, we find that a number of small towns had completed plans for new enterprises and institutions of public utility. Some of them had already begun the realization of these plans, others were investigating the possibility of floating loans, others were contemplating various schemes for improvements. The results of the inquiry quoted above show that in the year of the outbreak of the War the towns of Barnaul, Volsk, Izmail, Minsk, Perm, Troutsk, and Tobolsk were constructing waterworks, electric power stations, sewers, etc. But most of the towns (67) were kept from even starting the work in contemplation. It appears from the answers given by the municipalities to the "questionnaire" that among the enterprises that had to be abandoned were plans for the construction of waterworks, sewers, electric power stations, tramways, slaughterhouses, cold-storage houses, dams, harbor works, bridges, hospitals, dispensaries, schools, theaters, gardens, parks, market-halls, establishments for baths, and for mud baths, health resorts, public pharmacies, community halls, street railways, etc.

An investigation into the conditions of a group of towns in the Volga district made by the Union of Towns in the summer of 1916 fully corroborates the results of the above inquiry. A few statements taken from it are given below.

Rybinsk—the center of the Volga grain trade, the winter station of the Volga fleet, and the terminus of the railway that links the Volga district with Petrograd—"had to abandon the idea of laying a sewer system, as a result of the conditions created by the War; for the same reason a scheme for the building of a dry dock for the repair of vessels moored in the harbor could not be proceeded with."

Yaroslavl. "The decisions taken by the municipality which had provided for the expansion of the local system of water supply, the building of an electric power station and the construction of sewers, had to be canceled on account of lack of funds and the impossibility of floating a loan under war conditions."

Kostroma. "In the years preceding the War the activities of the municipality had greatly increased. It was intended to begin the construction of sewers and the building of a street-railway line; but these plans had to be abandoned, the War having prevented the issue of debentures."

Nizhni-Novgorod. "The War halted the carrying out of the town's school-building program. Of the twelve schools the erection of which had been authorized, two only were completed before the outbreak of hostilities; the building of the remaining ten had to be delayed, as the Ministry refused the subsidy required for this purpose. The extension of the system of water supply, the completion of the sewage system, and the reëquipment of the power station had to be suspended, partly because the machinery ordered in Switzerland could not be delivered until the end of the War."

Kazan. "The War has almost entirely brought to an end all those works for the improvement of municipal services, which were being carried on with great success. All enterprises of importance have had to be suspended."

Samara, which possessed municipal services superior to those of any other town on the Volga, had to abandon the works for the extension of the electric power system, and the completion of its sewage system, because it became impossible to obtain delivery of fittings and machinery ordered abroad; the War also prevented the completion of the street-railway line. A good many towns in European Russia, Siberia, and Central Asia were similarly affected. Voronezh was prevented by "the general conditions due to the War" from putting into effect a plan for the extension of the sewage system to the entire city. The best school buildings were converted into hospitals, and the children of two or even three schools were often crowded into the same building. Some of the educational institutions had to suspend their work and dismiss their pupils as a result of the rise in the cost of living. The completion of a proper system of waterworks in Tashkent was prevented by the War. These examples could be multiplied; they are not exceptions, but only illustrate the general tendency. The municipal Duma of Kiev intended to open an institute for the training of municipal and zemstvo workers. Perm was proposing to open an institute of forestry. Kostroma had petitioned for the establishment of a teachers' college. Five cities in Siberia were competing for the privilege of being made the site of an agricultural institute. . . . Russian towns were anxious to encourage the development of institutions for the popular betterment. Petrograd had in view the sanitary treatment of the soil, rivers, canals, and drinking water; an elaborate program provided for the construction of waterworks, sewers, street railways (a second line), hospitals, schools, docks, the planning of parks, the reëquipment of slaughterhouses. The cost of this was estimated at 145,000,000 rubles. The complete scheme of improvements required by the capital would have demanded an outlay of some 500,000,000 rubles. The municipality of Moscow was considering the construction of a third system of waterworks. A plan had been prepared for the development and extension of the principal municipal services (street railways, sewers, electric power station, etc.) and institutions (hospitals, maternity hospitals, dispensaries, orphanages), which would bring them up to the standard of the demands of the rapidly growing population. A scheme of school building provided for the construction of fifteen schools with sixteen classrooms each (twelve schools of this type were already completed), and thirty-six schools with twenty-four classrooms each. The cost of these schools, together with the cost of eight other buildings intended for educational purposes, was estimated at 14,-500,000 rubles. In order to relieve the congestion of the street traffic the municipality of Moscow was to enter in 1916 upon the construction of the first Russian underground railway. It had been hoped that its first section would be completed by 1920.

The War and the subsequent Revolution frustrated all such plans, and brought the rapid progress of Russian municipal development to an end.

CHAPTER IV

THE FIRST EFFECTS OF THE WAR

WAR was declared by Germany on 19th July 1914.[1] The Imperial manifesto summed up the causes of the War and its true character as follows:

The task now before us is not only to intervene in favor of a kindred people who have been unjustly attacked, but is also that of defending the honor, dignity, and unity of Russia and her position among the Great Powers. Let us forget in the hour of trial our internal disputes. May the ties that unite the Tsar and his people become even stronger, and may Russia rise as one man to repulse the insolent attack of the enemy!

The official declaration of war was preceded by a period of anxious waiting when the inevitability of the impending storm came generally to be recognized. An extraordinary meeting of the municipal Duma of Moscow was held on 18th July to allow the ancient capital to express her feelings on this historic occasion. The Duma unanimously adopted a resolution expressing its deep indignation at the action of those who had dared to break the peace, and its complete faith "that in the face of coming events, the people of Russia would be inspired by a deep and unfaltering sense of their duty both to the past and to the future of their native land, and would rally together and rise unanimously in her defense." The Duma called all the forces of the nation to action and urged them to support the Government in the struggle for the preservation of the country. Following ancient tradition, Moscow again gave expression to feelings shared by the entire country. To her fell the honorable task of unifying all popular forces for the struggle that had just begun, and her appeal was generously answered by the whole of Russia. She became the rallying point for the towns of Russia in their desire to assist their country; what she was to bear during the War and the part she was to play in its organization were recognized from the beginning. She became a symbol of unity, the real heart of Russia, which was beat-

[1] All dates in this monograph are given in accordance with the Russian calendar.

ing in sympathy with the army. Both the Union of Zemstvos and the Union of Towns originated in Moscow, and they developed the work of public organization for the War throughout the Empire.

The War with Germany swept away a complex network of economic and material conduct which in the course of many years of peaceful and neighborly relations had come to be the normal condition of everyday life. An important factor that had been deeply rooted in Russian life and had a considerable influence upon many aspects of the political and economic organization suddenly disappeared. The passage from peaceful intercourse to a state of war was bound to produce a complicated psychological and technical process of adaptation to new conditions, brought about at a moment's notice. This process was made particularly difficult by the fact that the War of 1914 took Russia by surprise. The masses of her population have no aggressive tendencies. In political and social circles, and among those of Russia's business and commercial world, the approaching war was regarded as a fatal event, for they knew how unprepared the Government was for it, and how incapable of organizing the country to face it. Hence when the irrevocable step was taken, and the War became a reality, it was generally felt to be a great and unforeseen calamity. But a sense of the immensity of the danger to which the country was exposed, a deep feeling of bitterness against the Germans, who were held to be responsible for the War, the recognition of the fact that in Germany Russia had an enemy exceptionally strong and well-prepared, produced general enthusiasm, which soon spread throughout the whole country and reached its remotest corners. It found voice in the words: "Russia is in danger! We must defend Russia, we must defend ourselves!" It resulted in the marked orderliness of the mobilization, the exceptionally high percentage of men who answered the call to arms, and the feverish organization of public forces in order to make easier the task of the Government. Finally, the country's attitude was settled by the reports of cruelty with which the Germans carried on the War from the very beginning.

The recognition of the great responsibility that was laid upon Russia's towns and cities by the War was general, unanimous, and genuine.

The Moscow Duma defined the field of its activities by resolving to undertake any work that might help in the struggle being waged by the army and navy or that might be made necessary by the development of events. In the meantime the Duma decided to enter at once upon the organization of medical and sanitary aid for sick and wounded soldiers at the front and for those already in Moscow. An initial credit of one million rubles was voted for this purpose, and the sum was put at the disposal of the *uprava*, or executive board. A special Committee consisting of all the members of the executive board and fourteen members of the Duma was founded and intended to begin its work without delay. Later this committee came to be known as the "War Committee."

The war activities of the municipality of Moscow form an intricate system. The first duty undertaken was, as has been said, the relief of sick and wounded soldiers, and they began to arrive in Moscow immediately after the outbreak of hostilities. This work was organized with extraordinary rapidity, and revealed the flexibility and elasticity of municipal institutions. They showed themselves quite able to adapt themselves to these new problems, demands, and conditions. The growth and development of the work born in Moscow marched in equal pace with the development of military operations. At a meeting of the Moscow Duma on 28th November 1914 the Mayor declared, "There is only one limit to our work, to our efforts: it is the extent of the demand." But in addition to the needs of the War it was also necessary "to safeguard that mighty cultural inheritance which was the result of the labors of the municipality of Moscow during many years." These words seem to indicate the two-fold program of municipal work: the satisfaction of the new demands due to the War, and the carrying on of the city's customary work at the pre-war level. The municipality of Moscow began with the relief of sick and wounded; eventually, without any decrease in the standard of its municipal services, it undertook the manufacture of munitions and of war supplies in general.

The example set by Moscow in meeting the emergencies caused by the terrible events of the War was followed by other Russian towns and cities. The Duma of Petrograd voted the same amount for military purposes as had Moscow. The main lines of the general program drawn up by Moscow were followed by the majority of towns, and they began to feel the effects of the War in the course of a few weeks. All the towns organized hospitals to receive the wounded, though the lack of adequate funds made the result of these efforts insignificant. Nevertheless, the municipalities were not frightened by the greatness of the problems confronting them; they early realized how much more could be accomplished by the coördination of separate efforts and activities, and by a closer coöperation between those engaged in the same work with the same object in view. This idea was embodied when all Russian towns and cities united in a single union.

The All-Russian Union of Zemstvos, which coördinated the work of the zemstvos, was created in Moscow a few days after the declaration of the War. The zemstvos had a certain experience in the organization of work in common, having gained it during the Russo-Japanese War, and also during Russia's famines. The Zemstvos Union rapidly outlined a scheme of combination work, and developed it on a huge scale with extraordinarily good results. The Union of Towns came into being a little later, a union which had no previous experience. The work of these two Unions was closely coördinated. They differed neither in aims nor in methods, though the elements included in the respective Unions were not the same. The Zemstvos Union was an organization which comprised the zemstvos and their personnel. The Union of Towns was made up of the administrative personnel of the municipalities.

It is exceedingly difficult to draw a clear line between the war activities of the municipalities and those of the Union of Towns, which was created to meet the demands arising out of the War, and which acted through the municipalities themselves or through the committees formed by municipal Dumas. The Union of Towns and the municipalities should be considered together in so far as they aimed at the solution of the same problem. Their work was part of the same scheme, was directed toward the same purpose, and financed from the same source.

The work of the Union of Towns and of the municipalities during the War—that poignantly tragic and heroic period of the life of Russian towns—has not yet been investigated. It was suddenly halted when it was under full headway. No data dealing with it have been collected, and much information relating to the period is probably wholly lost, in part as a result of the transfer of the archives of the old municipalities to the new authorities, and in part through the actual destruction of a vast number of valuable documents, archives, and books belonging to the old municipalities and to the numerous organizations of the Union of Towns. The reconstruction of any complete and exhaustive picture of the work of Russian municipalities, which was ruined by the War and the Revolution, and of their activities during the War, is made impossible by the scarcity of data within Russia, and by their complete absence in the world outside.

The information gathered together in this monograph may afford some idea of the social and economic effects of the War upon the municipalities. And it may be said at once that the Union of Towns embodied all those vital forces within Russian communities which had hitherto been suppressed. In the hour of the State's great need they rose to its defense.

In the chapters that follow all the leading features of the war activities of the municipalities will be treated in connection with the work of the Union of Towns, to which they are closely related.

CHAPTER V

HISTORICAL OUTLINE OF THE ALL-RUSSIAN UNION OF TOWNS

THE idea of a closer coördination of the war activities of Russia's municipalities arose simultaneously in various quarters. The initiative and the actual execution of the scheme are both due to Moscow. As early as 19th July 1914 (old style) during the first meeting of the War Committee appointed by the Moscow Duma, it was shown how desirable it was that all Russian towns should unite under the leadership of Moscow to make their war work easier. On 24th July the same idea was expressed in resolutions passed by the Dumas of Ufa and Baku.

A regional conference of the representatives of the towns of central Russia was called in Moscow on 31st July. The conference discussed the problem of evacuating the wounded and also the "necessity of establishing direct and effective ties between the municipalities." The district organization which took form in different municipalities during this conference may be considered as the model on which the All-Russian Union of Towns was formed. The question of a union was brought before a congress of mayors held in Moscow on 8th and 9th August 1914, on the initiative of the Moscow Duma; and this congress decided to proceed with the organization of the union. "The success of the War," it was said, "will not depend on the strength and organization of the army alone; it will depend directly upon the efficient organization of public forces, on the organization of society."

The amalgamation of Russian towns into an All-Russian Union was inevitable. It was dictated by the force of events. And the necessity for such an organization was further emphasized when the Government announced its plan for supplying the army and evacuating the wounded. The districts directly affected by the War were to be cut off from the rest of the country. No organization, with the exception of the Red Cross, was to be allowed to cross the line of demarcation. But public organizations were entrusted exclusively with the task of the relief and care of those sick and wounded soldiers who had been sent from the army to the clearing stations situated on this line of demarcation. The military authorities had come to see that they would be unable to fulfil their task without such assistance. The carrying out of the plan naturally called for the creation of strong and at the same time flexible organizations, which would be able to fill up all gaps, and prepare the whole country for the reception of the wounded. The Unions of Zemstvos and Towns undertook the work.

Once the provisional organization of the Union of Towns had been instituted and had drawn up a scheme outlining its future labors, one thing became clear: the Union would be absolutely unable to fulfil its great obligations if it was limited solely to the funds under municipal disposal. That the Government itself should assist in this work of national importance became imperative.

The imperial consent allowing the towns to join the All-Russian Union of Towns was given on 16th August 1914, on an application made by the Provisional Committee of the Union. It was the act of recognition of the Union and of its inclusion in the number of officially sanctioned organizations. The purposes of the organization were defined by the same document. They were notably curtailed as compared with the original scheme of work drafted by the organizers of the Union. Its activities were limited to the *relief of sick and wounded soldiers "during the present War."* At the same time the Central Committee of the Russian Red Cross, on the demand of the Committee of the Union of Towns, included the Union among the Red Cross organizations, thus giving it the right to recover from the Treasury all expenditures incurred in connection with the relief of wounded, permission to use the railways, free of charge, for the transport of freights, the right of exemption from the payment of stamp duties, and all other privileges enjoyed by the organizations of the Red Cross. The Union was also given the right to use the sign of the Red Cross, and henceforward all its activities went on under this flag. On 26th August the Government made the Union its first grant, one of 3,000,000 rubles.

On 14th September, Moscow saw the meeting of a new conference of representatives of municipalities. The conference of August had brought the Union into being; the conference of September gave it a definite form. The first conference consisted of 76 members, representing 36 provincial and 9 district towns of European Russia. When the second conference met there were 126 members; and 195 towns, of which 70 were provincial and 125 district, expressed their desire to join the Union.

In the course of the month that elapsed between the two conferences the municipalities which joined the Union began to feel that they had solid ground beneath their feet. The towns of Russia, with their limited possibilities, their absence of adequate status, their helplessness resulting from the lack of financial means, soon realized all the advantages that come from combined coördinate work, and though face to face with the new and complicated problems of the War, began to have new confidence in themselves.

This conference gave the structure of the Union its final shape. It was agreed that all townships that expressed a desire to join the Union should be admitted to membership. The administration of the Union was formed; the High Commissioner and the fifteen members of the Central Committee were elected. In addition to the settlement of administrative matters, the conference outlined and laid down a program of material work that was to be done. The problems with which the Union was confronted were summed up in the following eight paragraphs:

(1) aiding the municipalities to establish and maintain the necessary number of hospital beds;

(2) arrangements for the distribution of the wounded among the districts appointed to receive them, and the creation for this purpose of special local committees and bureaus of inquiry;

(3) the equipment of hospital trains;

(4) the building and equipment of suitable premises for the reception and evacuation of the wounded;

(5) the organization of army canteens along the routes chosen for the evacuation of the wounded;

(6) the organization of central depots of medical goods, surgical instruments, underwear, and winter clothing; the organization of similar depots attached to the clearing stations; and the establishment of a central workshop for the manufacture of surgical instruments;

(7) the provision of medical staffs for the various towns and cities concerned;

(8) the raising of funds for the work of the Union.

Outlining the program of the work of the Union, the conference declared that it should be closely coördinated with the activities of the Union of Zemstvos and of other organizations with similar objects. The conference also approved the general scheme for the evacuation of the wounded into parts of the country outside the war zone, and passed a budget of 30,000,000 rubles.

Following the lines above, the Union immediately set to work; but practical considerations and the conditions created by the War soon led to new demands and to the extension of its sphere of action.

As early as September 1914, the Union of Towns crossed the line that separated the country in the rear from the area of military operations, and came to the relief of sick and wounded soldiers in the actual trenches. Its depots, trains, medical detachments, hospitals, field-hospitals, canteens, bathhouses, and laundries began to appear in the army itself. Its work in the military area in time became essential, and as such was officially recognized. In the districts adjacent to the war zone the Union worked not only for the army, but also for the unhappy civil population.

A number of new departures were soon made in connection with the relief of sick and wounded soldiers. Some of them may be mentioned: the organization of sanatoriums and health resorts for those suffering from tuberculosis and other diseases; the organization of dental hospitals; the organization of special treatments; the manufacture of artificial limbs, etc. In October 1914 the question was raised as to whether the municipalities should take part in the relief of the families of men who fell in the War. A special department offered legal assistance to all those affected by the War. It gave professional advice on the rights and duties of mobilized men, of the wounded and of their families. The outbreak of epidemics brought to the fore the problem of the participation of the Union in the struggle against these diseases in the army and in the country at large. This in turn called attention to the need of improving the sanitation of towns, and of general conditions of public health.

The terrible events of the spring of 1915—the withdrawal of the Russian Army from the Carpathians and Galicia in consequence of the inadequacy of the supply of munitions and small arms—plunged the whole country into the greatest anxiety. Russia was confronted with a new problem: to supply the army with the equipment and munitions it needed. The Conference of the Representatives of Trade and Commerce sent forth an appeal to Russian industry, calling upon all to make special efforts in order to provide the army with "everything it needed for the defeat of the enemy." The All-Russian Union of Towns immediately responded to this appeal and, together with the Union of Zemstvos, business men, and the representatives of science and technology, took a direct and active part in the organization of army supplies. The first practical result was the appointment of a Central Committee for supplies and equipment, a committee nominated jointly by the Unions. This Committee became known as the *Zemgor:* it developed into an independent organization, which did not work under the flag of the Red Cross; it had a production that amounted to millions of rubles, and became the owner of various business enterprises.[1]

The retreat of Russian armies on the Western Front was accompanied by a mass migration of the population from the districts adjoining the battle area to the central regions of the country. The question of refugees, including their maintenance during their journey and their settlement in new places, became the most pressing and acute problem of the moment. The spontaneous movement of refugees assumed overwhelming proportions, and to cope with the situation, the assistance of public organizations became absolutely necessary. At the end of July 1915 the Central Committee of the Union of Towns outlined a general scheme for the evacuation of refugees, and, together with the Union of Zemstvos, took part in the work of refugee relief.

Thus the Union was extending its sphere of action always more and more, and penetrating farther and farther into the very center of war work. It became always more necessary to the army and to the towns. The military authorities appealed to it for assistance with ever increasing frequency. The municipalities, closely associated with the Union, sought its advice upon all new questions which affected their common work. An instinct of political self-preservation induced the towns to labor unceasingly; and such work, aided by the conditions which were created by the organization of the Union, led them out of their former state of confusion and helplessness.

"The political instinct of Russian people," it was said during the

[1] *Cf.* Polner, Prince Obolensky and Turin, *The Zemstvos and the All-Russian Union of Zemstvos during the War,* in this series of the *Economic and Social History of the World War.*

conference of the Union of Towns held on 12th-14th March 1916, "induces the humble local representatives, who are accustomed to the narrow limits of local finances, to the restricted freedom of action imposed by an obsolete municipal legislation, and to the strict supervision of innumerable authorities—this instinct induces them to undertake without hesitation this great and responsible work which is so new to them and for which they have no adequate training. . . . It is work, too, to which the municipalities are being gradually committed more and more deeply. They are being carried away by the force of events. The work of the Union is the voluntary or compulsory support of those developments demanded by war conditions, developments, moreover, which the Government is unable or unwilling to comprehend. We are led, therefore, to the conclusion that, on the one hand, it is wholly necessary to carry on the work, and that, on the other, it is work that must now be continued under abnormal, impossible conditions. They are conditions which are due to the relations that exist between the Government and the municipalities and zemstvos, and they ought to be altered."[2]

Purely military problems were soon further complicated by the disorganization of the country's economic life. And this assumed the scale of a national calamity. The satisfaction of every new demand arising from conditions in the army and the requirements of the War was frustrated by the disorganization of all economic functions. A country which had a surplus of everything was in want of everything. The speeches and addresses delivered before the fourth conference of the Union of Towns, held on 12th-14th March 1916, disclosed the complicated and tragic situation with which the country was confronted at the beginning of the second year of the War. The conference discussed the economic conditions of the country, the food crisis, the organization of the civilian population. "If Russia desires to win the War, the country should adapt itself to war conditions, it should become an efficient and active seconder of the army, it should supply the army with all that an army must have, to fight and win. In addition to the sacrifices which the people of Russia are prepared to make with resignation, and even gladly, a war of attrition requires a tremendous and active effort of the mind, of the will, of the creative powers, an honest desire on the part of all those con-

[2] *Izvestya Soyuza Gorodov,* 1916, No. 27, p. 11.

cerned to put into practice all the varying measures which conditions make necessary." These words voiced the feelings of all those present at the fourth conference of the Union. The conference laid down, as its leading principle, words which it embodied in the work of the Union, and they were these: "Together with her Allies, Russia remains ready for further sacrifices and a further struggle for a victorious end. The final blow to German imperialism depends on the coördination, skilful organization and sound utilization of all the resources of the country." And, in line therewith, the Union of Towns entered upon an extensive investigation into the country's economic condition and into any methods by which it could be improved.

The Union was not only a technical mechanism for the solution of technical problems; it remained until the last an organization with a public spirit which responded to every appeal made by the country in its emergency. It was accomplishing a great technical task, and this in itself entitled it to express an opinion. Its words of appeal and warning were addressed to the Government and to the country. The Government and the country listened to them. And as for the country, there was no doubt as to its sympathy.

But in the case of the Government, here the attitude was very different. The Government, in its dealings with the Unions, did not conceal its hostility. It did not hesitate to apply restrictions reminiscent of the ancient principle of blocking the development of popular institutions. The whole history of the Union is a continuous struggle for the right to carry on, for the defense and extension of the privileges obtained. It had to fight for each new inch of work and to pay for it by obstinate efforts. Only with reluctance and hesitancy did the Government increase the field of its operations. For the attitude of the Government was determined by secret apprehensions, by a fear of this organization of the country, even though the sole aim of the organization was the winning of the War. The Unions were often put in a most difficult position by delay in the payment of money required for the carrying on of works already in progress and of recognized necessity. The officers commanding minor military units and the commanders of whole armies voiced their gratitude to the Unions, and their complete satisfaction with the work being done for them. They asked them to undertake extensive new work. But the central Government delayed the granting of the requisite money, or even refused altogether the applications made by the Unions. In spite of repeated demands the Unions never obtained the money required for the organization of a systematic campaign against epidemic diseases. Precious time was wasted and these epidemics caused enormous losses.

From the beginning of the War it was the firm belief of the leading spirits of Russia's towns and cities that the army would succeed in its endeavors, and that the decision of the nation to win the War, in coöperation with its Allies, would triumph over all obstacles, provided that a complete mutual confidence between people and Government could be achieved. In the opinion of a conference of the Union of Towns held on 7th-9th September 1915, this could be obtained through the abandonment by the Government of the old attitude of aloofness, of lack of responsiveness, and by an honest and decisive acceptance of new conditions. To bring this to pass, men must be called to office who enjoyed the confidence of the nation. Without further delay the interrupted work of the legislative chambers must be taken up again. And within the country there must be created that peace and spiritual unity which could be brought about only by forgiving and forgetting the political animosities of the past. It was decided that these views of the conference of the Union of Towns, which were fully shared by a conference of the Union of Zemstvos, should be made known to the Emperor, and the two Unions appointed a special deputation for this purpose.

But the audience sought for was refused; and in the meantime internal conditions were rapidly becoming worse. The Government continued deaf to the opinion of the majority of the State Duma, and to the clearly expressed wishes of the public organizations working for the army, even while its isolation was day by day becoming more dangerous. The public organizations felt that salvation from approaching anarchy could be found only in a Government responsible to the representatives of the country. "The power should not remain in the hands of those who are unable to resist secret influences, who refuse to struggle against influences hostile to Russia, and who cannot organize the resources of the country for the War," declared the Union of Towns in October 1916. The Government answered by new repressions and obstructions. Meetings of the representatives of the Unions—and even meetings called to settle pressing technical problems—were prohibited. The conferences of the representatives of Russian towns were dispersed by the police.

Such were the last spasmodic acts of the old régime. It had lost the confidence of the nation and had nothing it could rely upon.

The Tsarist Government fell on 3rd March 1917. Tsarism was overthrown. And, in the midst of the storms of War and of general disorganization, the country entered upon a new period in its history.

New conditions led to considerable changes in the constitution of the Union of Towns. The sixth semi-annual conference of the Union, held on 8th April 1917, fully reflected the changes that had taken place in the country after the eventful days of February and March. The make-up of this conference was very different from that of previous conferences. The 174 representatives of local committees were now supplemented by 213 delegates of newly created bodies. These delegates were chiefly the representatives of Soviets of Soldiers and Workmen which had sprung up all over the country. The previous conferences of the Union of Towns had been composed almost exclusively of liberal and democratic elements; the sixth conference had a strong socialist majority. But these changes make only more noteworthy the attitude of this wholly new conference toward the War, toward the new developments in the life of the country, and toward the former labors of the Union; for the conference directed the Central Committee of the Union "to continue its work of relief, and its efforts to meet the needs created by this war for the liberation of peoples." And the conference likewise called on the Committee "to support and assist the Provisional Government in every possible way." The conference further gave its sanction to all the former work of the Union, both in the army and throughout the country, and decided to continue it "in accordance with requirements."

This attitude of the new conference toward the former work of the Unions clearly indicates that, in spite of the sharp line of demarcation drawn by the Revolution between the old and the new, the Union of Towns had succeeded during the very short term of its existence in creating lasting and vital traditions, and forms which corresponded to the demands of the country's altered conditions.

At the same time the conference stressed the need of an effective support by the Union of the purely municipal activities of the towns, particularly in the organization of the coming municipal elections, and of the elections to the Constituent Assembly.

Meanwhile, too, upon the Union fell the full consequences of rapidly developing events, of new shocks and breakdowns, of the collapse of the front, and of the anarchy in the country. While it went on with its war activities, the Union was soon totally absorbed in the problems brought into existence by the internal chaos of the country.

The Union's final conference was held on 14th October 1917, when, in 643 towns out of 798, municipal elections had taken place under the new Municipal Act of the Provisional Government, an Act which widely extended the suffrage. Few of the 271 representatives who took part in this conference had participated in the former work of the Union. The majority of its members represented the newly elected democratic municipal councils; 184 members belonged to socialist parties, 87 to other parties. This conference asserted in its turn that the "Union was to fulfil its honorable duty to the last, was to carry on the work of the former Union and, together with the National Army, was to defend a Russia newly liberated." Anticipating the approaching end of the War, the conference took up the problem of demobilization, and the coming work of the Union of "free towns."

A few days later the Bolsheviks seized power, a Revolution that was accompanied by the breakdown of these newly established democratic institutions and the collapse of the new municipalities.

CHAPTER VI

ORGANIZATION OF THE UNION OF TOWNS

THE earlier history of Russian towns tells of no organization of municipalities for the pursuance of common purposes. Scattered over the country, without a common program, without experience in public work on any large scale, with limited material resources and still more restricted powers and independence—Russian towns were deprived of all opportunities of coöperation.

The first attempt to organize a union was made during the Russo-Japanese War. In 1905, the mayors of the chief cities and towns met in Moscow on several occasions growing out of the difficulties the country was experiencing as a result of the failure of its military operations in the Far East. An officially recognized organization of the zemstvos was already in existence. In Moscow, in May 1905, as a consequence of the loss of the Russian fleet in the battle of Tsushima, the representatives of the towns and zemstvos met together for the first time. This conference made the celebrated appeal to the Emperor through a special delegation headed by Prince S. N. Trubetskoy. In June of the same year a great gathering of all the mayors of Russia was held in Moscow in the quarters of the Moscow Duma to discuss the general conditions created by the War. In the months that followed the representatives of towns took part in the conferences on the same footing as the representatives of the zemstvos. These conferences had considerable political importance; and their influence is chiefly responsible for the creation of the State Duma and the organization of the representative system. The conferences did not deal with local needs and economic problems. They accepted as the fundamental principle of their work the view that the satisfaction of local requirements and a progressive policy for Russian towns was possible only under normal conditions of political life, and these were unthinkable without popular representation.

The first attempt to bring about a joint consideration of purely municipal problems was made at a conference of representatives of towns held in Odessa in 1910. A similar conference met in Kiev in 1913 to discuss the improvement of municipal finances.

In 1914, the year of the Great War, the towns of Russia met again

and created an organization by which they could give support to the
country during the emergency, an organization that would make
for mutual assistance in the fulfilment of those new obligations
brought forth by the War which they could not face alone.

The formation of the Unions was due to "the conditions created
by the War." The existing legal code did not anticipate the appearance of organizations of this kind and they came into being without
any sanction of law. The organization of the Unions, the ceaseless
and irresistible expansion of their activities, and the great number
of institutions controlled by them were the result of the special conditions created in Russia by the War. The leaders concerned themselves little with the legal aspect of their work. Administrative traditions did not permit of the formation of associations that were
fundamentally opposed to the whole centralized machinery of the
State and to its policy of close supervision of municipal activities.
The method, therefore, by which the All-Russian Union of Towns
was brought into being presents considerable interest from the view-
point of public law, and likewise differentiates it from the municipal
associations of western Europe.

The powers of the Union of Towns, originally limited to the relief
of sick and wounded soldiers during the War, were expanded gradually but persistently until they embraced all the many departments
of national life that were particularly affected by the War. In this
respect the Union of Towns is essentially different from the inter-
communal organizations of western Europe, which were created for
the accomplishing of some definite object.

Another peculiarity of the Union is the fact that its activities
were not confined to any particular district. From the moment of its
establishment it became an All-Russian organization and extended
its work over the whole country. Only for the first few weeks was its
sphere of action limited to the area outside the military zone; this
restriction was soon dropped, and the Union rapidly developed its
work in the army.

Unlike the unions of western Europe, which usually include only
towns with a certain specified population, the Russian Union of
Towns was open to any city or town that chose to enter it.

Generally speaking, unions outside Russia are recognized by public law. They acquire the status and privileges of individuals in the

eyes of the law by a process of legalization and registration carried out by complying with certain fixed formalities, such as the drawing up of articles of association. These set down definitely and clearly the purpose of the organization, its sources of revenue, and the fundamental principles directing its work. The creation and the further development of the Russian Union of Towns was very different. It came into being as the result of an agreement entered into on 8th-9th August 1914, by the representatives of thirty-seven provincial and nine district towns. Their representatives assembled in Moscow. No legislation was introduced to legalize the work of the Union, and its articles of association were never officially sanctioned. The legalization of the Union of Towns must be found in the imperial assent permitting municipalities to join the Union, granted on 16th August 1914. The original purposes of the Union—the relief of sick and wounded soldiers, and the families of mobilized men—were, in accordance with the suggestion of the Council of Ministers, limited (as already stated)[1] to such relief only "during the present War."

The Union of Towns was formed immediately after the creation of the Union of Zemstvos. The latter had the same legal character, and was organized for the same purposes and under the same conditions. On the initiative of the Executive of the zemstvo of Moscow an extraordinary meeting of the Moscow zemstvo, held on 25th July 1914, decided to create an organization for the relief of the wounded. That the zemstvo of Moscow had taken this step was communicated by telegram to other zemstvos. A few days later telegrams were received in reply from almost every part of Russia, and the conference of the representatives of the zemstvos which created the Union of Zemstvos was held on 30th July. The Union was joined by forty-one zemstvos and by the Cossacks of the Don. On 12th August this proposed work of the Union of Zemstvos for the relief of sick and wounded soldiers received the sanction of the Emperor.

M. Stürmer, the Minister of the Interior, at a later period pointed out in a memorandum to the Council of Ministers that the organizers of the Unions had started their work before the attention of the authorities could be drawn to what must be the limits, or even to the essential desirability of such work. The Minister of the Interior,

[1] *See supra,* p. 172.

continued the memorandum, was faced with the necessity of taking official cognizance of the existence of the Unions. At the same time it was his duty to define, and, if possible, curtail the scope of their activities by submitting to the Emperor a report suggesting that their work be sanctioned during the present war, always on the condition, however, that it should be *limited*, as above, to the relief of the sick and wounded.

The legal standing of both Unions partook therefore of a twofold character: The *agreement* or voluntary association of towns (or zemstvos) and the *sanction* of this agreement by an act of the supreme executive power. But both these factors—the agreement as well as the sanction—were only responses to a public demand that had been most clearly expressed. And any delay in responding to it was obviously impossible.

The name of the Union of Towns, as also its purposes and the period over which its work could be extended, was defined by the Executive. With the end of the War, that is, upon the termination of the task for which it was created, its labors were to be brought to an end.

The Union received large sums of money from the Treasury in accordance with estimates which it periodically submitted. Military authorities and government departments entrusted it with the execution of various missions. Finally, following the provisions of the Acts of 17th and 20th August 1915, "the representatives of the All-Russian Unions of Zemstvos and Towns—one representative from each Union—were elected by their respective committees" as members of the Special Councils dealing with national defense, fuel, supply, transport, and refugees, such councils being a recognized part of the central administrative machinery of the country.[2]

These facts make it clear that the Unions of Zemstvos and Towns were not only recognized, but were included in the number of the institutions sanctioned by law. Their existence ceased to be a mere fact and became a right, acknowledged by the State. But although this official recognition fully safeguarded their external legal existence, it did not give them any definite internal legal organization. The Unions themselves were not anxious for any legislation to sanction the principles on which their work was based. They had ample

[2] *Cf.* Gronsky, *The Effects of the War upon the Central Government of Russia*, Chapter II.

proofs of their own ability to ensure the internal stability of their organization, and they themselves solved all problems and legal controversies arising in the course of their work. Yet if their work itself did not suffer from the absence of a clearly established legal status, the necessity of such a status was occasionally felt in their relations with the outside world. The Unions, as such, had no standing before the law, which was a serious drawback from the point of view of the civil code.

A special bill giving legal recognition to the Unions, with the object of facilitating their work, was submitted to the State Duma on 4th April 1916. The promoters of this Bill explained that it was desirable to alter a state of affairs in which the Unions, though they performed the functions of important government departments, were denied any real legal status. In the field of relations governed by the civil code the Unions were not sufficiently safeguarded against dishonest contractors, or against having their positions brought into question in the courts of law on purely technical grounds. The legal acts which formally recognized the existence of the Unions proved inadequate to confer upon them, for instance, the power to acquire real property, to be parties to a contract, or to enforce their proprietary rights in court.

When dealing with this bill the Government suggested a number of amendments designed to curtail the independence of the Unions, and these amendments were held to be essential to the consent of the Government to their complete legal recognition. The Unions could not accept these amendments and the question of legal recognition was left unsettled. The Union of Towns was, therefore, never officially sanctioned, in a legal sense.

With reference to the problem of the status of the Unions before the law, the representatives of the Government maintained that such status could be bestowed on them by an act of the Government, because, in their opinion, the Unions "were not Government Departments in the strict meaning of the term," but "should be rather treated as private associations governed by *jus privatum*." There is no doubt, however, that the Unions of Zemstvos and Towns could not be considered as organizations governed by *jus privatum*, since they did not aim at obtaining profits from their undertakings, either for themselves or for their members. They could not be treated as associations formed by private initiative and designed to carry on their work only as long as their members so desired, according to the definition set forth in the Regulations on Associations and Meetings of 4th March 1906. As was rightly pointed out by Prof. Elistratov, the Unions were associations of State institutions—the zemstvos and the municipalities—which fulfilled important public functions. The Unions themselves were engaged in work of undoubted public value, which conferred upon them the definite character of institutions coming under the *jus publicum*, not the *jus privatum:* and they were the instruments through which the zemstvos and municipalities exercised their powers.

Judicial practice closed the gap, made the position of the Unions virtually legal, and recognized their right to own real property. For instance, when in Ekaterinodar a gift of land was made to the Union of Towns, a decision of the District Court declared the gift to be valid. The question of the precise sanction under which they worked was a rather intricate part of the problem of the legal character of the Unions, and it led to numerous controversies. But the willingness of the municipalities to join together was quite clear and definite.

Admission to the Union of Towns became possible when the Duma of the town in question passed a resolution in favor of joining it. Towns, therefore, became members only if they chose to do so. Membership meant participation in the work organized for the relief of sick and wounded soldiers. No special obligations were imposed upon new members. The amount of the contribution to the funds of the Union was, originally, left to the will of the municipality; but later on a certain uniformity was introduced by Regulations of the Union of Towns. The advantages conferred by membership of the Union were enjoyed not only by the towns that contributed to its funds, but also by those which had hospitals equipped and maintained by it, or had expressed the desire to have them, even though they did not subscribe to the common fund. There were even towns which neither had hospitals nor contributed to the funds and yet held themselves to be members of the Union, and shared in the benefits derived from such membership.

The part taken by the towns of Russia in the Union is illustrated by the following figures: In September 1914, 195 joined it. At the end of the first five months of the War, that is, at the beginning of January 1915, its membership was increased to 428. It was 468 in

January 1916, and 495 on 1st May of the same year. When we remember that before the War the total number of Russian towns— provincial, regional, *gradonachalstvos*,[3] district and smaller townships—was 1,011,[4] we find that 48.9 per cent became members, even when we include the towns of Finland, Caucasus, and Siberia. If we deduct the 116 towns of the Kingdom of Poland, most of which from the very beginning of the War were situated in the zone of military operations, then the percentage will rise to 55.2 per cent. By 1st September 1917, the membership of the Union had become 630. At that time 179 towns were occupied by the enemy and the members of the Unions represented 75 per cent of the total number of towns still free from foreign invasion. The keenest interest in the work of the Union was displayed by the towns of Finland, which were represented by 63.2 per cent of their total number; the towns of European Russia were represented by 58.2 per cent; Caucasus, 53.2 per cent; Siberia, 41.4 per cent; and the towns of the steppes and of Turkestan, 23.1 per cent.

Considering only provincial and regional towns, European Russia gives a membership of 98 per cent; the Caucasus, 78.6 per cent; Siberia, 70 per cent; and Finland, 50 per cent,—these figures being for January 1916.

As stated above, the Union of Towns possessed no written constitution that had been sanctioned by any competent authority. Nevertheless, the fundamental organization outlined by the conference of 7th-9th September 1914, and confirmed by the fourth conference held on 12th March 1916, was preserved as a kind of unwritten constitution, until the downfall of the old régime. Certain changes in the organization of the Union took place after the Revolution, at the conference of 8th-10th April 1917. The statute of the Union of Towns was finally accepted by the last conference of the Union, held on 14th-17th October, a few days before the Bolshevik *coup d'état*.

In accordance with the principle steadily maintained throughout the whole period of the existence of the Union the supreme power was vested in the conference of the representatives of the towns which

[3] *Gradonachalstvo*—urban settlements which constituted separate administrative units.

[4] Data of the Central Statistical Committee.

joined the organization. These representatives were not necessarily members of local municipal councils (Dumas); any local resident duly elected by the Duma or by a special committee could act as such. Towns and cities with a population of less than 100,000 were represented by one member; the number of representatives increased in proportion to the size of the population, and reached ten each for Moscow and Petrograd.

Conferences had the general supervision and direction of the work of the Union; they examined and approved estimates and reports; they controlled the activities of the Central Committee and local institutions. The work was closely connected throughout with the course of events in the army, and required an organization capable of prompt and decisive action. This led to the creation of an executive machinery, all sections of which worked in close coöperation and at the same time enjoyed a considerable degree of independence. The executive machinery was divided into three parts: the central administration, the administration in the military zone, and local organizations throughout the country.

The central administration consisted of the High Commissioner, his Deputy, the Central Committee, and the Executive Bureau. The High Commissioner was the representative of the Union; he presided over the Central Committee and in case of emergency could make personal decisions, which, however, he had to report to the Committee. The Deputy High Commissioner presided over the Executive Bureau and conducted all the routine work.

The Central Committee of the Union, in the beginning, consisted of 17 members: the High Commissioner, his Deputy, and 15 members. The membership of the Committee was eventually extended, and in 1916 was raised to 72. The Committee included all responsible heads of separate branches of the Union's work, representatives of large local organizations, of Petrograd and Moscow, and a number of public men, some of them prominent in various departments of technical knowledge. The Central Committee of 1916 had among its members 8 doctors, 10 lawyers, 6 engineers, 12 scientists, 7 members of the State Duma, and 16 mayors.

It became customary to hold meetings of the Central Committee with the participation of the mayors of provincial towns. These meetings maintained the internal link between the central and local organizations. The Central Committee, in spite of the large number of its members, was a thoroughly efficient organization, and through-out its existence it enjoyed unquestioned authority among the public institutions and forces which supported the work of the Union.

The Executive Bureau was an auxiliary body attached to the Central Committee. The Central Committee met every fortnight; the Executive Bureau met several times a week in order to exercise an effective control over the current work. It included representatives specially elected by the Central Committee from its own members and residing in Moscow, and all the heads of the separate departments of the Union's work. A Financial Board was attached to the Executive Bureau in October 1916, and was concerned with the preliminary examination of all financial problems.

The work of the central organization of the Union, which developed rapidly, was distributed among twenty-one departments: (1) the medico-sanitary department, with the following subdepartments: hospitals, sanitary work, and medical staff; (2) evacuation, with subdepartments on statistics and the Caucasus; (3) inquiry; (4) surgical and bacteriological; (5) the supply of medical goods and bandages; (6) the supply of materials and underwear; (7) the sanitary-technical department with the motor-car and building subsections; (8) hospital trains; (9) army canteens; (10) work in the military zone; (11) liaison; (12) food supply; (13) economic; (14) legal department; (15) relief of prisoners of war; (16) raising of funds by voluntary contributions; (17) the editorial boards of the Bulletin of the Union of Towns; (18) the information department; (19) the secretariat; (20) bookkeeping and the preparation of estimates department; (21) the controlling department. Each of the above-mentioned departments was headed by a member of the Central Committee; but no salary was attached to the position.

The downfall of the old régime brought about a change in the constitution of the local organizations of the Union. This took place even before the election of the municipal Dumas under the new Municipal Act making it possible for all citizens to participate in the conduct of municipal affairs. Almost all the municipal Dumas, with a few exceptions (among which was the Duma of Moscow), were "democratized," i.e., the right to sit on the municipal council was extended, without any legal formalities, from professional associations of workmen and other public bodies to the representatives of Soviets of Workmen and Soldiers. The sixth conference of the Union, which was representative of the new tendencies, outlined a new by-law for the control of the Union of Towns. It was immediately made operative and was sanctioned by the seventh conference of the Union held in October 1917. This by-law abolished the office of High Commissioner; the membership of the Central Committee was limited to seventy-six; every forty members of the local Dumas had to be represented at the conferences of the Union by one delegate; but the municipalities of Petrograd and Moscow were, as before, each to be represented by ten members. The sixth conference originally elected the Central Committee on the basis of proportional representation of the so-called "census" group[5] of the former leaders of the Union, and of the Socialist Bloc. But the principle of proportional representation soon gave place to a method dictated by the real needs and requirements of the work, and it was not revived in the governing by-law adopted by the seventh conference. The local municipalities formed the nucleus of the chief organization of the Union of Towns outside the military area. The towns which joined the Union appointed local committees of the Union of Towns; these committees were special organizations, formed during the War. The local municipal committees for the relief of sick and wounded soldiers were elected by the municipal councils from their own members. But the limited number of persons who were eligible as members of local Dumas proved incapable, without outside help, of coping with new war problems. The local committees, therefore, extended their membership to various groups outside the municipal Dumas, such as physicians, engineers, and others of technical training. Many local committees gave good evidence of their vitality; they developed great activity, and showed much initiative and creative power.

The regional organizations occupied an intermediate position and served as links between the central administration and local committees. They were originally created for the purpose of organizing the evacuation of the wounded, and covered the districts along the railway lines used for the evacuation; they were afterwards reorganized on lines suggested by economic and national considerations. In 1915 and 1916, when the activities of the Union of Towns were at their height, the number of regional organizations was thirteen. The most important among them was the Committee for the Region

[5] That is, members possessing a property qualification.

of Petrograd, which gave proof of considerable independence in the coördination of the work of municipal organizations in the north of Russia. The Regional Committee of the Caucasus, of the Union of Towns, sprang into life on the isolated Caucasus front. It was financed partly by the State Treasury and partly by the Union of Towns. The towns of Siberia also created a united organization for the relief of sick and wounded soldiers. They became members of the Siberian association for the relief of the victims of the War, which collected a large amount of money, and was especially distinguished for its work at the front. The towns of Finland likewise formed an independent Union associated with the All-Russian Union of Towns. After the Revolution, the regional organizations were given a more definite form, and the towns of the Caucasus, of East and West Siberia formed autonomous Unions of Towns. The future constitution of the Union of Towns was, therefore, outlined as a kind of federation of regional unions.

The two capitals occupied a peculiar position. Moscow and Petrograd were formally members of the Union. It had been organized on the initiative of the municipality of Moscow, and the largest sums toward its expense were subscribed by Moscow and Petrograd. But the scope of the activities of the capitals, particularly of Moscow, was so wide and their administrative machinery was so powerful, that it was natural for them to conduct their work independently, with funds supplied directly to them by the State Treasury.

The work of the Union at the front by its very nature demanded a certain degree of decentralization and independence. The organizations of the Union attached to the army were controlled by three Committees of the Front, each being headed by a special commissioner. All their work was carried on in accordance with instructions specially issued by the Central Committee of the Union. Individual sections of the Union were put under the charge of commissioners. The Committees of the Front were connected with the central organization by a special central department assigned to work at the front. The alteration of the whole administrative machinery of the Union that took place in the year of the Revolution affected also the membership of these Committees of the Front. The office of special commissioner was abolished; members of Committees of the Front were now divided into two groups, one elected by the Central Committee, the other by the employees of the Union, by hospital workers, and by workmen. Committees of the Front also included two representatives of the Soviet of Soldiers. The Chairmen of Committees of the Front were appointed by the Central Committee, and they become *ex-officio* members of Committees of the Front. They were also necessarily coöpted to the Central Committee.

The Union of Towns was a voluntary association. The decisions of its officials did not have the value of commands binding upon the local Dumas. They could be submitted to discussion, criticism, and correction by them. The Union endeavored to coördinate the work of local institutions, to direct the efforts of separate municipalities toward a common aim, and to bring about closer coöperation by the aid of periodic discussions of matters of common interest. The public organizations which joined the Union preserved their full independence and their complete freedom of action. There was no means of enforcing a decision of the Union which one of its members chose to disregard.

The work of the Union was conducted openly and under the control of public opinion so far as this was possible in war-time conditions. The country and the army knew the work of the Union. It was a fact of common knowledge and could be seen everywhere—at the front and in the adjoining districts, in every town, every railway station, along the routes of the evacuation of wounded and refugees. Famous scientists and men of outstanding reputation in various branches of technical knowledge took part in the labors of these institutions set up by the Union, in its conferences on medical and technical questions, on economic and legal subjects. Wide opportunities were open to private initiative. These features of the work of the Union greatly contributed to its authority and popularity.

The Union of Towns and the Union of Zemstvos displayed most friendly coöperation in practical work. Not only was the Central Committee of each represented on that of the other, but they even created common organizations for the settlement of certain problems. Such joint organizations were the Committee on Tuberculosis, the Administration for the Relief of Refugees, the Administration for the Relief of Prisoners of War, and, finally, the Central Committee for the Supply of the Army, or the Zemgor.

Some idea of the scope and the scale of the work of the Union of

Towns may be gathered from the number of persons employed in its central administration, in local institutions, and at the front.

On 1st September 1917, the figures were as follows:

	Men and women	Women	Percentage of women
(1) Local and district committees	30,000	16,000	53.33
(2) Central Committee and Administration	2,636	876	33.23
(3) Committees of the Front	21,500	5,420	25.20
Total of persons permanently employed by the Union	54,000		
Number of noncommissioned soldiers attached to the Union	16,000		
Total	70,000		

Of the total number of men employed by the Union of Towns on 1st September 1917, 3,161 were liable to military service under the law of conscription. Of these, 1,603 were officially transferred to the medical service, and 1,558 were granted exemption. These men were permitted to remain in the service of the Union after their cases had been given careful consideration by specially appointed government commissions, which came to the conclusion that it would be impossible or exceedingly difficult to find skilled specialists who could replace them. The Union of Towns thus enjoyed a privilege conferred upon all the organizations working for national defense; members of their technical staffs could claim exemption from conscription on the ground that they could not abandon their work without damage to the national interests.

As already stated, the representatives of the municipalities, during their first meeting held in Moscow in connection with the War, found themselves compelled to acknowledge that the financial resources of the towns were quite inadequate to meet the new demands resulting from the outbreak of hostilities. They pointed out that they could not undertake to carry out their new obligations except on the clear understanding that only a small fraction of their modest revenue should be devoted to War purposes, and that the necessary funds should be provided by the State Treasury. Treasury grants were in fact the chief source of the money spent by the Union of Towns on the relief of sick and wounded soldiers, on the prevention of epi-

demics, on the organization of the relief of refugees and other charitable work. The donations of private persons and institutions, the
subscriptions of the municipalities as members of the Union, and,
finally, the proceeds from the sale of goods in its warehouses, formed
a very insignificant part of its total revenue. Private donations of
money and goods continued to be made throughout the whole duration of the War; but this stream of contributions was by no means a
steady one. It was very large during the first few months, but fell
when the War began to be looked upon as a part of the natural course
of things. Then, on occasion, it would rise again under the pressure
of a new calamity, such, for instance, as the tide of refugees flung
upon the country in the summer of 1915. The total donations in cash
to the central and local institutions of the Union of Towns during
the first year of the War reached 1,800,000 rubles. Gifts were also
made in kind and ranged from a piece of homemade cotton cloth
presented by a peasant to precious works of art. In March 1916 the
sum total of donations—both in cash and in kind—amounted to some
4,000,000 rubles. But by the end of 1916 and in 1917 such support
had fallen almost to nothing.

The size of the contributions which should be made by the towns
that joined the Union was not, at first, definitely prescribed. It was
suggested that they should contribute from 0.1 per cent to 1 per cent
of the amount of their budgets. The actual sum paid varied considerably, running from 25 rubles (Krasnik, province of Lublin) to
100,000 rubles (Moscow and Petrograd). A uniform rate of subscription—0.25 per cent of the municipal budget—was adopted
only by the last conference of the Union. Not all of the towns
that joined the Union were in a position to pay their contributions
regularly. Those close to the front, which had to bear the full consequences of their nearness to the war zone, were of necessity irregular in their payments. And this, of course, applied even more to those
which were presently within the German lines. In certain provinces
the decisions of the municipal Dumas to subscribe to the funds of
the Union were set aside by the governors on the ground that expenditure of this kind had not been provided for by law.

In May 1916, of the total number of towns (495) which joined
the Union, 364, or practically three-fourths, subscribed to its funds.
Of the total number of cities and large towns (including the capitals,
the provincial and regional towns) that had become members, the

following percentage paid their allotted subscriptions: in European Russia, 95.9 per cent; in the Caucasus, 81.8 per cent; in Siberia, 85.7 per cent. The Union occasionally registered as payment of subscriptions the advance of money by the municipalities for the organization and maintenance of its institutions, seeing that it granted subsidies to its members for this purpose.

On 1st August 1915, the total contribution of the towns to the funds of the Union amounted to 1,282,543 rubles. On 1st January 1916, the sum voted by the municipalities that were members of the Union, toward its expenses, was 1,411,000 rubles, of which 1,329,000 was actually paid. This contribution of the municipalities represents about 0.34 per cent of their total pre-war budget.

The ratio between the amount of the government grants and the revenue from other sources may be seen from the following data, taken from a report of 1st January 1915:

	Rubles
Government grants	32,099,000
Subscribed by the towns	1,282,543
Donations	1,846,619

A report, dated 1st August 1916, shows that during the first two years of the War the Central Committee alone effected payments to the amount of 125,000,000 rubles. Of this sum, 117,000,000 rubles represented government grants (32,000,000 rubles in 1914 and 1915, and 84,000,000 rubles in 1916), and only 8,000,000 rubles came from donations, subscriptions, or from other sources.

The estimates of the Union of Towns for the second half of 1916, ending on 1st January 1917, included the following principal items:

	Rubles
Treatment of sick and wounded	29,460,611
Transport, army canteens	1,825,558
Sanitation	2,869,050
Other expenditure	7,208,821
	41,364,040

For the same period the estimated expenditure of the Union on the three military fronts was 31,000,000 rubles.

The report submitted by the head of the accounting department of the Union of Towns to the seventh conference of the Union, held on 14th-17th October 1917, shows that the cash expenditure of the Union in 1917 up to 1st September amounted to 232,000,000 rubles. Of the 232,000,000 rubles that constituted the revenue, 106,000,000 rubles represented government grants, and the remainder was derived from various investments and transfers, subscriptions and other miscellaneous receipts. The sums quoted do not include the revenue and expenditure of the two capitals and the Caucasus, the addition of which would probably double the figures given above. This may give the reader some idea of the scope of the work of the Union.

Grants from the Treasury were obtained through the Union's Central Committee, which, every two months, submitted its estimates to a special interdepartmental committee for the consideration of all applications for grants in connection with the War. This committee was attached to the General Staff and consisted of representatives of the War Office, the Home Office, the Ministry of Finance, and the State Audit Department. If an order was placed with the Union by the Army Supply Department of the War Office or by some other military authority, the credits necessary for its carrying out were occasionally opened by the authority that placed it. An additional sum of 3 per cent on all Red Cross expenditures was granted to the Union in order to defray costs of administration.

The large scale of the Union's financial operations and its very nature as a public organization entrusted with the accomplishment of a task of vital national importance and conducted with funds obtained from the Treasury, caused the Central Committee to devote particular care to bookkeeping, the audit of accounts, and inspections. The books of the Central Committee were audited by a special permanent Commission appointed by the Conferences of the Union. The books and accounts of local institutions of the Union were examined and passed by the audit committees of the respective municipal Dumas. But the audit of the books after payments had been made did not present sufficient guarantees that the very large sums which passed through the hands of the central and local committees of the Union were actually spent for the purposes and in the way intended. The necessity of an effective control before the transaction took place led the Central Committee to establish an audit department, which had the task of examining and checking all accounts presented for payment before actual payment should take place. The audit department had also to examine all documents relating to advances made to or by the Union. It took part in the examination of the supplies belonging to the Union, and it was represented when new supplies were delivered. It was also the duty of this department to draw up reports which incorporated such data as had been furnished by the controlling committees throughout the country.

As early as September 1914 the Central Committee requested the Prime Minister to appoint a representative of the State Audit Department to be present at the meetings of the Central Committee dealing with financial estimates and affairs. This request was complied with, and accordingly the whole activities of the Union were, thereafter, conducted under the supervision of a representative of the Government. At the further request of the Union, special representatives of the State Audit Department were attached to the control department of the Central Committee and to the boards of audit of some of the Committees of the Front. A representative of the State Controller, specially appointed by him to investigate certain charges made against the Union by the enemies of independent public organizations, declared in December 1915 that the books and accounts of the Union were in perfect order and that he was fully satisfied with them.

CHAPTER VII

PUBLIC HEALTH

WAR was declared by Germany on 19th July,[1] and on 6th August the first train containing wounded reached Moscow. Moscow, as the largest city and the junction of ten railway lines which connected all parts of the country with the front, was certain, in the nature of things, to receive great numbers of wounded. And it did. Immediately after the outbreak of the War it became the largest of clearing stations for wounded. About 60 per cent of the whole number of men invalided from the front passed through the city. It likewise became the largest hospital center in the country, equipping and maintaining a large number of beds. At the same time Moscow provided a kind of great protective screen for the front, by isolating the men suffering from infectious diseases. For this department alone more than 10,000 hospital beds were maintained. The work of the municipality of Moscow for the evacuation of the wounded was intimately connected with that of the All-Russian Union of Towns. This link was created not only by the common purpose and character of the work, but also by the fact that it was organized and conducted to a large extent by the same men. The Mayor of Moscow was the High Commissioner of the Union, and the representatives of the Moscow Duma were among the most zealous and permanent members of the staff of the central organizations of the Union.

For the first two weeks this work of evacuation of the wounded disclosed an appalling lack of organization. Hospital trains, hastily and inadequately equipped, and consisting mainly of overcrowded luggage vans, arrived without notice. The wounded were unloaded upon the platforms, and often occupied all the available space in the railway stations. Railway lines were blocked by hospital trains. The number of hospital beds was inadequate. And while some towns and cities were sent too many wounded, others received none at all. On 23rd August the Union of Towns sent out a circular note to the municipalities, asking them to make the necessary preparations for the receipt of wounded and to supply the Union with a periodical

[1] Russian calendar.

record containing data as to the number of beds immediately available, which data was to be followed by notifications of all vacancies as they occurred, and of the establishment of all new beds.

The first estimate of the number of beds controlled by the Union was made on 20th August; it showed that along the line of ten railways it already had 6,628 available. This reserve of beds in various towns allowed the Union to set up an organization for the evacuation of the wounded from Moscow, and to draw up a general plan for carrying it out. The plan was prepared and approved by the Conference of 14th-15th September 1914. It emphasized the necessity of a common organization for the relief of the wounded. It pointed to the need of special committees for dealing with the evacuation, in which public organizations should be duly represented. It also dealt with the creation of registration centers, army canteens along the railway lines, the adequate equipment of hospital trains, hospitals for epidemic diseases, health resorts, and establishments for mental treatment.

The plan for the evacuation of the wounded was to a greater or less degree put in operation at all the clearing stations that were opened in Moscow, Petrograd, Orel, Kursk, Kharkov, Ekaterinoslav, Rostov-on-Don, and Tiflis. To each of the provinces of European Russia was assigned one of the above-mentioned clearing stations, and from this station it obtained its wounded. Siberia and Central Asia were not originally included in the scheme. But after the retreat of the Russian armies in the summer of 1915 the influx of wounded became so great that Moscow, with its thousands of beds and its seven clearing hospitals, found it difficult to stand the strain. It had to convert into hospitals, barracks, schools, and other public buildings. Later on, the curtailment of the number of hospital beds in the western part of Russia and the advance of the front line made imperative some change and improvement of evacuation methods. And the conference of the Union of Towns held on 7th-9th September 1915, decided to open new clearing stations in Perm and Chelyabinsk and to extend the organization of military hospitals to the towns of Siberia.

The reception of the wounded on their arrival at the clearing stations, with their further evacuation, was entrusted to special mixed committees consisting of representatives of the War Office, the Red Cross, and of both Unions. Various statistical bureaus attached to the Union of Towns recorded the movements of the wounded, and collected data on the number of beds available in each area.

The application of this scheme materially improved the situation. The towns provided with clearing hospitals were given preliminary notice of the arrival of hospital trains, which allowed them to give medical examination to the arriving men, to arrange to bathe them, to provide them with clean underwear, and to disinfect their belongings. The plan of evacuation provided for the equipment of hospital trains and for the organization of army canteens along the railway lines. The inadequacy of the equipment of hospital trains, which often had no kitchens, resulted in deplorable irregularity in providing whole detachments of wounded with hot food. The Central Committee of the Union of Towns, as early as September 1914, held an inquiry into the condition of railway stations between the important railway junctions, such as Kiev, Minsk, Vilno, Petrograd, and Moscow. All over the country private organizations and associations sprang up spontaneously and did what they could to provide the evacuated men with food and tobacco, also, in some cases, with underwear, bandages, and clothing. The necessary funds were raised by voluntary subscriptions and donations, and the work was carried on by the free labor of thousands of volunteers. On 30th September 1914, the Central Committee decided to give support to all the canteens so organized on condition that they would accept the control of the Union over their expenditures and accounts, and comply with certain general rules. And the question of joining the Union was a vital one for private organizations; the work carried on by voluntary contributions had gradually to be cut down because of the increasing cost of living, until finally it ceased altogether. In October 1914 the flag of the Union was flown by six canteens attached to railway stations. In November they numbered 32; in December, 81. In February 1915 the number of railway canteeens was 118; in December, 133. In 1916 the number of canteens had begun to grow fewer. It was 110 in January, 102 in July, and 99 in December. Some of the canteens were closed down; some were transferred to other organizations.

These canteens were divided into three classes: small canteens providing cold food, light refreshments, and tea and tobacco; canteens that were more elaborate and which provided hot food; and, finally, canteens located in large centers, which possessed stores of underwear, clothing, and medical supplies. Of this third type of canteens there were 39.

In the summer of 1915, when tens and hundreds of thousands of refugees flooded the railways, the railway canteens undertook to relieve and feed them. And the machinery of these railway canteens, quickly adapting itself to the emergency, rendered invaluable services. In August 1915 such relief was administered by 98 canteens.

The number of meals distributed by the canteens of the Union of Towns up to 1st January 1916, was as follows: 4,870,076 to the wounded, and 8,642,676 to refugees, a total of 13,512,752. The expenditure on foodstuffs amounted to 1,344,877 rubles; the maintenance of canteens in 1916 cost the Union 616,034 rubles. During this period the canteens of the Union provided food for 3,278,229 men and women.

In August and September 1914, the Union of Towns entered into an agreement with the War Office: the Union undertook the complete equipment of hospital trains, including the provision of medical staff, instruments, and stores, the maintenance of personnel and of the sick and wounded while in transit, the laundry expenses, etc.; the War Office undertook to provide the Union with rolling stock and to defray all railway charges. In the spring of 1915 the Union of Towns had thirteen hospital trains; two of them bore the name of the Municipality of Moscow and one was equipped entirely by private donations. Some of these trains were employed outside the military area in conveying the wounded from the clearing stations to their ultimate destination; others, known as field hospital trains, were attached to the section of the railway between the front and the clearing stations. One train was transferred to the Caucasus and was controlled and provided for by the town of Baku. Each train consisted of a permanent section of 8 or 9 carriages and comprised quarters for the staff, berths for seriously wounded men, a dispensary, departments for medical and general stores, and a kitchen. The permanent section was supplemented by a provisional one, which consisted of some 13 to 20 carriages in the trains working away from the front, and of 24 to 30 carriages in the field trains. A field train could receive about 700 men, a train of the other type about 400. The equipment of a train cost between 22,000 and 26,000 rubles. The combined staff of all hospital trains of the Union on 1st

November 1915 consisted of 806 persons, including 32 doctors. The total number of journeys was 326, covering 490,231 versts (326,-800 miles) ; the number of men evacuated was 159,157. In March 1916 the number of men carried by the trains of the Union was 200,-000, and in October 1917 the total number stood at 340,000.

On 30th August 1914, the Union accepted a scheme for organizing hospitals and increasing the number of beds. The number of beds in the interior of Russia was estimated by the War Office to be 280,000; of these, 258,920 beds, or 92.5 per cent, represented those of the two Unions, together with those in Moscow and Petrograd. In order to make easier the establishment of new hospitals, the Union of Towns sent to the municipalities concerned all necessary information as to the distribution of wounded, estimates for hospital organization, and detailed schedules of the expenditure involved in the equipment and maintenance of hospital beds. These were divided into three classes according to the seriousness of the wound or disease. The estimates for September 1914 were as follows: the equipment of a bed of the first class, 100 rubles; second, 80 rubles; and third, 50 rubles. The monthly expenditure for the maintenance of a bed was reckoned at 40 rubles for a hospital, and 25 rubles for a *patronage*.[2] According to a report for September-December 1915, the average expenditure for one bed was 25 rubles. The largest items of expenditure were the salaries of the medical staff and food for the patients, which absorbed 62.2 per cent of the total. The greatest deviation from average figures occurred in the cost of medical staffs and medical and sanitary stores.

The task of providing for the equipment of 65,000 beds out of the total number of 258,920 mentioned above was turned over to the Union of Towns; that of providing the remaining beds was divided between the Union of Zemstvos and the municipalities of Moscow and Petrograd. The appeal made by the Union of Towns to the municipalities led not only to a speedy fulfilment of its obligations, but even to a surplus in the number of beds actually established; there were three times the number assigned to the Union under the original scheme. Large cities and small towns took an equal interest in the organization and equipment of hospitals. Military hospitals were established in August 1914, in 10 towns; in January 1915, in 98

[2] *See infra,* p. 207.

towns; in August 1915, in 169; in January 1916, in 248 towns of central Russia; and in 12 towns of the Caucasus. The increase in the number of hospital beds recorded with the Union of Towns may be illustrated by the following data; Moscow, Petrograd, and the towns of the Caucasus are not included:

Date	Number of beds
August 1914	6,628
January 1915	38,967
July 1915	45,994
August 1915	45,899
October 1915	47,343
January 1916	55,958
August 1917	80,894

The geographical distribution of hospitals on 1st January 1916 was as follows:

Region	Number of beds
Moscow	19,299
Orel	6,690
Petrograd	5,227
Ekaterinoslav	4,305
Rostov-on-Don	2,967
Kharkov	2,769
Kursk	2,465
Finland	2,179
Kiev and the provinces not included in the regions named above	10,057
Total	55,958

To which should be added:

Moscow (the City of)	73,248
Petrograd (the City of)	25,198
The towns of the Caucasus	23,963

Moscow had 1,075 hospitals with 76,580 beds, of which 3,332 were maintained at the expense of the Red Cross, the Union of Zemstvos, the imperial family, etc. The remaining beds were registered with and provided for by the municipality of Moscow. The total number of hospital beds in Petrograd on 20th December 1915 was 39,173; the hospitals managed by the War Office are not included in this number. Of the total number of 23,963 beds in the towns of the

Caucasus, 20,162 were controlled by the Union of Towns and 3,800 by local organizations.

The total number of hospital beds under the control of the municipalities of Russia on 1st January 1916 amounted to 178,364.[3] If we add to this figure the 3,500 beds in sanatoriums, and 10,000 beds in isolation hospitals and at the front, the total number of beds controlled by the Union of Towns in the autumn of 1916 reaches something like 200,000.

They were distributed among the towns of Russia (omitting the two capitals and the towns of the Caucasus) as follows: Kiev, 6,480; Kazan, 4,895; Nizhni-Novgorod, 2,666; Saratov, 1,316; Voronezh, 1,220; Tula, 1,103; Kharkov, 1,107; Rostov-on-Don, 1,065. Seventeen towns had from 500 to 1,000 beds; 60, from 100 to 500, and the remaining 173, less than 100 beds each.

The number of sick and wounded who passed through the hospitals of the Union, from the beginning of the War until January 1916, is shown in the following table:

	Number of patients	Percentage of the total number
Moscow	348,000	27
Petrograd	152,000	12.1
European Russia	566,000	45
The Caucasus	186,000	14.7
Finland	8,000	0.6
Total	1,260,000	

The most rapid increase in the number of the beds controlled by the Union took place at the end of 1914 and the beginning of 1915. The subsequent development of the hospital work of the Union was chiefly connected with local hospitals, that is, hospitals which were registered with the Union for the purpose of aiding in the evacuation of the wounded, but which were maintained at the expense of local municipalities or by private subscriptions. In 1916 and the beginning of 1917 the Union concerned itself principally with special phases of relief, and engaged in an energetic struggle against epidemics; and this called for an increase in the number of beds for

[3] Report presented to the Central Committee by the Deputy High Commissioner of the Union of Towns on 17th January 1916.

patients suffering from infectious diseases. The total number of beds for surgical treatment, however, remained, generally speaking, unaltered. The newly established beds had little effect upon the total figure as they merely filled up the gaps left by the closing of existing hospitals. The facts quoted above are meant to convey to the reader an idea of the scale of the hospital work undertaken by the Union of Towns and by the municipalities of Russia.

The work performed by the municipality of Moscow in this department was exceptionally important. It began with the grant of one million rubles voted for hospital purposes by the Moscow Duma on 18th July 1914. But as early as 2nd September the municipality of Moscow applied to the Government for a grant of 11,000,000 rubles for the development and expansion of its work for the relief of the sick and wounded. From the beginning of the War until 1st July 1916, the Government granted Moscow 60,500,000 rubles for hospital work, and the estimates for the second half of 1916 amounted to 30,000,000 rubles. During the first months of the War the number of sick and wounded received by Moscow was 52,495, the arrival of wounded increasing greatly during the periods of heavy fighting. The average was five hospital trains a day. The total number of trains, from the beginning of the War to 1st May 1916, was 3,327; one of the worst days was 21st July 1915, when twenty-one trains brought in 9,601 wounded soldiers. When the fighting was bitterest, and during the evacuation of the population in western Russia in the summer of 1916, Moscow had to deal with an average of more than 10,000 wounded soldiers a day. In the first seventeen months of the War, up to 1st January 1916, 1,191,169 men passed through her clearing stations; of this number, 737,219 were wounded, 348,481 were suffering from diseases, and 105,469 were prisoners of war requiring medical treatment.

Up to 1st March 1916, Moscow's clearing stations received and evacuated 1,415,218 sick and wounded men. Of this number, 176,206 passed through a clearing station attached to the War Office; 145,-676 through that of the Red Cross, 1,004,139 through the clearing stations—six—of the municipality of Moscow, and 89,197 through the depots established at railway stations at an early stage of the War. Of the total number evacuated, the clearing stations controlled by the municipality received 75 per cent. And, on 1st April 1916, Moscow's clearing stations were equipped with 8,503 beds.

About 30 per cent of such sick and wounded men remained in the hospitals of Moscow; 50 per cent were sent on to other parts of Russia, 16 per cent were transferred to the hospitals managed by the War Office. At the municipal clearing stations the evacuated men were divided into groups and registered; they had their hair cut, were given baths, and supplied with clean underwear; their clothes were disinfected and they were sent to various hospitals in Moscow and elsewhere. As a rule, they did not remain at the clearing stations for more than thirty-six hours.

The largest numbers passing through the clearing stations of Moscow were registered in the following months: July (134,179), August (121,547), and September (102,538), 1915; October and November 1914, and March 1915, each of these months gives more than 80,000 wounded soldiers; February, May, and June 1915, more than 70,000 each; August 1914, and April 1915, more than 50,000; September and December 1914, and January and October 1915, more than 40,000 each; November 1915, 22,772.

The purely hospital work of the municipality of Moscow was conducted on the same large scale. In peace-time its hospitals could accommodate 6,000 patients. Under the original scheme drawn up by the military authorities the number of beds assigned to Moscow was 10,000; but this figure was soon exceeded. On 10th August 1914, three weeks after the outbreak of hostilities, Moscow had already opened 35 hospitals with 2,448 beds; by 1st September, there were 219 hospitals with 15,816 beds; on 1st October, 527 hospitals with 38,116 beds; and on 1st January 1915, the number of hospitals registered reached 896, with 49,389 beds. On 1st January 1916 this number had increased to 1,075 with 76,580 beds; in August 1916 the number of beds was 80,229, and in 1917 it was estimated at 105,-000. Only about 15 per cent of the total number were endowed by private persons; most of them were maintained at the expense of the municipality alone, or at the expense of the municipality and private persons. In all the number of men who were cared for in the hospitals of Moscow during the War was more than 500,000.

Among the hospitals maintained by private subscriptions we may mention 46 maintained by the Stock Exchange of Moscow, with 4,822 beds, and the Hospital of the Municipal Credit Association with 1,000 beds.

During the first months of the War the establishment of new

hospitals could not keep pace with the demand, and the municipality, to meet overcrowded conditions, had to appeal to private initiative, and urge the citizens of Moscow to provide the wounded soldiers with accommodation in their houses and apartments. This led to the creation of a new form of relief for the sick and wounded, which came to be known by the name of *patronages*. At the early stage of the War about 5,000 men with slight wounds were distributed among the patronages. At a later period these patronages were reorganized as a special group of small hospitals with not less than five beds each. All these small hospitals were registered with the nearest large hospital, and were under the supervision of a special physician attached to it. They were mainly intended for the use of convalescent patients. Hospitals were housed in municipal buildings, schools, charitable institutions, orphanages, in the premises of restaurants and cinemas, and in newly erected blocks of apartments and offices.

Some of the hospitals were designed for special purposes. For instance, eight were hospitals for diseases of the nervous system; five, for diseases of the ear and throat; four were ophthalmic hospitals; seven were for skin and venereal diseases; nine were for tuberculosis; one was for plastic surgery of the jaw. Eleven hospitals were devoted to the treatment of disabled men. The manufacture of artificial limbs was conducted in a workshop established by the municipality. Large hospitals were equipped with X-ray apparatus; small ones used movable X-ray cabinets installed in motor-vans.

The municipality organized a special department which provided hospitals with equipment, linen, instruments, and foodstuffs. Orders for articles of clothing, underwear, and various materials required for hospital equipment were placed with the city's institutions for the relief of paupers, and with other municipal enterprises. From the beginning of the War until January 1916 municipal stores furnished more than 10,140,000 articles of various kinds, valued at over 10,500,000 rubles; half of these were articles of clothing and underwear. During the same period the municipal medical depot supplied to the municipal and other hospitals medical goods to the value of 2,500,000 rubles.

The Duma of Moscow appointed 418 visitors to supervise the work of the hospitals. The staff of the municipal hospitals numbered 14,401 persons, including 1,855 doctors, 708 clinical assistants,[4]

---

[4] *Feldshers.*

3,351 nurses, 7,398 attendants and orderlies, and 1,089 others. The wounded were moved in 53 auto trucks and in specially adapted street cars—30 hospital trains made up of two street cars each.

Large municipal hospitals organized courses for the training of nurses and orderlies. The number of men and women who qualified for hospital work amounted to 2,025. There were altogether seventeen training centers. Special courses were instituted by the municipality for the training of attendants at the disinfecting stations. The students who passed their examination immediately found employment with the municipalities or with the Unions.

Unlike the municipality of Moscow, which organized and carried on the relief of sick and wounded under the joint control of the municipal executive and a special committee of town councillors which became known as the War Committee, Petrograd entrusted the whole of her relief work to a Municipal Committee, and it adhered to the scheme drawn up by the All-Russian Union of Towns. This Committee, which was created on 15th October 1914, largely took the place of a committee appointed at an earlier date to assist the Mayor in the organization of relief work; it received funds directly from the Treasury. The Petrograd Committee of the Union of Towns, of which the Mayor of Petrograd was Chairman, acted in close co-operation with the Central Committee of the Union of Towns, and adopted the same methods of work as the municipality of Moscow and the Union of Towns.

Two clearing stations were opened in Petrograd in connection with the railway stations of Warsaw and Finland. The former consisted of ten huts; and each hut could accommodate about 200 lightly wounded or 65 seriously wounded men. From 25th September 1914 until June 1915, 186,582 men passed through this clearing station. The clearing station attached to the terminus of the Finland Railroad consisted of four huts, which were in a position to deal with the wounded brought by an average hospital train.

During the first months of the War Petrograd was included within the area of military operations, and, therefore, had no share in the systematic evacuation of wounded from the front. But by the turn of events, Petrograd in her turn was forced to assume a prominent part in the work of sick and wounded relief. As early as August 1914 the municipality was compelled to establish 5,000 hospital beds and to address an appeal to the public; this called forth an immediate response from some 500 persons and institutions. They expressed their willingness to assist in the work. On 19th November 1914, Petrograd was required to provide 40,000 hospital beds. Of this number, 26,000 were allocated to the municipality; 2,500 beds were installed in the already existing municipal hospitals and a similar number in school buildings. One hundred and seventy-nine small hospitals with 4,750 beds were equipped and maintained by voluntary subscriptions. On 1st January 1915, the Municipal Committee of Petrograd was in charge of 19,334 beds; on 1st April, 21,410; on 1st June, 24,256; on 1st January 1916, 25,298. The task assigned to Petrograd was not merely fulfilled; it was more than fulfilled. If we add to the number of hospitals opened by the municipality those of the Red Cross, the War Office, and the Union of Zemstvos, the total hospital accommodation of Petrograd on 1st March 1915 amounted to 40,168 beds. On 1st August 1915, 43,000 beds were actually occupied within the city and its suburbs. At the same time about 47,000 beds were fully equipped and ready for the reception of patients. Of this number, 24,000 were opened by the Union of Towns, 1,800 by the Union of Zemstvos, 12,400 by the Red Cross, and 8,700 by the War Office.

The general plan drawn up by Petrograd for the relief of the wounded was the same as that of Moscow. The evacuated men were similarly distributed among the towns of the north of Russia; the same program was followed in the organization of special hospitals, in the establishment of stores of underwear, clothes, medical goods, surgical instruments, etc. The inadequacy of available accommodation necessitated the erection of temporary huts for the wounded. For example, the sum of 1,313,479 rubles was spent on the building of hospital huts for 3,000 men at Sosnovka.

The total expenditure of the Petrograd Committee of the Union of Towns from the beginning of the War until 1st October 1915, was 14,206,000 rubles; on 1st June 1916, it reached 26,339,339 rubles. The grants from the Treasury for the same period totaled 24,244,709 rubles.

The hospital work for the relief of sick and wounded soldiers in other towns of Russia was conducted on the same lines as in Moscow and Petrograd. It differed only in scale.

The Union of Towns opened clearing stations of 500 beds each in Orel, Kursk, and Ekaterinoslav and in Tiflis one of 2,000 beds.

No other industry in Russia was so overwhelmed by the War as the drug industry, nor did any other suffer such dislocation. Before the War almost the whole business of supplying the market with pharmaceutical goods and with the materials required for the dressing of wounds was concentrated in the hands of a few firms and they obtained their stocks from Germany. A large number of drugs were manufactured abroad and could not be produced by the home industry. In the course of the first few weeks after the outbreak of the War the prices of medical supplies and dressing materials rose sharply. For instance, the price of a kilogram of quinine, which, before the War, was from 8 to 10 rubles, rose to 120 and 140 rubles; caffein from 5-6 rubles to 70-80 rubles; aspirin, which was quoted at 1 ruble 50 copecks in September 1914, went up to 100-200 rubles. A similar rise occurred in the prices of all dressing materials.

Public organizations were confronted with a new and stupendous task. The Unions arranged for the purchasing of medical goods in allied and neutral countries. They supported local manufactures, and created new establishments for the production of drugs and dressing materials. For instance, the Union of Towns, with the assistance of the municipality of Moscow, organized its own cotton-batting factory; this had an excellent effect upon prices and stimulated private initiative. A special workshop for the preparation of dressings was established in Moscow by the Union of Towns; dressings were rendered aseptic at the municipal disinfecting station, and were sent to the army in sealed packets. At the same time the Union was supplying the army with phials of stimulants and local anaesthetics. Drugs were purchased in Sweden, Japan, England, in the island of Java, etc. The value of the purchases made during the first months of the War amounted to some 500,000 rubles (c. £50,000). The Union of Towns also established in the Shaniavsky People's University a laboratory for the production of Galenic infusion and for the purification of chloroform.

The value of drugs, including vaccines and serums, supplied by the dispensary of the Union of Towns in the course of six months amounted to 1,700,000 rubles. The Union of Towns subsequently expanded its activities in the purchase of drugs, etc., and suggested the formation of a special organization for this purpose. Forty municipalities united to establish it. On 1st August 1916, the value of drugs and dressing materials which had been supplied by the central dispensary of the Union exceeded 3,000,000 rubles.

The question of surgical instruments and the medical equipment of hospitals presented similar difficulties. The production of surgical instruments, of microscopes, stains for bacteriological, pathological, and anatomical research, thermometers, and other instruments for medical purposes was unknown to Russian industry. A special department was created by the Central Committee of the Union of Towns in September 1914, in order to organize a scheme for supplying such things. On the initiative of this department the manufacture of surgical instruments was entrusted to the cottage industry (*kustari*) of the villages of Pavlov and Vorms in the province of Nizhni-Novgorod. The experiment proved very successful and Russian craftsmen soon produced forty varieties of various surgical instruments, which were generally acknowledged to be excellent substitutes for the instruments of foreign manufacture. By stimulating the activities of private firms the Union succeeded in bringing about the production of vessels, thermometers, thermostats, microscope slides for bacteriological research, etc. The Sanitary-Engineering Department of the Union of Towns established a station where experiments were made with water-filters; and refrigerating plants were manufactured to order for the municipalities.

As early as October 1914 the War Office had asked for the Union's assistance in supplying hospitals with underwear and bed linen. Measures were taken to organize a mass production of underwear, clothing in general, goat-skin coats, shoes, felt boots, and fur caps for the men who left the hospitals. A number of workshops in Moscow and provincial towns were working for the warehouses of the Union. The turnover of the general store and foodstuff department of the Union, for the period of two years ending in August 1916, reached 27,247,000 rubles. In October 1917 the turnover of the underwear section exceeded 67,000,000 rubles. The cost of such things when manufactured by the Union was considerably below the market price. For instance, a leather coat cost the Union 23 rubles, whereas its market price was 125 rubles.

In the process of the organization of a large number of hospitals all over the country, local committees often applied for the assistance of the Union in engaging doctors and other members of the medical staff. The inadequacy of the number of doctors in Russia

had been felt even in peace-time; and under the first pressure of the
War, it became an acute problem. The mobilization of a large number of medical men for service in the army and the great demand
created by the establishment of new hospitals soon exhausted the
available reserve of doctors in many localities, and above all in small
communities. The Union of Towns acted as a link between the members of the medical profession and the local committees of the Union.
It determined the number of the medical staff of each hospital and
the amount of their salaries, made provision in case of their illness
or death, organized courses for the training of nurses, orderlies, and
attendants for disinfecting stations. Special courses of training in
the prevention of epidemics were opened in the spring of 1915 and
many physicians attended them. In November 1916 the Union of
Towns, in collaboration with the Union of Zemstvos, established special courses of orthopaedic surgery in Moscow; these were made
necessary by the fact that many of the mobilized doctors had little
knowledge or experience of surgery. The results of an inquiry held
on 1st November 1915 show that the number of the medical staff
employed by the Union amounted to 5,738 men and women, of whom
798 were physicians. The two capitals and the Caucasus were not
included in the inquiry.

An important group of men, evacuated from the army, were in
need of a protracted course of treatment at sanatoriums and health
resorts. The after-effects of infectious diseases, nervous breakdowns,
neuritis, chronic rheumatism, tuberculosis, and mental diseases ac-
counted for a considerable number of patients. An inquiry held in
the hospitals of Moscow and Petrograd made it clear that 17 per
cent of the inmates required special treatment. The organization of
sanatoriums for the patients suffering from tuberculosis and requiring other special treatments began to develop rapidly in the
second half of 1915. In the summer of that year the Union of Towns
had already 1,112 beds for men suffering from tuberculosis in sanatoriums and in nursing-homes which provided their patients with the
koumiss[5] treatment, 925 beds at the balneotherapeutic establishments of the Caucasus, and 500 beds in establishments which gave
mud baths. Sanatoriums were opened in the Crimea, the Caucasus,
in Finland, and the provinces of central Russia. The Petrograd

[5] Koumiss, kumiss, a Tartar word; a fermented alcoholic drink prepared
from mare's milk.

District Committee of the Union of Towns equipped a hospital ship on the Volga, which made a number of voyages in the summer of 1915.

The scheme prepared by the Union of Towns for the relief of the sick and wounded included also the treatment of men affected with mental diseases. In view of past experience and of the character of the Great War it seemed advisable to keep 7,000 places for mental cases. The two Unions appointed a joint Committee to deal with this problem and the preliminary scheme was duly approved by the Central Committees; but the important measures it provided for were never put into practice, as the Government chose to adopt another course of action, that excluded the Unions from any share in the treatment of cases of this kind.

With the assistance of the Union various towns established dental clinics with special laboratories for plastic surgery. This sort of medical relief was particularly important, because even in peacetime about 70 per cent of the total strength of the army suffered from dental troubles; during the War the percentage was still heavier. At the end of 1914 and the beginning of 1915 the Union equipped a central dental clinic in Moscow and opened other such clinics in Petrograd, Orel, Kursk, Kharkov, Ekaterinoslav, Tambov, and Tver.

The Central Committee of the Union equipped with X-ray apparatus the Union's hospitals at Kursk, Voronezh, Vladikavkaz, Kazan, Vyatka, Tula, Kharkov, Penza, etc. It also lent financial support to the special X-ray committee which was working in Kiev.

The Union of Towns, taking as it did a keen interest in all the developments of the War, could not remain indifferent to the sudden appearance of a new offensive factor against which the army of the Allies and of Russia could make no defense. The use of poisonous gas by the Germans necessitated the taking of immediate measures against a method of warfare totally unknown to military history. The first news of the gas attack made by the Germans reached the Union through a telegram of the head of the Petrograd Detachment of the Union, Prince Obolensky, on 18th May 1915. The total loss of men during this attack was 12,000, and about 30 per cent of them died from poisoning, or subsequently in hospitals from gangrene, often after long suffering. Fighting men and medical corps were equally powerless to meet the new species of warfare. The action of the gases was so strong that even the personnel of the hospitals who had to care for the poisoned men often experienced a certain amount of discomfort. The whole country took up the manufacture of gas masks; they were held to be the one means of safety. For a time it would have been impossible to find any household that was not endeavoring to prepare a gas mask or an anti-gas bandage. Private associations for the manufacture of such masks sprang up all over the country, and the providing of troops with these articles became entirely a question of private charity. Gas masks were sent to the army without being submitted to any preliminary test and without any guarantee that they would serve their purpose.

The Union of Towns undertook the manufacture of gas masks with respirators. The work was done on a large scale; for instance, the Union supplied more than 22,000 arshines (c. 18,000 yards) of gauze alone, and, by 15th October, 175,000 respirators had been produced. In addition, the Union carried out a detailed scientific investigation into the nature of asphyxiating gas, its effects upon the organism, the various methods of treating gassed men, and of the counter-measures which would neutralize or minimize the effects of chemical warfare. A special committee was created for this purpose at the beginning of June 1915. It consisted of Russian scientists, medical men, engineers, and representatives of all public organizations. The experiments, organized on a large scale, produced notable results; and they were put at the disposal of the Supreme Sanitary Board. The committee examined various gas masks and eye protectors, studied the effects of poison gases upon animals, and inquired into the neutralizing value of certain chemicals, among them being hyposulphite, soda, glycerine, aniline, and urotropine, as also moss and charcoal. Important experiments were likewise carried on with chlorine and phosgene, their presence being evident in the gases in question.

A special hospital was reserved at Moscow for gas-poisoning cases, and secondary treatment was given at the Sevsky-Sanatorium in the province of Orel.

The massing in hospitals of hundreds of thousands of sick and wounded soldiers, some of whom were convalescent, necessitated the taking of special measures in order that their enforced idleness might be turned to account. The first steps were taken toward teaching the illiterate to read and write, and in opening manual training courses. Hospitals organized lectures, debates, and theatrical performances. In the hospitals of Moscow, Ekaterinoslav, Simbirsk, and in many other towns, the manual training work was very extensive. Some of the municipalities instituted special courses for the training of instructors to supervise the work of the sick and wounded men. This work was carried on in one form or another in all hospitals either by their staffs or by local organizations.

As the War went on the number of men in the hospitals who were permanently unfit to return to the ranks grew steadily. This group consisted of the patients who had lost a limb, men with amputated legs or arms, those who were blind or deaf, or suffering from incurable nervous disorders and other disabilities. The hospitals were crowded with such disabled men. More and more men were declared unfit for further service and invalided home. The country was thus confronted with a new problem. The scale on which the War was conducted excluded the possibility of solving it by private charity, widespread and enthusiastic as was the support of these charities. The disabled men had to rely upon the protection of the State, and the assistance offered them had to take the form of providing them not merely with charitable relief, but with the proper medical treatment, and with work. By September 1915 the number of disabled men was estimated at 25,000, and the number accepted by the Treasury as a basis for determining the sum to be allocated to their relief was 40,000.

An investigation into the condition of 85,000 sick and wounded men in the hospitals of the province of Moscow at this time gave the following data: 3.4 per cent were suffering from tuberculosis; of the total number of wounded, 51 per cent had wounds in the arm, 35 per cent in the leg; almost one-quarter of the men who left the hospitals were disabled and unfitted for military service. Of this number 21.6 per cent required further care in order to recover the complete use of their limbs; 7 per cent as the result of nervous breakdowns and affections of the nervous system were in need of protracted hospital treatment; 3.8 per cent had suffered amputation and required to be provided with artificial limbs and trained in some gainful occupation; 3.1 per cent were suffering from tuberculosis,

0.5 per cent from mental disorders, 0.4 per cent from complete and 1.1 per cent from partial deafness, 0.2 per cent from complete and 0.5 per cent from partial loss of sight.[6] Of the patients who left one of the large hospitals in Petrograd, 34.2 per cent were certified as unfitted for military service. Enough that however great the number of disabled men, all alike had a right to demand relief and the chance to earn a living under the new conditions they must face.

In accordance with the Act of 22nd November 1911, each disabled man who lost a limb in the War was entitled to an artificial limb, to be provided at the expense of the Treasury. The Orphanage of Empress Marie in Petrograd took charge of this work and produced about 4,500 artificial limbs a year, a number obviously inadequate, and of necessity workshops and factories were organized for their manufacture in quantity.

The Act of 25th June 1912 established five classes of pensions for disabled men. But these pensions were too small to provide even the bare necessaries of life. The largest, which was granted for 100 per cent disability involving the necessity of permanent treatment, was 216 rubles a year; and for partial disability the amount might be as little as 30 rubles. The relief of disabled men on a large scale was first suggested at the third conference of the Union of Towns held in September 1915. The scheme presupposed the complete, or at least partial, restoration of the physical fitness of the disabled men. To put the relief plan into effect it was decided to open, first in large cities and eventually everywhere in the country, appropriate institutions and hospitals, and particularly physio-therapeutic establishments for the treatment of the sick and wounded after they had left military hospitals. Institutions of this type were to be established in Moscow, Petrograd, Kharkov, Odessa, Kiev, Kazan, Saratov, and Tiflis.

The creation of factories and workshops for the manufacture of artificial limbs, and the training of disabled men in various crafts that would enable them to become self-supporting in the future, were questions no less important than that of medical treatment. The problems presented by the care and the training of the blind, the deaf, and those who were deaf-mutes, required special attention. A plan was outlined which included the establishment of labor ex-

[6] Report presented to the Medical Section of the Central Committee of the Union of Towns on 22nd-23rd February 1916.

changes for the convalescent, of special organizations for the sale of articles made by disabled men, and of various types of homes for men suffering from incurable diseases and for such unfortunates as could not rightly be allowed to go at large. This plan was to be put into operation under the direction of a special central administration consisting of representatives of the Government, the Red Cross, and public organizations. Local committees were to be in charge of local work for the relief of disabled men, and the plan was based on the compulsory registration of all such men by the hospitals. The Union of Towns estimated that it would call for a necessary expenditure of some 16,066,000 rubles, to be distributed as follows: 6,000,000 rubles for the organization in eight towns of physio-therapeutic institutions, workshops for the manufacture of artificial limbs, and homes for men completely disabled or requiring isolation; 2,108,000 for the equipment, and approximately 8,000,000 rubles for the upkeep, of various institutions. The Central Committee of the Union of Towns appealed to their members to assist in the relief of disabled men, and thirty-eight towns responded. Eleven of them offered to organize workshops with living quarters for the training of disabled men; seven towns agreed to take charge of those who were absolutely unable to work; six, to organize homes for patients requiring isolation. Orel and Kharkov opened homes for the blind. The municipality of Orel undertook the organization of a labor exchange for disabled men and a home for those requiring isolation.

This plan and the estimates required were duly approved by the government department in charge of the relief of disabled men, and it was decided that the funds necessary for carrying it out should be entrusted to a Special Committee of the Supreme Council. But the further development of the relief work was hindered by a kind of friction that was only too common under the conditions then prevailing. Government departments, while admitting the soundness of the principles on which the scheme suggested by the Union of Towns was based, at the same time sought to exclude the Union from the organization of the relief work. The funds required for the execution of the scheme were withheld from the Union and were sent directly to local organizations which often were not even connected with the municipalities, but had a purely private character. These methods deprived the whole undertaking of the systematic organization which it needed, introduced into it an element of uncertainty, and reduced responsible government work to the level of a private charity. The complete plan for the relief of disabled men was never therefore put into operation, and a communication to this effect was made to the conference on disabled men held in Moscow on 31st October 1916; certain parts of the plan were nevertheless carried into effect by the Union of Towns, and also by separate municipalities.

In February 1916 the Central Committee of the Union approved an agreement between the Union and the municipality of Moscow dealing with the establishment of a Traumatological Institute with a hospital for 1,700 patients. The Institute was planned for special treatment of those who had been injured in the War, and who were detained in the hospitals managed by various organizations. It was intended for the treatment of wounded who were suffering from injury to nerve centers, which affected the control of the use of the limbs, and for patients who needed diagnostic or surgical treatment that for one reason or another could not be obtained at the local institutions of the Union. The Institute was to take charge of particularly difficult cases and accordingly became an important center for research in traumatology. The distribution of beds among the various departments was as follows: surgical, 200; orthopaedic, 600; nervous diseases, 600; experimental department, 100; and hostel, 200. The Union of Zemstvos joined in the agreement. The Institute was under the control and supervision of the municipality of Moscow and had already begun its work in November 1915.

In order to improve the organization for the relief of the disabled, in May 1915 the municipality of Moscow appointed a special municipal relief board composed of representatives of the citizens of Moscow. This board undertook the establishment of homes for disabled men and their training for various trades; it also endeavored to provide them with suitable employment and distributed allowances in cash. The municipality opened a special hospital with 322 beds for the treatment of the most serious cases. In addition, it maintained the following institutions for such relief: a temporary home with 150 beds, for men who needed a shelter after leaving hospital; a hostel and training school for men—it could care for 48—who had lost one arm; an elementary school which could accommodate 116, for training students in the work of coöperative societies; a home for the blind, for 25 patients; a hostel for 24 men; a workshop equipped to give 100 disabled soldiers manual training; classes in bookkeeping and railway work for 320 men; a school and hostel for 300, and three small hospitals. The problem of providing disabled men with suitable employment was in the hands of a special bureau attached to the municipal relief board. Up to 15th August 1916, the municipality of Moscow spent 738,048 rubles of its own funds on this form of relief work. The means required for carrying on the work were derived from the grants of the municipal duma, the Supreme Council, and from voluntary subscriptions.

A State Committee for the relief of disabled men was appointed by a decree of the Provisional Government dated 20th June 1917. To ensure a closer coördination of all the relief measures instituted by the zemstvos and towns which joined the two Unions, the decree established a joint conference of the representatives of the Central Committees of the two Unions and of the delegates of the Association of Disabled Men.

CHAPTER VIII

WORK IN THE ARMY

THE activity of the Union of Towns at the front developed gradually. Neither the scheme nor the scale nor the general trend of the work was settled in advance. The government order which excludes unofficial organizations from the military zone was soon rescinded; hard facts showed that such restrictions could not stand. The stagnation and exclusiveness of the army medical service, its bureaucratic routine, its obsolete sanitary rules and regulations, were utterly inadequate to meet the requirements of a modern war. It was essential that some more elastic and adaptable organization should have a share in the work. A few weeks after the outbreak of the War the Government itself was compelled to invite the Unions to come inside the area of military operations and to commission them to take up whatever work was most urgent. The Unions began by assisting the Government in the solution of such problems as were clearly defined. But they soon expanded their work, outlined a general scheme of action, and with their establishments they covered the whole fighting line from the Baltic to the Black Sea, as well as the isolated Caucasus front.

The work of the Union of Towns for the immediate relief of the needs of the army was centered in certain sectors[1] behind the fighting line, and originally in three, the sector of Galicia and Bukovina, the sector of Warsaw and Suvalki, and the sector of Keletsk. Later on, when the front was altered and extended, the partition of the work of the Union coincided with the main military divisions, that is, in Europe, the Northern, Western, and Southwestern, and the Rumanian fronts, and, in Asia, that of the Caucasus. The work on each particular front was concentrated in the hands of a special commissioner appointed by the Central Committee of the Union and assisted by a Front Committee. At a later date a body of commissioners served as liaison officers between the Union's Committee of the Front and the various headquarters. A special department of the Central Committee supervised the work of the Committees of the Front.

The problems which the Union had to meet in the military zone

[1] *Napravlenya.*

were twofold. In addition to giving direct assistance in the evacuation and care of the sick and wounded, the Unions found it absolutely necessary to undertake the relief of civilian sufferers. This work had to be undertaken in the interest of the troops themselves to safeguard them from epidemics and the effects of the complete collapse of normal conditions in the districts immediately adjoining the front.

The Union's first work was that of evacuating the sick and wounded, organizing depots of underwear, winter clothes, drugs, and dressing materials, and establishing army canteens and field hospitals, the latter being used equally by the wounded, the refugees, and the local population. As a result of the development of military operations and the pressure of new demands from the army, the Union next went extensively into sanitary engineering. It erected bathhouses and laundries, cleaned up foul areas, cleaned and sunk wells, dug ditches, and drained and cleaned trenches. In 1916, not only was the number of the Union's various enterprises within the military zone increasing, but it was still embarking upon new works. In the districts adjoining the military zone, it set up workshops and factories wherewith to supply the army with articles of which the shortage was particularly felt. In 1916, indeed, its activity reached its culminating point. In 1917 it lost its systematic character, and under the influence of the disorganization of the army began to show signs of that weakening and deterioration which were then becoming very evident in both the army and the country as a whole.

The main features of the activities of the Union of Towns at the front are described in the following pages. Their character was determined by the peculiar nature of the Russian front, with its enormous distances, the insufficient development of its system of roads and railways, and the general inadequacy of all technical facilities.

One of the main auxiliary services organized by the Unions within the military zone was the establishment of army canteens in connection with the field hospitals. The experience of the Russo-Japanese War had demonstrated the extreme usefulness of establishments of this type; they served as a flexible link between the fighting line and the sometimes very remote railheads with their ambulance trains.

Each field ambulance with its refreshment station consisted of a whole system of smaller units acting in close collaboration. Each sent forward two or three advanced dressing stations, where the troops were also supplied with refreshments. They established themselves as near the fighting line as circumstances would permit, and were organized in such a way as to ensure the highest degree of mobility; they could go to work, or move to a new spot, at a moment's notice. The wounded were conveyed on stretchers from the trenches or from the regimental ambulances to the advanced dressing stations, where they received first aid; their wounds were dressed, they were given refreshments, and sheltered from bad weather. From the advanced dressing stations they were conveyed by horse-drawn ambulances or by motor ambulances to field hospitals some 8 to 15 versts (5 to 10 miles) from the trenches. Field hospitals were also preliminary casualty clearing stations, where wounds could be given a more careful examination and dressing. From these hospitals the patients were moved to railhead. Field ambulances, in addition to their medical work and their part in the evacuation of wounded, had also to serve as army canteens. They were accordingly furnished with the necessary equipment, including field kitchens, to provide the troops with tea and hot meals; and to allow of their performing their twofold task they maintained, at their bases, large stores both of foodstuffs and medical supplies.

The main feature of field detachments was their adaptability. The new and continually changing conditions of the War, and the varying demands of the troops, often compelled the units forming a field detachment to change the whole character of their work. Field detachments were often obliged to take up work for which they were not originally intended, such as the prevention of epidemic diseases, the organization of dispensaries, the lending of medical aid to the civilian population, the repair of boots and clothing, the establishment of bathhouses and laundries for the troops, etc. To be in a position to deal with all these problems large field detachments had a numerous personnel, often of two hundred or more, with possibly two hundred and fifty horses. In the beginning the equipment of a detachment cost about 80,000 rubles, and later as much as 100,000 rubles. The organization of such field detachments was a popular form of public charity, and the name of the donor was often given to the detachment. The Central Committee of the Union made a rule that donors should subscribe the difference between the total sum subscribed by municipalities, public bodies and private persons, and the actual cost, provided that the donor need not subscribe more than 60 per cent of the total. On 1st January 1916, the flag of the Union

of Towns covered twenty-five field detachments. They included: a
large and well-equipped detachment maintained and provided by
the municipality of Moscow; nine detachments maintained by the
towns of Siberia; detachments from the city of Petrograd, from the
towns of the Petrograd district, and detachments given and maintained by various persons and institutions, among them being the
Bar of Moscow, Petrograd, and Kazan; the Petrograd Societies of
Popular Universities, of Russian Engineers, of Merchants, the children of Petrograd, and certain private individuals. These detachments were organized in 1914 and 1915. The first field detachment
left for the front on 21st November 1914, the detachment of the
city of Petrograd on 31st December 1914, and the detachment of
the city of Moscow on 15th March 1915. In parts where the front
line remained unchanged, and where the operations took the form of
trench warfare the large field detachments lost their original character, and their mobility; hospitals were organized on permanent lines;
and sanitary engineering, the building and management of bathhouses and laundries, and the erection of workshops and other establishments providing for the comfort of troops became outstanding
features of the detachment's program. These large field detachments
became important centers around which the Union inaugurated other
work. As for sections of the front where the lines were advancing,
field detachments preserved their original organization, and fulfilled
their functions with conspicuous success, a fact recorded in the numerous expressions of gratitude and appreciation forwarded to the
Union by military authorities.

The energetic activities of the Union in establishing bathhouses
and laundries deserve special mention, for these were sanitary measures for the prevention of epidemic diseases. These sanitary detachments showed great capacity to adapt themselves to the peculiar
conditions of front-line life. The bathhouses, a most important re-
quirement for the welfare of the troops, were of great variety; they
ranged from primitive makeshifts in abandoned cottages and huts,
costing a few rubles, to expensive establishments provided with
disinfecting stations and special equipment for the destruction of
parasites. The building of bathhouses led to the organization of laundries and repair workshops. It soon became necessary to furnish
underwear for the men who used bathhouses and washhouses. This
branch of the activities of the Unions developed to such a degree that

presently almost all army units were using the washhouses and bathhouses of the Union of Towns or of the Union of Zemstvos.

In addition to the field and the sanitary detachments, the Union of Towns maintained a number of permanent institutions in the military zone for the comfort and well-being of the troops and of the civilian population. These institutions included dispensaries, stationary hospitals, isolation stations, hospitals for infectious diseases, detachments for the prevention of infectious diseases, dental clinics, depots of medical stores, etc. For instance, all the measures connected with sanitation and with the prevention of infectious diseases on the Northern Front were entrusted to the Union's Committee of the Front. It became possible, therefore, to create three zones of hospitals for infectious diseases on the main lines of communication leading from the front to the interior of the country. A special hospital for patients suffering from scurvy was among the institutions opened in this section. The energies and activities of the Union were directed in accordance with local needs and conditions. On the Northern Front attention was largely concentrated upon the zone adjoining the fighting line; and on the Western Front most thought was given to the trenches themselves. There thirty detachments for the prevention of infectious diseases were at work. The Committee of the Caucasus Front, working under conditions of exceptional difficulty, had to meet the needs both of the front and of the adjoining areas.

Large masses of the population of the military zone were constantly abandoning their villages and moving eastward; and as for the Jews, at times they were given only a few hours' notice in which to leave the district. A portion of the civilian population, nevertheless, remained by their ruined homesteads and near the army. In the interests of the army it was essential to take care of them, and to provide them with foodstuffs and medical help. A new and unforeseen problem was the maintenance of men employed in the digging of trenches; these were sent to the front in large numbers by the War Office. The local population was also employed in digging trenches, as well as a special labor corps consisting of the non-Russian population of Siberia and Turkestan, which was exempt from military service. The Union of Towns provided for this part of the population of the military zone, realizing that it was a hygienic necessity. The care of the local population and the labor corps was undertaken at the request of the military authorities and at the earnest desire of the people concerned. The administration of such relief was made difficult at times by local customs and prejudices. For instance, at the beginning the population looked with great suspicion upon free medical aid, the Jews refused to eat food provided by Gentiles, etc.

The growing activities of the Union at the front necessitated the development of their supply work. The organization of field and other detachments, of army canteens, the building of bathhouses, and the distribution of underwear on a large scale, called for front-line depots of underwear, clothing, foodstuffs, household articles, medical supplies, surgical instruments, dressing materials, etc. The Union established a number of depots, and could often supply articles not then obtainable from the Army Supply Service. Goods from the depots of the Union were furnished at cost price, that is, considerably below the market prices. And such Union depots became very popular among the troops. They could obtain from them certain things which they most urgently needed, such as winter clothing, felt boots, and goat-skin coats, as well as minor articles of equipment. The first depot of the Union was opened in October 1914 in Brest-Litovsk. Its turnover up to 1st August 1915 amounted to 1,344,000 rubles. When the front line moved eastward the stores of this depot were transferred to Gomel where a new depot to provide for the needs of the Western Front was formed. At the end of October 1914 a similar depot was established at Skarzhisko, and moved later to Keltsy. The turnover of this depot up to 25th June 1915 (when the town was evacuated) stood at 882,623 rubles. On 15th January 1915, a base depot, which also supplied goods to the civilian population of the devastated areas, was opened at Lvov. The turnover of this depot up to the time of its transfer to Kiev (15th August 1915) amounted to some 500,000 rubles. The base depot of Warsaw began its work on 1st March 1915; with the alteration of the fighting line it was transferred to Belostok, Smolensk, and Pskov. The turnover of the depot of Warsaw up to 1st August 1915 had reached 521,396 rubles. At the end of 1916 the stores of the depots of various institutions of the Union of Towns on the Northern Front were valued at, 1,903,726 rubles; at 3,400,000 rubles on the Western Front; and at 1,402,727 rubles on the Southwestern.

The Union's Committees of the Front did not limit their labors to the organization of depots and stores. They also set up a number of workshops. These produced various articles needed for the equipment of hospitals, medical convoys, and bathhouses—from horseshoes and plain kitchen chairs to elaborate formalin disinfecting chambers and laundry machinery. Among the enterprises organized and managed by the Union were soap-works, tanneries, works for the building of army huts, mills, bakeries, shoe-repair shops, forges and locksmiths' shops, ironworks, workshops for the manufacture of bedsteads, boiler tubes, boilers, baths, apparatus, of the Japanese and other types, for disinfection and for the destruction of parasites, and so on.

In response to the requests of military units on active service and of the officials responsible for the organization of the Army Supply Service it opened a number of shops in the neighborhood of the trenches for the use of officers and men. As an illustration of the enormous range of the activities of the Union within the military zone it may be mentioned that it owned its own herds of cattle, and in certain instances its officers and institutions had to take care of the local harvests. In the summer of 1917 about 50,000 deciatines (c. 135,000 acres) situated within the military zone of the Northern Front were cultivated by the Union. This measure proved particularly valuable, and enabled the army to carry on through the difficult time at the end of August and in the beginning of September, when the supply of foodstuffs was almost entirely cut off.

At the front the Union's work was above all valuable and productive. There the common aims of the army and of such public organizations were realized more clearly than anywhere else; the necessity of their work was irrefutably demonstrated. When sharing the hardships of the army the Union workers could truly feel that they were obeying the call of duty. They often had to carry on their work under fire, and they suffered as much as the troops from the effects of poisonous gases; not infrequently they withdrew at the last moment, behind the retreating troops, and railway lines and bridges were blown up immediately after they had left them. They constantly faced the danger of infection. And many of them made the supreme sacrifice. "There was no work which the Unions would have feared to attempt if it had been demanded for the good of the army and the people of the front line zone. We were working without legal status, and were guided solely by our desire to be useful," said M. Schepkin, addressing a meeting of mayors. The character of the work of the

Union and the devotion of its staff were known to and appreciated by the army, from commanding officers down to the private soldiers. Many proofs of this appreciation may be found in the letters sent— in numbers—by men and officers; letters which expressed their gratitude in the plainest sincerity, and in the official tributes paid to the Union by commanding officers.

The work of the Union of Towns at the Front was closely coordinated with that of other public bodies. There was an active collaboration with the Union of Zemstvos, which was similar to the Union of Towns in its organization and spirit, and with the Red Cross; all the humanitarian institutions of the two Unions flew the Red Cross flag. Their spheres of action were defined by agreement; there was no friction or overlapping, and in case of emergency every organization could rely upon the support of the others.

The scope of the work of the Union of Towns in the military zone may be inferred from the following summaries taken from reports of the Committees of the Front.

The Northwestern Front.

(From April 1915 to October 1916.)

Hospitals:

Number of hospitals (according to the time)	from 27 to 41
Maximum number of beds	3,419
Sick and wounded soldiers admitted	17,710
Patients of all kinds admitted (of whom 11,299 were suffering from infectious diseases)	29,699
Total number of days spent in hospital	310,399

Dispensaries:

Number of dispensaries	from 36 to 63
Number of visits	275,622
Number of patients (including 16,526 soldiers)	212,567
Number of wounds dressed	26,450
Number of inoculations	38,694

(From November 1915 to October 1916.)

Dental clinics:

Number of clinics	from 13 to 22
Number of visits (including 53,996 soldiers)	127,825

Chemico-bacteriological laboratories:

Number of investigations completed (of which 4,864 were made for the Army Medical Service)	5,537

Bathhouses:

Number of bathhouses (according to the time)   from 30 to 79

Average number of men who used a bathhouse in the course
of one day   264

Total number of men who used the bathhouses   2,290,368

Number of pieces of underwear distributed   2,376,710

Number of pieces of soiled underwear received   2,162,225

Laundries:

Number of laundries   from 7 to 13

Number of articles washed   3,265,413

Number of articles repaired   855,154

(From April 1915 to October 1916.)

Tea rooms:

Number of tea rooms   from 29 to 45

Average number of meals served daily in each tea room   736

Total number of meals   10,456,928

Meals supplied to soldiers   5,278,823

Meals supplied to refugees   5,178,005

Army canteens:

Number of canteens   from 77 to 128

Average number of men daily supplied with food at each
canteen   484

Total number of meals served   19,011,604

Including:

Number of meals supplied to refugees   9,670,204

Number of meals supplied to soldiers   653,333

Number of meals supplied to men engaged in the digging of trenches   8,688,067

The Western Front.

(To 1st June 1916)

Dispensaries:

Number of dispensaries   42

Number of visits   107,026

Disinfecting stations:

Number of articles treated at disinfecting stations   2,061,167

Bathhouses:

Number of bathhouses   160

Number of men who used the bathhouses   2,497,153

Number of pieces of underwear distributed   871,841

Laundries:
Number of laundries   51
Number of pieces of underwear washed   513,320

Canteens:
Number of meals served at the army canteens   6,032,247
Number of meals served at the tea rooms   4,351,285

The Southwestern Front.

(Up to 1st June 1916.)

Dispensary visits   54,216
Number of articles treated at disinfecting stations   2,976,695
Bathhouses   172
Number of men who used bathhouses   2,200,897
Number of pieces of underwear distributed   920,763
Meals served, canteens   5,322,538
Meals served, tea rooms   3,875,534

The total amount of work done by the Union of Towns on all the fronts may be gathered from the following summary dated 14th October 1917, and presented to the seventh and last conference of the Union of Towns held on 14th-17th October 1917.

All European Fronts.

	Number
Hospitals and Evacuation:	
Hospitals	247
Hospital beds	57,742
Field detachments and ambulance convoys	68
Hospitals for out-patients (dispensaries, dental clinics, etc.)	254
X-ray apparatus, bacteriological and other laboratories	16
Patients admitted to hospitals	622,240
Days spent in hospitals	4,628,222
Men conveyed by ambulances	964,862
Dispensary cases	1,795,504
Inoculations	186,796
Dental cases	510,080
Canteens, tea rooms and meals:	
Canteens	263
Tea rooms	125
Meals served, canteens (including full day ration for 14,242,504 men employed in the digging of trenches)	36,611,150
Meals served, tea rooms	80,158,779

Number

Sanitation:

Engineering detachments	49
Sanitary detachments	24
Disinfecting stations	424
Bathhouses	833
Laundries	263
Convoys for the collection of refuse	21
Bathhouses were used by	53,900,715 men
Number of pieces of underwear distributed	35,638,614
Number of pieces of underwear washed	45,144,349
Number of disinfections	52,779,099 cases
which were distributed as follows:	
Houses	280,045
Miscellaneous	21,567,479
Underwear and clothing	30,930,775

The expenditure of all institutions of the Union engaged at the front was estimated at 10,800,000 rubles a month. On 1st September 1917, their staff—of both men and women—numbered 21,500.

CHAPTER IX

RELIEF OF REFUGEES

THE retreat of the Russian army in July 1915 was followed by the movement eastward of a great tide of refugees. At the approach of the invaders hundreds of thousands of people left their native villages, abandoned their property, and fled toward an unknown fate. The districts which the Germans pressed especially hard were, of course, cleared of population for strategic reasons, and all buildings and other property that could not be carried away were destroyed. The rapidity of the retreat made a systematic evacuation impossible. The tragedy of the refugees, unexampled in number, with no organization, was something too appalling for any adequate description. It came to be known in Russia as "the great exodus." The wave of refugees moving eastward flooded all the roads and railway lines leading from the front to the interior, and continued to advance for nearly three months. Not till November was there any falling off. Railway trains were crowded with refugees. A telegram sent by one of the commissioners of the Union of Towns, on 1st September 1915, stated that "some 15 versts (10 miles) of the railway lines leading to Gomel were blocked with trains conveying refugees" and that in the trains "living men and women were mingled with the bodies of the dead." The highroads were crowded with innumerable refugees in horse-drawn carts and on foot. These people were moving forward with no definite destination, leaving behind what property they could not carry, losing their children, covering the road with sick and dead. This tide of humanity flooded the towns that found themselves in its way, and spread disease and infection. At the beginning the refugees preserved their organization as village communities, and advanced under the leadership of their clergy and elders (*starosta*), who acted as their representatives in all negotiations with local authorities and with the relief organizations. But eventually the character of the movement changed. Those who had horses pushed on ahead; and the mass of people who followed were no longer members of an organized community, but a mere mob, tired, hungry, and almost beyond restraint. In September from 100,000 to 192,000 men and women passed daily through the registration stations; in October, from 14,000 to 205,000. In November and December the daily average was 300. Often a group that had numbered a hundred when it left its native village was reduced to ten by the time it reached its final destination, the remainder having perished or lost themselves on the way. It was a terrible and a national calamity.

This tragedy of the refugees, like many other problems arising during the War, had not been foreseen by the Government. It was only when the population had already abandoned their villages and were flooding the roads that the Unions began to receive alarming telegrams from the military authorities, asking for immediate help. On the lines of communication there must be some immediate organization of refreshment stations, canteens, and sanitary stations, and an examination of all refugees by sanitary officers. Similar requests were received from the civilian administration, for instance, from the Governor-General of Kiev and the Governors of Grodno, Podolia, Lomzha, Volhynia, etc. Still more urgent appeals were made by the municipalities and the local committees of the Union.

The Union of Towns was among the first to respond to these appeals; as early as the beginning of July it outlined the first plan for the relief of refugees along the lines of retreat, using for this purpose the already existing institutions of the Union. A conference of its commissioners was held on 18th July at Brest-Litovsk, the Special Commissioner being in the chair. The conference drew up a general scheme of relief, which was eventually approved by another conference, called by the Central Committee of the Union, a conference in which the principal cities, the Union of Zemstvos, the municipality of Moscow, and other public organizations were represented. This scheme proposed two zones of registration stations. The station of the advanced zone was to supply refugees with meals and direct them to the stations of the second zone. The latter had a preventive function; they were to detect and detain all cases suspected of infectious diseases, carry out a preliminary registration of refugees, and direct them to the clearing stations at the rear. It was also proposed to organize refugee clearing stations in the central provinces, these to be charged with a systematic distribution of refugees over the eastern provinces of European Russia and Siberia. It was hoped that with the assistance of the Union of Zemstvos a large proportion of the refugees could be accommodated in rural districts. The Union of Zemstvos, submitting this plan to the approval of the Government, begged the military and civil authorities to take proper measures for the regulation and systematization of refugee relief, to put an end to a purely automatic system of distribution, to prevent, so far as possible, the separation of families and the scattering of the members of one village commune among various provinces, etc. The attention of the authorities was drawn to the necessity of regulations concerning the transfer of refugees by rail, the need for alarm bells in the trains conveying refugees, the desirability of keeping together trains carrying refugees from the same districts and so on. Finally, attention was also called to the drawbacks of a compulsory evacuation.

In the meantime the uncontrolled streams of refugees had penetrated to the very heart of the country and were spreading cholera and typhus. On the Western Front, in the small Bobruisk section alone, the medical establishments of the Union of Zemstvos registered in the course of three months (August, September, and October 1915) 10,697 refugee cases of epidemic diseases, of which 5,342 were cholera. Five thousand cases of cholera among refugees were registered in September in the province of Minsk, 3,000 in the province of Mogilev, and 1,000 in the province of Smolensk.

The Union of Zemstvos began its work for the relief of refugees at the same time as the Union of Towns.[1] Their common aims and methods led to the amalgamation of the activities of the two Unions and the creation of a joint committee of relief. The scheme outlined by the Unions was not, however, put into operation in its entirety. This was partly due to the stupendous scale of the retreat, which upset all estimates and plans, and partly to the hostility of the central Government, which refused the grants of money needed. For it desired to keep the entire control of this work in its own hands. Under these conditions the Unions were compelled to abandon their plans and confine themselves to endeavoring to solve particular problems, such as the moving on of refugees crowded at railway junctions or in the towns they came to on their way; the organization of canteens, refreshment stations, dispensaries, and hospitals for infectious diseases.

A number of smaller organizations joined in this work of refugee relief. Among them were national organizations—Polish, Lettish,

[1] For the participation of the Zemstvos and their Union in the relief of refugees, see Polner, Prince Obolensky, and Turin, op. cit., Chapter X.

Lithuanian, Jewish, and Armenian. An all-Russian association was established for the special purpose of helping refugees of only Russian nationality. The Committee of the Grand Duchess Tatiana Nicholaevna had charge of registration and general work. Finally, on 30th August, a special Act created authoritative machinery for "providing for the needs of the refugees." Under the provisions of the Act the administration of the relief of all refugees in the Empire was concentrated in a Special Council presided over by the Minister of the Interior. This Council, however, was unable to systematize the relief work in its entirety, and prepare a general scheme. It endeavored to settle the problem without the assistance of the Unions; and it acted through the local organizations of the zemstvos and municipalities, as also through private societies and persons. As a result, the Council was inundated with demands and applications, and with contradictory suggestions and estimates from various organizations. Local organizations sometimes obtained their funds from more than one source. Some of them were well provided with money, others got nothing at all. And the appointment of Special Commissioners for the Northern and Southern Fronts by the Council of Ministers did little to improve the situation.

Up to 18th October the Special Council distributed more than 64,000,000 rubles for the relief of refugees. Of this sum only 8,000,-000 rubles (13 per cent) passed through the organizations of the Unions. The remaining sums were allotted to the Special Commissioners, to Governors, and to various organizations. The sum granted to the Unions was far below the estimates prepared at the beginning of 1916. These estimates asked for an immediate grant of 5,500,000 rubles and for an allowance of 16,000,000 rubles during the course of the next three months. They were based on the expenditure to be incurred in connection with the following forms of relief: the provision of meals, lodgings, clothing, footwear and underwear; the prevention of epidemic diseases among the refugees and the spreading of diseases among the population; the organization of bathhouses, laundries, disinfecting stations; medical help in cases other than those of infectious diseases, and, finally, the relief of children and the providing of refugees with employment. In asking for this grant the Unions prepared detailed estimates of the expenditure per head, of food, lodging, clothing, etc. Only partial grants were allowed by the Treasury, and the plan, therefore, could be executed only in part and without system.

In the meantime the refugees had spread themselves all over the country, and their position in new places of settlement was exceedingly difficult, in spite of general sympathy, and great and unselfish efforts of the local population to help them. The American scholar, Professor Whittemore, whose name is gratefully remembered by many Russians, in his report of his visit to Russia in November and December 1915, gives a grim picture of the condition in which he found the refugees, and of the overcrowding, disorder, and utter wretchedness of their dwellings. He points out the lack of bathhouses and laundries, the insanitary state of the premises occupied, the general idleness, and the part which refugees played in spreading infection among the people around them. Professor Whittemore investigated the conditions under which the refugees were living in Nizhni-Novgorod, Penza, Pskov, Kursk, Kharkov, Tambov, Saratov, Samara, Orenburg, Tashkent, Ufa, etc., and he was driven to the conclusion that to improve their condition, certain measures were urgently needed. He advocated the establishment of huts, bathhouses, washhouses, and disinfecting stations, the institution of compulsory sanitary regulations, vaccination, and the like.

The condition of refugees in other districts was no better. The hardships suffered by the great majority of them were further emphasized when contrasted with the position of a certain number who were well-to-do, and who were often the cause of an increase in rents and in the prices of the necessaries of life.

At the beginning of 1916 the problem presented by refugees was still further complicated. Those who had just settled in certain districts were removed to other parts of the country. For instance, it was decided, as the result of an outbreak of epidemic diseases in Turkestan, to move the refugees from that region. The evacuation of refugees from the cities was made necessary by a rapidly developing economic crisis. It was among the measures suggested in July for the relief of congestion in Petrograd; and similar measures had to be taken in other cities of European and Asiatic Russia. This evacuation from the cities was intended both to relieve congestion and—as a measure of social policy—to induce the refugees to seek employment in agriculture.

Both Unions undertook the systematic refugee registration. But this work was soon handed over to the Committee of the Grand Duchess Tatiana Nicholaevna, and the Unions were compelled to suspend their activities, though they were already conducting them on the largest scale. The obvious desire to exclude the Unions from participation in such work led to its complete abandonment by the Union of Zemstvos in March 1916. The Union of Towns continued to carry it on, managing finally to overcome the obstacles put in its way by departments of the Government. And it played its part as follows.

During the early stage of the retreat of the refugees the joint organization of the two Unions had equipped a number of detachments of "guides," who had the task of looking after the refugees *en route*, of furnishing them with food and medical help, and of conveying them to their ultimate destination. From September to December 1915 the guides accompanied about 1,000 trains, and provided assistance for some 1,000,000 refugees in all. A statement made by the Deputy Special Commissioner of the Union (April 1916) shows that the 133 canteens belonging to the Union distributed 9,000,000 meals.

By November 1915 the movement of refugees was practically over. They had scattered throughout the country, as far as Archangel, Tashkent, and Vladivostok, and it then became plain that they had brought with them all manner of epidemic diseases. The arrival of refugees was commonly accompanied by outbreaks of cholera, typhus, and smallpox, and contagious children's diseases such as measles, scarlet fever, and diphtheria. A report on epidemic diseases among refugees, submitted to the Executive of the Union of Towns in February 1916, enumerated eighty-five towns and cities in the Volga district, along the Siberian railway, and in the north, center, and south of Russia, where outbreaks of epidemics had been recorded. Of the total number of cases of illness registered among refugees, about 20 per cent were cases of infectious disease. A report by the Union's Sanitary Bureau gave the death rate from various diseases as follows: typhus, 12 per cent; typhoid fever, 25 per cent; cholera, 10 per cent; dysentery, 20 per cent. The number of beds maintained by the Unions for refugees suffering from infectious diseases was 1,640 on 1st January 1916; in March it had become 2,075. The total number of beds which the Unions proposed to equip for this purpose in various towns was 10,331. In March 1916 the Union maintained 2,715 beds for cases other than those of epidemic diseases and proposed to equip 3,552 additional beds for the same purpose. To add to this, 25 towns opened dispensaries and medical stations and 166 other medical stations were to be opened. The organization of bathhouses for the refugees, the washing of their linen, and the disinfection of their clothing, formed part of the sanitary policy of the Unions. Districts where refugees accumulated were supplied with drugs and with the equipment required for disinfecting stations.

A Central Labor Exchange was established at the end of August 1915. It had the task of organizing local labor exchanges, of coordinating their work, of "redistributing among them the surplus of demand and supply." In March the Central Labor Exchange had formed connections with 140 national organizations and with local labor Exchanges which had been opened in various towns (56) and townships of Russia. The Labor Exchange supplied workmen to the railway companies, to the labor detachments engaged in the digging of trenches, to factories and workshops working for national defense, etc.

A Special Inquiry Bureau recorded the names of refugees who had lost their relatives; during three months it had to deal with 80,000 applications. It assisted refugees in tracing the missing members of their families, and registered deaths. The legal department of the Union of Towns provided refugees with legal services. Till then they had had to live in conditions approaching outlawry, their various rights being continually infringed. This legal department took steps to obtain payments on the vouchers given refugees for goods requisitioned and for work performed; finally, it published a handbook containing the acts and regulations referring to refugees.

The Union paid special attention to refugee children who had been separated from their parents in the disorder of the retreat, or who had been orphaned. The reports of the representatives of the Union give an appalling picture of the death of hundreds of children from disease, from exposure to cold, and lack of food. The agents of the Unions collected children who had lost their parents, and brought them in numbers to the clearing station in Moscow. With the consent of the municipality the orphanages of Moscow took care of children who passed through the city. By 10th January, 3,970 had been registered. And not all were registered. Similar clearing stations for the distribution of orphans among appropriate institutions were estab-

lished in Gomel, Bryansk, Kiev, Mogilev, Zhukov, and other places;
and from these clearing stations children were sent to the orphanages of adjacent towns. Up to 12th January 1916, 1,418 children
were admitted to the orphanages situated in the provinces; 58 orphanages with accommodation for 3,714 children were opened in
towns and cities of Russia, besides those of Moscow. About 2,000
children were maintained in the Union homes in Mogilev, Minsk,
Bryansk, Rovno, etc., and 1,223 children were accommodated in such
homes in Moscow itself. The vast majority of unweaned children
died on the way to new places of settlement. The children of refugees
who passed through the institutions of the Unions were registered;
over 7,000 children were registered up to 10th January 1916. Particular attention was paid to the protection of girls between the ages
of 10 and 16. A special home was organized for deaf-mute children.
Up to 1st June 1916, 2,775,735 refugees were registered by the
public organizations alone. The influx of refugees was particularly
large in the following provinces: In Ekaterinoslav it was 7.01 per
cent of the pre-war population; in Livonia, 6.95 per cent; in Samara, 4.39 per cent; Tambov, 3.60 per cent. Excluding the capitals,
the largest numbers of refugees registered by the Unions in towns
were: in Ekaterinoslav, 50,000, or 23.7 per cent of the normal population; in Kharkov, 45,000 or 18.37 per cent; in Samara, 41,000 or
28.6 per cent, etc.

The figures given above show only the work of the two Unions,
and do not represent the full extent of the movement of refugees,
considered as a problem of the Great War. The relief of refugees,
their registration, and the whole handling of the problem, as has
been stated, was not under Union administration, but was concentrated in the hands of a Special Council.

Moscow played a leading part in the organization of refugee relief. Here, too, it became a great clearing station, as well as an important center for refugee colonization.

The first wave of refugees, from Kalish, arrived in August 1914,
immediately after the declaration of War. But the number who then
sought relief in Moscow did not exceed 1,500. A very different picture might have been seen a year later, in the weeks following mid-
July 1915, when the populations of whole provinces had to leave their
homes. The total number who settled in Moscow and were registered

by a census held in November 1915 was 141,649.[2] The railway junction of Moscow, which could deal with 800 coaches a day, was sometimes completely blocked by refugee-filled trains. The records of the municipality show that during the period from 1st August 1915 to 1st September 1916, 442,987 refugees were registered in Moscow; of this number, 272,371 were transferred to more distant destinations; the rest remained, provisionally, in the city. The average monthly figures were 34,076 arrivals and 20,951 departures. Those refugees who remained were provided with dwellings—about 500 apartments were leased for this purpose from private owners by the municipality—and food, the standard ration being 20 copecks per head. Accommodation for 9,100 refugees was provided in well-equipped huts erected around Moscow at a cost of 1,297,233 rubles. The administration of refugee relief was entrusted by the municipality of Moscow to a special committee, which included representatives of national and religious organizations, and to 16 district committees, which supervised the distribution of allowances and clothes, organized workshops, provided refugees with employment, assisted them in obtaining legal advice, and looked after their spiritual needs.

All possible medical and sanitary measures were taken by the executive board of the municipality to protect refugees both when detained at the railway stations of Moscow, and in their places of settlement. Medical stations were attached to the railway termini and ten doctors were appointed to oversee the care of refugees living in their respective Moscow districts. In spite of measures for the prevention of infection, 4,553 cases of infectious disease were registered in the course of five months (August to December 1915) among the 40,000 refugees who were in receipt of relief from public organizations; the highest figures were recorded in September and October. Of this number, 2,663 were admitted to various hospitals; the rest were accommodated in properly isolated flats and private houses. Between 9th August 1915 and 30th July 1916, the total number of serious cases of infectious disease among the refugees who remained in Moscow was 6,409.[3]

Special schools were organized for the children of refugees, and orphanages for those who had lost their parents.

[2] *Statistichesky Ezhegodnik goroda Moskwi (Statistical Year-Book of the City of Moscow)*, Moscow, 1916.
[3] Returns of the Executive Board of the Municipality of Moscow.

The total expenditure of the municipality of Moscow for refugee relief from 1st September 1915 to 1st September 1916 amounted to 4,750,345 rubles; of this amount the Government refunded to the municipality 2,947,198 rubles. At the end of 1915 the average monthly expenditure of the municipality of Moscow for such relief was approximately 600,000 rubles.

From 10th July to 31st December 1915, 42,037 refugees were registered in Petrograd. In July 1916 the district relief committees of the municipality of Petrograd, of national organizations, of the Union of Towns and of the Committee of the Grand Duchess Tatiana had on their registers 38,000 refugees. The Petrograd Committee of the Union of Towns organized canteens and provisional shelters. From these shelters, women with young children, those who could not earn their own living, chronic invalids, and old people were transferred to special homes. There were 83 of these homes, with accommodation for 3,950 people. About 5,000 children of various ages were provided with homes in temporary orphanages. Up to 1st January 1916, the Executive Board of the municipality of Petrograd spent 1,217,611 rubles on refugee relief.

The distribution of refugees in the various provinces was, in January 1916, as follows: Ekaterinoslav, 250,000; Samara, 204,000; Tambov, 155,000; Kharkov, 121,000; Saratov, 117,000; Vitebsk, 100,000; the provinces of Moscow, Ryazan, Nizhni-Novgorod, Penza, Petrograd, Ufa, Kazan, Kaluga, Orenburg, and the Territory of the Don Cossacks, had from 64,000 to 92,000 each; 18 provinces had from 16,400 to 47,000 refugees; and seven, from 1,000 to 7,500.

The problem of refugees on the Caucasus front may be illustrated by the following data: 105,000 settled down in the province of Erivan, 9,500 in the province of Elisavetpol, 7,400 in the province of Tiflis, 2,300 in the Black Sea province, 6,200 in the province of Stavropol, 3,500 in the Terek Territory, 10,000 in the Kuban Territory, 24,000 in the Kars Territory, 12,000 in the Batum Territory, and 2,900 in the Baku Territory. The total number of refugees in that part of the Empire was 182,000. The expenditure for the relief of refugees in the Caucasus during the first three months of 1916 was estimated at 1,900,000 rubles.

When the Russian armies on the European and Caucasian fronts began to win victories, they gave rise, among refugees, to an irresistible homeward movement. Its strength was greatly increased after the second occupation of the Bukovina by the Russian troops, and it was checked and taken under control only by a system of strict repressive measures. And how greatly they were needed was very plain, for reports of these homeward movements on the part of refugees came from Perm and Ufa, from the Caucasus, the valleys of the Volga and Siberia.

CHAPTER X

COMBATING EPIDEMIC DISEASES

EPIDEMIC disease is an invariable accompaniment of war, outbreaks being commonly observed not only among the troops but also among the civilian population. The history of former wars has established that the number of cases of infectious diseases and the mortality from them are always greater than the number of casualties in the field and the mortality from wounds. The conditions created in Russia by the Great War were particularly favorable to the development of epidemic diseases. The War involved large areas in the west and south of Russia; the front line of hundreds and thousands of miles passed through dozens of provinces. Millions of mobilized men moved toward the front, overcrowding cities and railway junctions. Tens of thousands of men employed in the digging of trenches gathered behind the fighting line and in the adjoining zone. On the other hand, the front sent to the country an unbroken stream of sick and wounded, of prisoners of war and refugees. They spread over the country and penetrated to the remotest parts of Siberia. The commixture of the population was further increased by the change in general economic conditions, and the abandonment of large factories and workshops in the districts endangered by the enemy. The continual shifting of great masses of population, and the resulting congestion caused a marked change for the worse in the already unsatisfactory sanitary conditions of towns and villages, and gave infectious diseases their favorite ground in which to develop and spread.[1]

Some information indicating the character of the problem of epidemic diseases in Russia during the War may be gathered from the report[2] covering the spread of epidemics in the Empire for the period from 1st July to 31st December 1915.

[1] For the details of the participation of the Zemstvos and their Union in the struggle against infectious diseases *see* Polner, Prince Obolensky, and Turin, *op. cit.*

[2] Presented to the fourth conference of the Union of Towns. The report is based on the official data of the Army Medical Service (*Upravlenie Verkhovnago Nachalnika Sanitarnoy i Evakuatsionnoy Chasti*).

	Number of cases	Percentage of total number of cases	Number of deaths	Percentage of deaths
Cholera	42,953	5.6	15,819	36.8
Typhus	43,823	5.8	4,135	9.5
Typhoid	177,947	23.4	16,768	9.4
Remittent typhoid	16,795	2.1	445	2.7
Dysentery	123,620	15.0	9,730	7.9
Smallpox	34,001	4.5	6,313	18.6
Diphtheria	104,097	13.6	7,323	7.0
Scarlet fever	153,129	21.7	19,667	12.9
Erysipelas, tetanus, and unknown species	63,012	8.3	2,520	4.0
Total	759,377	100.0	82,720	10.8

The distribution of infectious diseases according to the time of occurrence was as follows: The greatest number of cases of cholera were registered in September 1915; after that date they fell off rapidly. The greatest number of cases of dysentery, diphtheria, and scarlet fever were recorded in July. In the case of typhus and smallpox, both were steadily spreading during the period under investigation.

During the same period the distribution of patients suffering from epidemic diseases over the country was as follows:

Region	Number of patients	Percentage of total number of cases
Moscow	245,754	32.3
Petrograd	59,857	7.9
Finland	4,483	0.6
Orel	27,178	3.6
Kursk	28,575	3.7
Karkhov	54,832	7.2
Ekaterinoslav	39,369	5.2
Rostov-on-Don	13,018	1.6
Caucasus	49,440	6.5
The military zone	171,094	22.7
Siberia	49,051	6.5
Central Asia	16,726	2.2
Total	759,377	100.0

About one-third of all cases of infectious disease were concentrated in the district of Moscow.

The data quoted above seem to indicate that the number of cases of epidemic diseases in the army and the death rate among the men suffering from them were not so high as might have been expected under the exceedingly unfavorable conditions created by the War. This was, no doubt, due to the great improvement in the organization of the army medical and sanitary service which had been introduced since the Russo-Japanese War, and increased knowledge of the epidemiology of many infectious diseases.

The prisoners of war who were conveyed in large groups to the central districts proved a very dangerous element from the point of view of the spread of infection. A severe outbreak of typhus took place among the Turkish prisoners of war on the Caucasus front in the winter of 1915. The inadequacy of preventive measures resulted in the spread of this disease from the Turkish concentration camp to many towns of Russia. It was responsible for a severe outbreak of typhus in the towns of the Volga region, especially in Samara and Saratov, in Ufa, and along the line of the Siberian railway; 7,000 prisoners of war died in a concentration camp near Totskoë, a station of the Samara-Orenburg railway. An outbreak of remittent typhoid took place among the prisoners of war sent to the province of Moscow from various districts in January and February 1916 in connection with a scheme for the cutting of timber. Typhus developed among a group of 1,000 prisoners of war sent to Moscow in factories and in workshops manufacturing boots. Through the same channel typhus was brought to Kaluga, Nizhni-Novgorod, and other towns.

From the beginning of the summer of 1915 the towns of Russia were invaded by refugees. Suddenly thrown into the midst of the population, with whom they were in continuous intercourse, the refugees died in large numbers from infectious diseases and spread them among their neighbors. The rapid development of epidemics among the population may be illustrated by the following examples: 863 cases of typhus were registered in Kharkov in December 1915; out of this number, 249 were local inhabitants and 410 were refugees. In January 1916 the comparative relation of these figures was already altered: the total number of cases was 1,099, of which 542 were local inhabitants and 309 were refugees (the remaining cases were soldiers). In October 1915 two cases of typhus were reported in Ufa; in November, 7; in December, 631; and in January 1916, 755.

Three hundred sixty-five cases of typhus were reported in Saratov in January, of which 292 were refugees. During the period from 3rd January to 28th February 1916, 937 cases of typhus, remittent typhoid, and smallpox were recorded among the inhabitants of Moscow, which considerably exceeds the figures for the preceding years.

Frequent outbreaks of infectious diseases occurred also among the numerous army units located in various towns while awaiting their departure for the front. Similar outbreaks were reported from the military trains proceeding from Siberia and the east of Russia; they constituted a direct danger to the army by spreading infection among the troops.

An inquiry into the sanitary conditions of Russian towns, held by the Union of Towns in the spring of 1915, shows that 75,443 cases of infectious disease were registered during the spring months of 1915 in the 160 towns which provided information. Of this number 19,212 were soldiers, 11,597 were prisoners of war, and 44,634 were local inhabitants. About 30 per cent of the total number of cases therefore came from new elements of the population. In the second half of 1915, with the arrival of the refugees, the percentage of cases among the new elements of the population became still larger. Under these conditions the sanitary institutions of the municipalities and the hospitals for infectious disease had to devote about two-thirds of their work to new settlers, or even to persons on their way to some further destination. The towns of Russia with their inadequate sanitary equipment and their almost complete absence of experience in sanitation were totally helpless in the presence of these new and tremendous problems.

As stated above, only a small fraction of the municipal revenue could be devoted to medical and sanitary purposes; moreover, of the sums that appeared in the municipal estimates under the heading "Hospitals and sanitation" the greater part was spent on hospitals and only a very little on sanitation. If the organization of the medical and sanitary service in the capitals was more or less satisfactory, it was very poor indeed in the majority of smaller towns. The results of an inquiry held in 1912-1914[3] show that of 224 towns which took part in the inquiry—they included the two capitals and all provincial and regional towns except three—only 81 towns had their own mu-

[3] Published in the medical journal *Obshchestvenni Vrach,* 1915, Nos. 7 and 8.

nicipal hospitals, the inhabitants of 143 towns having to seek the assistance of hospitals belonging to the zemstvos and to other organizations. In Petrograd there was one hospital bed per 140 inhabitants; in Moscow, one per 180; in Odessa, Riga, Rostov-on-Don, one per 200; in Simferopol, one per 5,600, etc. A more or less complete system of sanitation was established in 45 towns only; in 41 towns it was still in a primitive stage of development. An investigation conducted by the Pirogov Society on the eve of the War disclosed that 96 of the larger towns, or 48 per cent of the whole number, had no municipal medical service, and 139 towns, or 62 per cent, had no system of sanitation. The expenditure for medical purposes per head was exceedingly small. The maximum figure was reached in Moscow and was only 4 rubles 60 copecks; it was 3 rubles 88 copecks in Petrograd. In 14 small towns nothing at all was spent for medical purposes. The expenditure per head on sanitation in the capitals averaged 35 copecks.

The majority of Russian towns were deprived of the benefits of sanitation essential to the health and welfare of the population. In 1912 only 241 towns had constructed waterworks, which ranged from up-to-date and excellent services such as, for instance, those of Moscow, the construction of which cost 50,000,000 rubles, to unpretentious and primitive systems worth a few thousand rubles. Twenty-six provincial and regional towns had no properly organized water supply; seven of them were in Poland, four in European Russia, four in the Caucasus, five in Siberia, and six in the Russian possessions in Central Asia. The removal of refuse was effected by special garbage wagons, but many towns had no such wagons. An inquiry held in 1907-1909 revealed that only 38 towns had systems of sewers, none of which covered the whole area of the town. Even in Moscow the sewers extended only to some five-sixths of the area of the city; in Odessa they covered half the area of the city; in Tiflis, one-sixth. Petrograd had no adequate system. It was not until just before the War that many municipalities undertook the planning of regular systems of water supply and sewers. In 1913 and 1914 thirteen towns began the constructions of new waterworks; ten towns extended the existing system of water supply, thirty-three prepared schemes for new waterworks. Plans for the laying down of sewers were drawn up in thirty-six towns, and the municipalities were seeking funds which would allow them to put these plans into execution.

The War suspended all work and all plans, yet at the same time necessitated urgent measures for the improvement of sanitary conditions; and many municipalities employed the funds granted to them by the Union of Towns on the improvement of their water supply, the maintenance of wells, the better organization of their control, and the extension and improvement of their methods of collection of refuse. All this was absolutely necessary, but was not a solution of the problem. The sanitary conditions of the average town continued to be very unsatisfactory. An inquiry held by the Union of Towns disclosed in many towns a high death rate, and extremely insanitary conditions of the soil and of wells. Many municipalities removed only a small fraction of the refuse; the rest was thrown into pits, drained into the rivers or buried in ditches. "Impurities are accumulating in the soil, in the water and in the air," says a report which covers the towns of the Volga, Siberia, and Central Asia.

The insanitary condition of Russian towns favored the development of epidemics. Outbreaks of infectious disease were reported from Kharkov, Poltava, Chernigov, Saratov, Samara, Ufa, Orenburg, Ekaterinoslav, Kishinev, and many other places. Among the victims were doctors and other members of the medical staff (Tashkent, Ufa, Saratov, Novocherkask, etc.). Municipalities organized on their own initiative urgent measures for the prevention of the spread of epidemic disease. Special sanitary municipal commissions were appointed in Moscow, Petrograd, Samara, Smolensk, Vyatka, and other towns; these commissions supervised the sanitation of business premises, markets, dwellings, etc. The municipalities mobilized the members of the medical profession, established new hospitals and increased the number of hospital beds (Saratov, Samara, Simbirsk, Kharkov, Ufa, etc.), opened temporary hospitals in army huts, set up isolation hospitals in private houses and flats, rented and constructed bathhouses, provided for the disinfection and washing of underwear and linen, and organized clearing stations which exercised medical control over arriving refugees and workmen.

Under these conditions heavy responsibilities were laid upon the Union of Towns, which undertook the important task of coördinating the policy of separate municipalities in preventing the spread of epidemic diseases. Russia at that time did not possess any legislation on sanitary questions, and had no officially recognized system of measures for the prevention of epidemic diseases. The regulations of the committees for the prevention of cholera and plague exhibited numerous important defects, which at the time of their publication provoked a unanimous protest from the zemstvos, municipalities, and medical organizations. The Central Committee on Plague gave little signs of activity and produced neither a scheme, nor general regulations for the prevention of the spread of epidemic diseases under war conditions. The Committee distributed the few million rubles put at its disposal among separate zemstvos and other bodies without any definite plan, and without taking into consideration all the conditions on which the spread of epidemics depended. Of the total sum of 17,200,000 rubles put in 1915 at the disposal of the Central Committee on Plague—the central organization for the prevention of the spread of epidemic diseases—only 5,600,000 rubles was allocated to the zemstvos and municipalities for medical and sanitary purposes up to 20th November 1915, in spite of the fact that their demands considerably exceeded the whole fund assigned to the Committee.

The conference of the Union of Towns held in September 1914 had already discussed the necessity of organizing detention and isolation hospitals in the area adjoining the front and connected with the main clearing stations. It drew up a preliminary list of towns where such hospitals should be established in order to prevent the spread of infection from the army; the list included: Belostok, Vitebsk, Vilna, Dvinsk, Polotsk, Gomel, Orel, Kursk, Kharkov, Samara. The Conference of February 1915 examined a more detailed scheme of preventive measures against epidemics, prepared by the Central Committee and coördinated with a similar scheme of the Union of Zemstvos. In accordance with this plan, hospitals for epidemic diseases were to be opened in towns, which were divided for this purpose into three categories. In the towns of the first category the number of beds for patients suffering from infectious diseases was fixed at 10 per cent of the total number of surgical beds and was estimated at 15,000. The second category was composed of towns some distance from the front and equipped with hospitals for wounded and sick; 5 per cent of the beds of these towns were to be used for the treatment of epidemic diseases (2,525). The towns of the third category were to provide 4,495 beds for cases of epidemic diseases; Caucasus and Siberia, 5,000 each. The scheme of the Union of Towns, therefore, proposed the establishment of 31,020 beds for cases of epidemic diseases. The estimates of the Union included, in addition to the provisions for the building of huts for temporary hospitals, grants for the equipment of bathhouses, laundries, disinfecting stations, etc. The estimates required an initial outlay of 18,120,250 rubles and 10,635,200 rubles to defray the current expenditure of the first four months. In asking the Government for the grant of these sums the conference pointed out that "immediate measures for the prevention of the spread of epidemic diseases among the troops, the population, the refugees, and the prisoners of war are essential for the preservation of national health as well as for maintaining the efficiency of the army, and should, therefore, be recognized as necessary for the continuation of the War."

Without waiting for the approval of the estimates by the Government the Union began the organization of hospitals for epidemic diseases in various towns, using for this purpose sums in hand and two government advances of 1,752,000 rubles and 1,000,000 rubles. Among these hospitals we shall mention the large hospital in Gomel for 1,655 beds. This hospital was opened in the spring of 1915 and grew into a small town, with its own water supply, sewage farms, washhouse, disinfecting stations, barracks for the staff, etc. During the violent outbreak of cholera in the summer of 1915 this hospital played an important part by detaining suspect cases among the troops and the refugees. In addition to the hospital of Gomel, the Union established and equipped during the same period the following hospitals for epidemic diseases: in Vitebsk, 250 beds; in Orel, 200 beds; in Samara, 500 beds; in Kursk, 200 beds; in Dvinsk, 250 beds; in Vilna, 250 beds. At the same time the Union was supporting the municipalities in their endeavor to improve their sanitary conditions and to organize the removal of refuse. These measures prevented the outbreak of epidemic diseases in many towns. The municipality of Archangel, which was at that time the only accessible port of European Russia, sent to the Union a complete list of its sanitary requirements; most of them were satisfied.

This was only the beginning of a partial execution of the scheme; it could not be put into effect as a whole unless adequate funds were obtained. But the Government followed in this case the same policy as in the question of the relief of disabled men, of refugees, etc., insisting that the whole work for the prevention of the spread of epidemic diseases should be concentrated in the hands of the Central

Committee on Plague appointed by the Ministry of the Interior. The scheme of the Union was set aside, and repeated demands for putting it into operation remained unanswered. Only in September 1915, when an outbreak of epidemic diseases created an alarming situation, did the headquarters of the Army Sanitary Service inform the Union that their scheme for the prevention of the spread of epidemic diseases, together with the estimates, which had in the meantime been reduced to an initial outlay of 10,235,185 rubles and 910,000 for current expenses, was at last approved; and a sum of 4,000,000 rubles was advanced by the Treasury on 19th September for the execution of the scheme. But the delay in obtaining the grants had unfortunate consequences. The cost of material and labor had risen in the meantime from 50 to 100 per cent. Whereas at the time when the estimates were prepared the cost of the equipment of a bed for infectious diseases was 425 rubles, with the rise of prices it had increased to 700 rubles. The cost of various sanitary installations had risen in proportion; but the worst was that epidemic diseases had by then had time to establish themselves in the country.

On 1st August 1915, the Union established 10,422 beds for patients suffering from epidemic diseases throughout the country (including the Caucasus). Of this number, 6,784 beds were distributed among the towns removed from the front. Under the Union's revised plan the total number of beds for cases of epidemic disease was fixed at 7,830 in 71 towns of European Russia, and 5,000 in Siberia, in addition to those already in existence.

The following hospitals for epidemic diseases were opened in the second half of 1915 and the beginning of 1916: in Kharkov, 1,000 beds; in Kursk, 800; in Kaluga, 500; in Syzran, 200; in Simbirsk, 200; in Rostov-on-Don, 200; in Voronezh, 158, etc. At the same time a scheme of installation of sanitary equipment in various towns was proceeded with. Bathhouses for the use of the general public and of the hospitals were opened in eight towns, public laundries in 18, disinfecting stations in 14, bacteriological laboratories in 8; in 87 towns the municipality organized the collection of refuse, and in 8, new systems of water supply and draining were laid out. On 1st March 1916, of the total number of hospital beds proposed by the scheme of the Union, 6,872 were already available in 46 towns, and 3,648 were almost ready. For the period from 1st February 1915 to September 1916, the government subsidy to the Union amounted to 8,802,996 rubles. A report presented by the Committee on Sanitary Engineering to the conference of the Union in November 1916 states that "in spite of the delay in obtaining the necessary funds from the Treasury and of the disorganization of local municipal workers, a great part of the plan for the creation of a preventive cordon of isolation hospitals, and the improvement of the sanitation of more or less important towns, is nearing its completion." The last conference of the Union, held in October 1917, was informed that 18,548 patients suffering from infectious diseases were detained in the hospitals of the Union (Petrograd and Moscow are not included in this number).

Among the measures taken by the Union for the prevention of epidemic diseases we may mention the organization of inoculation against typhoid and cholera. The Union undertook the supply of municipalities with vaccines. A special medical detachment, consisting of the medical staff and a bacteriological laboratory and provided with means of transport, was sent to the Caucasus front. On the initiative of the Union the committees of the Union in a number of large towns appointed special bureaus on sanitary engineering, staffed by local medical men and engineers, to attend to problems of sanitation. These bureaus, working in provincial towns, extended the benefit of their advice also to district towns, the sanitation of which was in a still more unsatisfactory state.

The municipality of Moscow repeatedly insisted on the necessity of preventive measures and the non-admittance to Moscow of men suffering from epidemic diseases; it urged the adoption of a scheme to limit the functions of the capital to those of a clearing station, for those cases of infection only which, in spite of all preventive measures, were brought to Moscow by the hospital trains. The representations of the municipality, however, were ignored, and the arrival of patients suffering from epidemic disease was not due to a mere accident; trains loaded exclusively with such patients were directed to the capital. Moscow, therefore, not only prevented the spread of accidental infection within the country, but became a great hospital for epidemic diseases, to which patients were deliberately sent from the front. From December 1914 to January 1916, ninety-one trains brought to Moscow 20,538 patients suffering from infectious diseases. On 1st May 1916, the number of trains was increased to 182 and the number of patients to 40,839. Nineteen thousand five hundred and ninety-seven patients suffering from infectious diseases were registered and detained in Moscow hospitals up to 1st August 1915. In January 1916 the total number of patients suffering from epidemic diseases registered in the hospitals of Moscow reached 35,000; in April 1916, 45,000. In order to deal with the rapidly growing number of cases the municipality was gradually increasing the number of hospitals and beds. On 1st January 1915, 1,486 beds in the municipal hospitals were assigned for the use of patients suffering from infectious diseases; on 1st April 1915, 7,128; on 1st December 1915, 10,000; on 1st March 1916, 11,947. Serious outbreaks of epidemic diseases among the population and their spread all over the country were prevented only by the energetic measures of the municipality in increasing the accommodation of the hospitals. This important function of Moscow was well understood by the Government as well as by the local organizations.

In order to prevent the spread of infection through the wounded evacuated from the front the Petrograd Committee of the Union of Towns took a number of measures, among which the following may be mentioned: organization of clearing stations and quarantine, disinfection, bacteriological investigations, establishment of a strict control over the boilers supplying the troops with water and over the refrigerators, sanitary inspection of hospitals, etc. Three thousand seven hundred beds were equipped in August 1916 for the use of patients suffering from epidemic diseases.

Various measures for the prevention of such diseases were taken by other towns, with the assistance of the Union of Towns. A decrease in the number of cases among the urban population may be noticed from May 1916; this was partly due to the measures taken by the Union.

CHAPTER XI

OTHER WAR ACTIVITIES

THE war work of the Union of Towns and of the municipalities was not limited to the relief of the sick and wounded. It was extended in many other directions and formed an intricate system.

Immediately after the outbreak of war the municipalities took upon themselves the care of the families of municipal officers and employees who were called to serve with the colors. About 10,000 employees of the municipality of Moscow were mobilized in the course of the first few months. The allowance made by the municipality depended on the size of the family of the mobilized man; a full salary was paid to a wife with three or more small children. A special committee was in charge of the distribution of allowances. By the beginning of 1917 the total amount of these allowances rose to 2,500,000 rubles. The relief of families of mobilized municipal officials and employees was not always organized on the same scale as in Moscow, but not a single municipality refused to fulfil this duty.

The families of the mobilized members of the "reserve" troops were entitled to an allowance from the Government under an Act of 25th June 1912. But the amount of this allowance—3 rubles 60 copecks a month for an adult and 1 ruble 80 copecks for a child—was absolutely inadequate in the capitals and large cities. The municipalities were compelled to bear the cost of increasing the standard allowance. In Moscow it was raised to 5 rubles for an adult and 3 rubles for a child; and the expenditure thus involved threw a new and heavy burden on the municipal budget. On 1st June 1915, the government allowance was raised to six and three rubles, respectively, and the necessity of a grant from the municipality, therefore, ceased to exist; but by this time the municipality of Moscow had already spent on allowances 841,665 rubles, drawn from the general municipal fund. Moreover, the municipality still had the care of certain categories of persons not mentioned in the Act. Such were, for instance, natural and adopted children, "civil wives,"[1] etc. The allow-

[1] *I.e.*, women living openly and permanently as the wives of men with whom they had gone through no form of marriage, civil or religious.

ances made by the municipality of Moscow to these categories up to October 1916 amounted to 1,162,470 rubles.

At the same time the municipalities were compelled to increase the usual subsidies contributed by them toward the expenses of district committees for the relief of the poor, committees which did splendid work in helping the most unhappy section of the population to overcome the additional hardships brought about by the War. Government grants and municipal subsidies amounting to 17,388,115 rubles passed through the hands of the district committees from the beginning of the War up to October 1916. The committees provided the families of the mobilized members of the reserve force with dwellings and meals at reduced rates, or even free of charge. They also showed great energy in obtaining employment for them, and in organizing crèches, kindergartens, playgrounds, etc. Special attention was paid to the question of destitute children. The War and the refugees created a strong stimulus for the development of this activity. A conference of some 300 members was called by the Union of Towns in March 1916, in order to discuss the problem of the relief of children in the new light thrown upon it by the War. The conference recognized that the State and the community as a whole had the duty of looking after destitute children, including the children of the refugees, and prepared a detailed plan of measures for the prevention of juvenile crime, the organization of the relief of children, their education and training, the protection of maternity and infancy, the prevention of juvenile prostitution, the supervision of juvenile labor, the appointing of guardians for destitute children, etc.

Municipal committees were particularly efficient in their endeavor to supply destitute persons with suitable employment. They organized a number of central workshops, where articles of clothing and underwear were cut out and distributed among women in need of work, who were sent to them by the municipal committees. During the period from 12th August 1914 to January 1916, 12,298,641 articles of clothing and underwear were distributed through the municipal committees in Moscow. The number of women employed was about 11,500, and a total of 1,117,857 rubles was paid to them in wages.

The system of relief of the poor was based on the following two principles: the relief was administered through small territorial units, such as the municipal committees for the relief of paupers and through societies for the promotion of the welfare of school children; free from the narrow character of private charities, this system included a number of far-reaching preventive measures, which formed an integral part of the general and social policy of the municipalities.

The number of families of mobilized men increased with the calling of new classes. In July-August 1914, the number in Petrograd was 35,913; a year later, in July 1915, it was 69,764; in November of the same year it had reached 83,848. Of this number, 53,942 were in receipt of allowances. By 1st December 1915, 2,700,629 rubles had been spent on the relief of families of mobilized men. The total expenditure of the district committees for the relief of paupers of Petrograd during the first year of the War, on the relief of children, the distribution of free meals, the supplying of infants with milk, the organization of labor exchanges and cheap dwellings, etc., amounted to 1,980,667 rubles.

Special interest is attached to the work of the municipality of Moscow during the tragic period when, in the spring of 1915, the Russian army, inadequately provided with arms and munitions, was compelled to retreat and to abandon to the enemy not only the territory previously occupied, but also Russian land, Russian towns, and fortresses. With the lack of munitions and supply, the absence of adequate organization also greatly contributed to the disaster.

In its resolution of 19th May 1915, the Duma of Moscow expressed its readiness to "do anything which would prevent the army from being short of supply or munitions," and gave voice to the necessity of creating a special public organization to undertake the production of equipment, etc., for the army. The passing of this resolution took place at almost the same time as the organization of the war industries committees, which undertook the task of coördinating the work of Russian industry for the War. The next stage was reached when, on 10th June 1915, the joint Committee of the Union of Towns and the Union of Zemstvos—the *Zemgor*[2]—began its work on the various technical problems brought into existence by the War, but unconnected with the Red Cross activities, and assumed the control and direction of the efforts of local committees of the zemstvos and towns for the organization of war industry. The municipality

[2] *See* Polner, Prince Obolensky, and Turin, *op. cit.,* Chapter XV.

of Moscow immediately undertook the production of munitions, the workshops of the municipal street railways being adapted for this purpose; and on 12th June the Duma was shown the first shell turned out. The development of the production of munitions was checked by the shortage of lathes and by the length of time required for making them. Some lathes were assembled and put into working order in Russia; some were ordered in America, England, Sweden, Denmark, and Japan. The lack of raw material for the production of munitions on a large scale and the almost entire absence of skilled labor—the majority of skilled workmen were mobilized—also greatly hindered the work. But all obstacles were overcome, and the municipality of Moscow succeeded in organizing a mass production of shells of the French type, Russian three-inch shells, six-inch shells, 4.8-inch shells, and fuses. The equipping of the municipal workshops was completed in February 1916. Their output was valued at about 20,000,000 rubles a year. At the same time the production of hand grenades, of bombs and mines, was got under way. A number of special furnaces were devoted to extracting from petroleum by-products available for the manufacture of explosives.

The output of these municipal workshops may be seen from the following data: up to 1st August 1917, they turned out 315,813 three-inch shell cases, 47,149 six-inch shell cases, 20,210 annealed six-inch shell cases. They produced 260,891 three-inch shells of the French type, 251,984 three-inch shells of the Russian type, 23,951 4.8-inch shells; 599,306 caps for three-inch shells, 99,184 caps for six-inch shells; 584,588 stamped cap-cases, and 45,000 plugs. They repaired 18,281 ammunition wagons and turned out 8,548 new ones. The municipal gas-works produced 25,848 kilograms of liquid ammonia and 180 puds (56 cwts.) of ammonia salts.

Still greater activity was developed by the municipality of Moscow in providing the army with equipment. It had been felt that a more economic treatment of worn-out articles of equipment would lead to a great saving of leather and cloth. The War Office fully endorsed this policy, sent to the municipal workshops large consignments of old army boots, overcoats, and other articles of equipment, and gave the municipality of Moscow the right to employ mobilized men and prisoners of war for this work. The sorting and cleaning of old articles of equipment were organized on a large scale. These were then sent to repair shops, which soon began to turn out large quantities of repaired military coats, tunics, army boots, and felt boots. A number of workshops engaged in the manufacture of winter caps, army wagons, harness, horseshoes, etc. All this work was done partly in the workshops set up by the municipality, and partly by private establishments commissioned for the purpose. Moscow distributed work in the provinces of Voronezh, Tambov, Tver, Kazan, and Vladimir. The number of men employed was estimated at tens of thousands. The yearly budget of the institutions of the municipality of Moscow engaged in supplying the army with ammunition and equipment reached 60,000,000 rubles, that is, a sum equaling the total normal budget of Moscow in pre-war time. The value of the daily production averaged 150,000-200,000 rubles. As many as 5,000 pairs of boots and 75,000 winter caps were turned out per day. The number of cleaned and repaired articles of clothing reached 4,000 a day. The output of horseshoes reached 2,000 and that of "vent sealing tubes" 5,000 per day. To 1st November 1915, the workshops controlled by the municipality repaired 409,000 pairs of boots, 800,000 trench coats, 220,000 felt boots, and made 1,400,-000 winter caps and 2,140,000 gas masks.

Various trades were taken up by different municipalities. For instance, the municipality of Kazan organized the production of pharmaceutical goods. A laboratory attached to the gas-works was engaged in the production of benzol, etc., for the army. The by-products of benzol were used for obtaining salicylic acids. The amount of aspirin produced at these works was large enough to meet the requirements of five adjoining provinces.

The deep and sincere interest taken by the towns in the fortunes of the army also found other ways in which to express itself. It became customary to send presents to the troops for Christmas and Easter. These presents were the result of public donations and subscriptions, and of special grants made by the municipal Dumas. By 1917 the municipality of Moscow had sent to the front more than 120 railway cars of presents, each consignment being accompanied by members of the Duma. The Union of Towns sent its presents to the army in its hospital trains when they returned to the front; 87 carloads of presents were sent in this way between November 1914 and March 1915.

We may also notice an interesting project which could only materialize in part. The municipality of Moscow acquired in the neighborhood of the city an old estate with a finely timbered park, for a war cemetery. In accordance with a plan approved by the municipal Duma, a memorial, which was to take the shape of a church and a war museum, was, likewise, to be erected in this park. It was hoped that the museum would house a collection of various souvenirs relating to the Great War. The cemetery was rapidly filling with graves, and a small church of attractive architecture was built by private subscription.

Among the people who suffered directly from the War two classes deserve particular attention: prisoners of war, and those who at its outbreak were abroad, especially in Germany and Austria. As early as September 1914 a special committee for the relief of Russian prisoners of war, and of Russians in foreign countries, was appointed by the municipality of Moscow. Agencies were established in Copenhagen, The Hague, Stockholm, and Berne. In November 1915 in connection with the decision of the Conference of Stockholm and the sending of a delegation to investigate the conditions of Russian prisoners of war in Germany and Austria, the Central Committee of the Union of Towns set up a special department for their relief. The duties of the department were these: assistance to relatives and friends in obtaining information as to the whereabouts of prisoners of war; assistance in establishing connection between prisoners of war and their relatives, and the transfer to prisoners of letters, parcels, and sums of money; information as to methods of communication and on the law relating to the subject; the collection of funds by subscription; and the relief of prisoners of war. Similar departments for dealing with the problem were established by local committees of the Union. In March 1916 the committee for the relief of prisoners of war of the municipality of Moscow was amalgamated with similar organizations of the Union of Towns and the Union of Zemstvos. This joint organization obtained through the Committee of the Empress considerable funds from the Treasury (700,000 rubles monthly), which allowed it to develop its work on a large scale. It became a center for inquiries about prisoners, for the transfer of letters and money, and for various other matters connected with prisoners of war and their relief. It standardized three types of parcels suitable for prisoners of war, and established a war prisoners committee. Finally, a special factory of biscuits for prisoners of war was started in Moscow. By 1st October 1916, more than 110 railway wagons of biscuits had been sent to Germany through the Swedish Red Cross. From September 1915 to October 1916 the joint organization dealt with 26,141 inquiries, and took charge of 156,981 letters and 69,828 parcels and books. Its work was connected with the activities of local committees, which invited the coöperation of the parties concerned, that is, the relatives and friends of prisoners of war.

The urgent need of obtaining legal advice for persons suffering from infringements of their rights during the War impelled the Union of Towns to establish a legal department. It consisted of members possessing authoritative knowledge of the theory and practice of military, administrative, and civil law; among such members were 15 professors, 22 judges, and 150 advocates and junior counsels. The department published a guide to the Acts and regulations relating to persons who suffered through the War. It drafted a form for the so-called "hospital will," which was extensively used in the hospitals. The work of the department rapidly expanded; it proved vital and necessary. It took the form of consultation on a great variety of questions asked in interviews or by letters. Inquiries were sent in by private soldiers, officers, their relatives, refugees, prisoners of war, and other persons whose legal position had been affected. The questions dealt with pensions, allowances, payments for requisitions, various problems raised by the evacuation, and by conscription, and with other matters of administrative and civil law. Together with national organizations for the relief of refugees, the Union of Zemstvos, and the municipality of Moscow, the legal department extended its help to refugees both while they were *en route* and in the localities where they settled.

Help was given also by legal departments opened in Petrograd, Tver, Ekaterinoslav, Orel, Samara, Ekaterinburg, Irkutsk, Minsk, Chernigov, Kiev, Kursk, Kharkov, Odessa, Voronezh, Rostov-on-Don, Ufa, Kazan, Nizhni-Novgorod, Orenburg, Tambov, Gomel, Smolensk, and other towns.

CHAPTER XII

REGIONAL ORGANIZATION OF THE UNION OF TOWNS

As was pointed out in Chapter VI, the regional committees of the Union of Towns were originally set up in connection with a scheme for the evacuation of sick and wounded, and were specially adapted for this purpose. It soon became clear, however, that intercourse between the smaller towns of one particular region and its center was often limited to the purely automatic distribution of wounded, and that no real link existed between them. In the meantime, since the creation of the Union of Towns even the small district towns of Russia, the large majority of which still preserved the leisurely and patriarchal habits of the past, had begun to show signs of animation, and were seeking to establish a more intimate connection with the large urban centers. It was suggested that the participation of district towns in the work of the Union should be increased by the creation of provincial organizations. They might not necessarily follow the strict lines of the administrative division; but they should take into consideration the geographical, cultural, and economic tendencies and sympathies of each particular district. A scheme for the organization of the Union after the War, embodying these principles, was outlined as early as May 1916. The last conference of the Union, held on 14th-17th October 1917, defined and formulated the already existing relations between the Union and the regional organizations. The latter were described in the charter as the "representatives ('collaborators') of the Central Committee of the Union of Towns, carrying out the common policy of the All-Russian Union of Towns within the limits of their respective regions." The work of the regional organizations, as outlined by the conference, was to be this: preliminary measures for the liquidation of the activities of the Union in the War and participation in the demobilization of the army; extensive assistance to the towns in the execution of various measures of municipal policy, and in the co-ordination of the work of the municipalities in this respect: it was proposed in detail, that the regional organizations, on the demand of the municipalities, should undertake the execution of various works, for instance, the preparation of schemes of sanitary engineering, the erection of public buildings, the organization of wholesale buying, the creation of regional municipal enterprises, arranging for credits, etc. It was suggested that the regional organizations might assist the municipalities by means of special consultations, and by the drafting of schemes of water supply and drainage; that they should undertake the establishment of special hospitals, for example, hospitals for nervous diseases, sanatoriums for tuberculosis, laboratories for the preparation of vaccines, etc. The necessary funds were to be supplied by the municipalities and by the zemstvos.

The activities of the regional organization of Petrograd may be cited as typical of the work of the regional organizations of the Union of Towns. The conference of the representatives of the towns of the region of Petrograd, held in September 1914, laid the foundations of the regional organization. The Regional Committee of Petrograd was elected from the representatives of the capital and of smaller towns; it included, besides the members of the municipal Dumas, a number of persons who were not eligible under the Municipal Government Act. It brought about efficient business collaboration with the municipal committee of Petrograd and the committee of the Petrograd zemstvo; and it was incorporated into the Union of Towns. The Regional Committee of Petrograd displayed great activity in the execution of the general plan of the Union of Towns, and gave proofs of its initiative and capacity by expanding its work to meet the new demands of a changed situation. A peculiar feature of the regional organization of Petrograd was the non-participation in it of the city of Petrograd. Petrograd, like Moscow, had its own budget and its own organizations. The transporting of wounded as far as the hospitals of Petrograd and their care within the boundaries of the city were under the control of the municipal committee of Petrograd; the Regional Committee, acting in close coöperation with the municipal committee, was in charge of the evacuation from the capital to the towns of the region. The area controlled by the Regional Committee of Petrograd originally extended to the provinces of Petrograd, Novgorod, Olonets, Vologda, and Archangel; it was identical, therefore, with the area assigned by the War Office for the reception of wounded from Petrograd. But eventually the jurisdiction of the Regional Committee was extended to the provinces which, for geographical and economic reasons, de-

pended on Petrograd as their center. Such were the provinces of
Pskov, Vitebsk, all the Baltic provinces, the provinces of Vyatka and
Perm, the northern districts of the province of Kostroma and the
town of Ostashkov in the province of Tver. Finally, to the regional
organization of Petrograd there was added that of Finland. Then,
too, there had been formed a Union of the Towns. And accordingly
the regional organization of Petrograd now covered twelve provinces
and the whole of Finland as well. It included 127 towns.

The first task of the Regional Committee was to establish close
collaboration with all the organizations in charge of the evacuation,
and to prepare the region for the arrival of sick and wounded from
the capital. Of the total number of hospital beds of the Petrograd
region, including those of the city itself, 35.4 per cent were controlled
by the Union of Towns, 23.2 per cent by the Red Cross, 20.9 per
cent by the Union of Zemstvos, 18.6 per cent by the Army Medical
Department, and 1.9 per cent by private persons.[1] The Central
Committee of the Union put at the disposal of the Regional Committee of Petrograd five hospital trains, each of which made 28 journeys during the first year of the War. By the beginning of 1916
the Regional Committee had established a tuberculosis sanatorium
and seven homes for convalescent patients, with a total of 437 beds,
an institution for mud-bath treatment, with 145 beds, and a hospital
ship on the Volga for 136 patients. Of the total number of 2,587 men
and 786 officers sent by the military authorities to the sanatoriums
of the Petrograd region, 1,405 men and 243 officers were admitted to
the establishments managed by the Union of Towns; and up to 1st
November 1915, 14,580 patients were treated in the dental hospitals
of the Regional Committee. It also took part in the equipment and
sending to the front of seven medical detachments with army canteens and field ambulances. With a view to preventing the spread
of infection, specialists were sent to the Baltic provinces and to
the Pskov-Dvinsk district to ascertain the conditions there, and to
plan preventive measures. These specialists visited various towns,
and assisted local authorities in preparing schemes and estimates
for the needed sanitary installations. Special courses were instituted
to train attendants for disinfecting stations. A new type of tem-

[1] *Ocherk deyatelnosti Petrogradskago Oblastnogo Komiteta V.S.G. za god
voini (Outline of the Work of the Regional Committee of Petrograd)*, Petrograd, 1916.

porary building for isolation hospitals was devised. Traveling exhibitions were assembled; such collections of sketches, plans, and illustrative examples of sanitary measures were sent from one town of the region to another; and this did much to increase the knowledge needed for the checking of epidemic diseases.

The systematic development of the work of the Regional Committee of Petrograd may likewise be traced in the organization of a hospital for the treatment of nervous diseases, as a department of the great Hospital of All Sorrows (*Vsekh Skorbyashchikh*). The Regional Committee likewise participated in the work of the relief of refugees. Winter clothes, underwear, etc., to the value of over 400,000 rubles was collected for the refugees in the towns of the region, and 56,000 refugees were so provided with clothing. Advice on legal matters was given by the Committee's legal department, which was organized with the aid of the capital's leading lawyers and judges. The membership of the department rose to 226, and local sections were opened in Vologda, Archangel, Vyatka, Perm, and Luga.

The scope of the work actually done by the organization may be gathered from the financial returns of the Regional Committee for the first year of the War. The total revenues amounted to 524,355 rubles; and they were made up as follows: grants from the Central Committee of the Union, 371,398 rubles; subscriptions, 126,963 rubles; and sundry receipts, 25,994 rubles. The chief item of expenditure was the formation of field detachments at a cost of 247,722 rubles; a total of 70,939 rubles was spent on hospitals for nervous diseases, 69,836 rubles on hospital trains, 22,821 rubles on sanatoriums and convalescent homes, etc. The total revenues of the institutions of the towns of the region, not including those of Petrograd and Finland, amounted to 1,420,755 rubles. The chief items of expenditure were: the equipment of hospitals, 399,150 rubles; maintenance of hospitals, 746,046 rubles; and the equipment and maintenance of quarantine stations, bathhouses, laundries, disinfecting stations, bacteriological laboratories, collection of refuse, etc., 116,-025 rubles. A grant of 1,285,906 rubles to assist in meeting these expenses was made by the Central Committee of the Union of Towns; the remaining costs were met by the subscriptions of towns, donations of private persons, and by loans.

After the creation of the All-Russian Union of Towns its Central Committee communicated with the municipal Duma of Helsingfors, and invited it to raise the question of the participation of the towns of Finland in the work of the Union. The Central Committee suggested that the towns of Finland could perhaps provide some 2,500 hospital beds in addition to the 3,500 beds already promised by the civil authorities of Finland. The All-Russian Union of Towns was of the opinion that the towns of Finland might create for this purpose an independent organization which could be connected with the All-Russian Union of Towns, and could act in accordance with a common plan. The population of Finland at the outbreak of the War was 3,231,995, the urban population numbering 497,914. There were 38 towns and cities, the largest being Helsingfors with a population, in 1913, of 167,083.

On 24th October 1914 the representatives of all the towns of Finland, with the exception of three, met in Helsingfors and approved the creation of a Union of Towns of Finland for the purpose stated above; and 24 towns and cities, out of the total number of 38, joined the Union at its formation. Finland's Union of the Towns became an autonomous organization of the All-Russian Union, but limited its activity to the relief of sick and wounded. During the first year of the War 21 hospitals with 2,674 beds were opened in Finnish towns, and eventually two of these hospitals were converted into convalescent homes. The contribution of the new Union to the funds of the All-Russian Union was 10,000 rubles. It expended during the first year of the War 1,119,685 Finnish marks, 410,095 being spent on hospital equipment and 709,589 on maintenance.

The towns of the Caucasus established an independent Union of Towns of the Caucasus, at a conference held on 12th-14th September 1914. This organization planned to care for the wounded, in case of a war with Turkey. The total number of hospital beds in the Caucasus was put at 50,000; and the Caucasus Union drew up a scheme for their distribution. It decided to join the All-Russian Union, preserving, however, its independence, and to open its hospitals for the sick and wounded on the Western Front only in the event of there being no operations on the Caucasus Front. But the amalgamation with the All-Russian Union of Towns became necessary as soon as the war against Turkey was declared, and as early as November 1914 the Union of the Caucasus joined the All-Russian Union, under the name of the Caucasus Department of the Union. By surrendering its independence, the organization of the Caucasus put itself under the protection of the Red Cross and obtained the support of the powerful central organization of the All-Russian Union; at the same time a certain uniformity was established in applying for and in obtaining grants from the Treasury.

In March 1916 the Caucasus section of the Union comprised 40 towns of the Caucasus and 22 local committees. The work of the Caucasus organization had to be done under exceptionally difficult conditions. It was often hindered by the fact that only one railway line linked this region with the center of Russia, by the difficulty of communications *via* the Black Sea in war-time, by the small number of wagon roads, and, finally, by the complete absence of roads in certain districts where military operations were being conducted. The lack of enough keen public workers, and the marked national feelings among the peoples of the Caucasus were other obstacles in the way of the creation of a really great organization.

On 1st February 1915, in eight towns of the Caucasus, namely in Tiflis, Baku, Elisavetpol, Derbend, Petrovsk, Vladikavkaz, Ekaterinodar, and Gory, 10,526 hospital beds were being maintained by the Union of Towns; 4,158, in 20 towns, were being maintained by private subscription, and 1,955 beds, in 14 towns, by the municipalities themselves. A large clearing station, originally for 1,100 beds, but eventually expanded to 2,000, was opened at Navtluga, near Tiflis. On 15th September 1915, the total number of beds was given as 20,835; on 1st March 1916, the beds for surgical cases numbered 16,380, and those for infectious diseases 4,356. All these hospital beds were registered with the Caucasus organization of the Union of Towns.

The Turkish prisoners of war brought with them an epidemic of typhus. Under a scheme devised for the prevention of the spread of the infection it was proposed to create hospitals for epidemic diseases, reserving 10 per cent of the number of beds in each for surgical cases; and provisionally such hospitals, containing respectively 1,000 and 600 beds, were opened in Tiflis and Baku. Similar hospitals were established in other places. The prisoners of war were subjected to a closer medical supervision, and a number of clearing stations and quarantine stations were created on the lines of com-

munication between Tiflis and the front. Special detachments for
dealing with epidemic diseases were sent to the areas from which
serious outbreaks were reported. They did excellent work in disinfection and in improving the sanitary conditions of Sarakamysh,
Erzerum, and the adjoining districts, which were in an appalling
state, and were hotbeds of epidemic diseases. The detachments removed bodies left unburied in inhabited neighborhoods, undertook
the treatment of insanitary areas, cleaned the wells, disinfected dwellings, etc. A large disinfecting station of the Japanese type, combined
with a laundry equipped with machinery of great efficiency, was
organized in Sarakamysh. The line of communication between Sarakamysh and Erzerum, which are separated by mountains with a few
primitive roads, was entirely in the hands of the Union of Towns.
And it organized, at various points along the road, tea rooms, hostels,
canteens, and hospitals.

After the battles of July 1915 a great wave of refugees from
Turkish Armenia—some 250,000—flooded the Caucasus. Thousands
of them, exhausted, died of hunger and disease, and from them there
also spread a violent epidemic of typhus. First aid to refugees was
entrusted to the Union of Towns, to which there was eventually
turned over all medical relief for refugees. In the districts where the
numbers of refugees were particularly great, such as the provinces
of Elisavetpol and Erivan, the region of Batum and in Persia, the
Union established bathhouses, laundries, disinfecting stations, etc. A
large bacteriological detachment was busy administering vaccines.
Altogether the Union opened 80 bathhouses, 4,000 hospital beds for
refugees, and a number of smaller medical units and dispensaries. A
home for lost children was organized in the district of Van, to which
such children were sent from adjoining areas. Refugees were supplied with articles of clothing and underwear; and meals were distributed to them by special canteens.

The Caucasus section of the Union of Towns had under its control
one hospital train and four field ambulances. These ambulances were
provided with horse-drawn ambulance wagons, stretchers adapted
for horse transport on the mountain roads, tents, and 230 horses
with their entire equipment. The bacteriological detachment was divided into mobile units, and by June 1916 it had administered vacci-
nations to the number of more than 266,000, against typhus, cholera,
and smallpox. This Union likewise had the responsibility of looking

after the health and providing food and housing for the men employed on new construction.

The estimates of the Caucasus organizations of the Union for September-December 1915 amounted to 4,967,375 rubles. They included expenditures for the upkeep of 20,835 hospital beds, four field ambulances, one detachment presented by the engineers of Russia, two depots, 45 refreshment stations and canteens, five dressing stations, 10 hostels, six detachments for the prevention of epidemics, 12 bathhouses, two disinfecting stations, a machine laundry, etc. The approved expenditure of the Caucasus organizations for the first half of 1916 amounted to the sum of 9,333,449 rubles.

During the period from the outbreak of the War up to the end of 1916 the Committee of the Caucasus front was in charge of 266 institutions of various descriptions. The total expenditures of the committee were over 20,000,000 rubles. On 1st July, the monthly expenditures of the committee were 1,268,000 rubles, and it had been granted a subsidy of 1,440,000 rubles. The expenditures for the relief of refugees from the outbreak of the War had reached 2,500,000 rubles. The staff employed by the organization of the Caucasus Front had risen to 15,000. And in October 1917 the institutions of the Union working on this front numbered 600.

Simultaneously with the work of the Union of Towns on this front, other work on a large scale was conducted by the Union of Zemstvos. The two Unions divided the whole front into sectors, and agreed that the activities of the Union of Towns should extend to the following districts: Sarakamysh-Erzerum, Adzerberzhan-Van, East Persia, and the coastal section.

CHAPTER XIII

THE REORGANIZING OF ECONOMIC LIFE

The War soon became a dominating factor in the life of the country, and produced a number of far-reaching changes in its economic and social conditions. They did not occur simultaneously, and did not affect in the same degree the various aspects of national life; but almost all normal development was changed or broken off by the declaration of war. The economic disorganization came commonly to be known under the familiar name of "high cost of living." And beneath these outward signs there were going on profound processes of economic decay. They were extending and growing, indeed, until soon they were a menace to the very life of the nation. In the end they brought on the Revolution, and made the continuation of the War an impossibility.

The rise in the cost of living had a most unfavorable effect upon the towns in which large numbers of consumers were concentrated. The municipalities displayed great energy and resource in the organization of the service of supply, under most adverse conditions, in spite of the fact that they had no experience in this kind of work, no funds, and no legal right to undertake it. For their right to establish fixed prices for commodities was limited by law to meat and bread; and, in every case, the consent of the representative of the Ministry of the Interior had to be obtained. And in equal pace with the prevention of this increase in the cost of living, municipalities had to find the means of meeting the tremendous problems brought forth by the War.

During its second year the acuteness of the economic crisis made the problem of the cost of living first of all. In its third year all the functions of the municipalities, and all their work for meeting the war needs and demands of the people were entirely dependent on the problem of supply, on the possibility of finding, purchasing, and delivering foodstuffs, fuel, and the necessaries of life. The struggle with the high cost of living became a struggle for existence, and the municipalities were soon involved in it. And in 1917 they found themselves completely at the mercy of the violent economic and financial depression brought about by the Revolution.

Meanwhile the Union of Towns continued to work without ceasing, and through its representatives on the various government committees it took part in the regulation of economic problems by means of administrative and legislative measures. At the same time it supplied the municipalities with information upon the general economic situation, assisted them to find methods of solving some of the most pressing questions, and endeavored to coördinate the too irregular methods of the municipalities in the domain of supply.

The Russian army during the Great War numbered from eleven to twelve millions, and the total number of those mobilized reached 15,000,000.[1] The original mobilization in 1914, and the further mobilization of various classes, considerably reduced the labor reserves of the country. By the spring of 1915 between 20 and 25 per cent of the working population had been mobilized in all.[2] This alone constituted sufficient cause for great changes in the economic life of the country.

The transport of large masses of men and goods for military purposes necessitated a revision of the whole system of communication. The Russian railway system was inadequately developed, inadequately supplied with rolling stock, and could deal with only a limited number of trains a day; it was entirely unprepared to face the new and unforeseen responsibilities thrown upon it by the War. The blocking of railroad lines and the utter disorganization of traffic were the natural results. Railways were powerless to maintain the supply of raw materials and fuel needed for the country's factories and workshops, of grain for its mills, and of the necessaries of life for its towns and cities. A constructive policy was made impossible by the dual control system maintained, for the railroads were now in the hands both of the War Office and of the Ministry of Transport.

The collapse of Russia's railroad system immediately affected other parts of her economic system. At the beginning, the fundamental factors of production were not as yet involved. The country

---

[1] *Trudi komissii po izsledovanyu sanitarnikh posledstvy mirovoi voini 1914-1920 gg.* (*Transaction of the Committee of Inquiry into the Effects of the World War of 1914-1920 upon Public Health*), Moscow-Petrograd, 1923, p. 125.

[2] S. N. Prokopovich, *Voina i narodnoe khozyaistvo* (*The National Economy and the War*), Moscow, 1918.

still had large supplies of raw materials and could maintain production at a fair level. The decrease in production could be met by a readjustment of its distribution among consumers. But by 1915 it had become clear that in certain industries production was inadequate to the demand. Indeed, the very foundations of production had been undermined.[3]

The disorganization of transport, the reduction of national production, the increased wealth of the rural districts, and, lastly, the growth of profiteering, contributed to the rise in the cost of urban living. The rise in the prices of commodities, and goods in general had begun by the end of the first six months of the War; the shortage of certain commodities was first felt in the middle of the second six months. By October 1915 the whole country felt the shortage. In their replies to the inquiries made by the Government and the Central Committee of the Union, almost all municipalities stated that their towns were suffering from this shortage of the necessaries of life. By 1916 life in the towns and cities had become a virtual ordeal, so great was the inadequacy of the food supply. The most essential commodities disappeared from the market one after another. The newspapers were filled with reports from all parts of Russia, all alike dealing with the crisis in foodstuffs. Large cities and small towns, the north and the south, the central districts, the regions of the Volga and the Caucasus—all were passing through a violent crisis. Shortages of bread and flour were reported from the Caucasus, from Nicholaev, Odessa, Kishinev, Mogilev, Smolensk, Ribinsk, Vyatka, Tambov, Ryazan, Vologda, etc. The flour mills of Nizhni-Novgorod, Yaroslavl, Ribinsk, Kostroma, and Tver, had no grain. Even in the wheat-growing provinces, such as the provinces of Simbirsk, Samara, Saratov, the work of the flour mills had to be periodically suspended for lack of grain. An acute shortage of meat was reported from Tiflis, Ryazan, Pensa, Kishinev, Perm, Tambov, Smolensk, Kharkov, Rostov-on-Don, Ekaterinburg, Dvinsk, Vitebsk, etc. Sugar disappeared from the markets of Kharkov, Kiev, Tiflis, Baku, Tagan-

[3] For a detailed treatment of this subject *see* Professor Struve, *Food Supply in Russia during the War;* Antsiferov, Bilimovich, Batchev, and Ivantsov, *Rural Economy in Russia and the War;* and Zagorsky, *State Control of Industry in Russia during the War* (Yale University Press, 1928), in this series of the *Economic and Social History of the World War.*

rog, Kishinev, Yaroslavl, Novgorod, Rostov-on-Don, Nicholaev, Ekaterinoslav, Kazan, etc.

The data of the Statistical Bureau of the Economic section of the Union of Towns show that the rise of prices in January 1916, as compared with the prices prevailing a year before the War, was 83 per cent for the five principal crops (rye, wheat, barley, oats, and buckwheat) and 74 per cent for thirteen other commodities, among which were foodstuffs and raw materials.

While the average increase in the price of foodstuffs ranged from 50 per cent to 70 per cent in England, from 20 per cent to 50 per cent in France, and from 30 per cent to 35 per cent in Italy, it was 114 per cent in Russia during the two first years of the War, as compared with the prices of 1913-1914; the average increase was from 89 per cent in the case of bread, to 232 per cent in that of meat.[4]

During the first eighteen months of the War the average increase in the prices of nineteen commodities (including flour, meat, potatoes, butter, salt, sugar, etc.), calculated for July and December 1914 and 1915, gives the following evidence that the cost of living was rising steadily. If its cost in July 1914 be put at 100 per cent, in December 1914 it was 107.1 per cent; in July 1915, 121.9 per cent; in December 1915, 148.7 per cent.[5]

The records of the Union of Towns[6] show that, from the outbreak of the War until June 1916, the prices of certain commodities in Moscow underwent the following changes:

	Increase in percentages
Sweet rye bread	143
Sour rye bread	150
Rye flour	195
Butter	220
Animal fat	273
Sugar	153
Coffee	271

[4] A. Shingarev, *Voina i finansi* (*The War and the Financial Situation*), in the yearbook *Rech,* Petrograd, 1916.

[5] *Statisticheskya dannya otnosyashchyasya k Petrogradu i k perogradskomu khozyaistvu* (*Data on Petrograd and Its Government*), Petrograd, 1916.

[6] *Dvizenie tsen za dva goda voini* (*Movement of Prices during the Two Years of the War*), Petrograd, 1916.

	Increase in Percentages
Eggs	193
Milk	171
Beef	371
Mutton	381
Potatoes	144
Rice	243
Fuel (anthracite coal and firewood)	224
Petroleum and candles	210
Matches	500
Textiles (average increase for cotton, linen and woolen cloth, and flannels)	262
Footwear (boots)	334

The prices of many goods and necessaries of life were higher in Moscow than in Berlin; for instance, the cost of sugar, bread, and meat, was from one-and-a-half times to twice as much as it was in Germany.

While the economic depression, which was felt most severely in the cities, was developing, the size of the urban population was undergoing considerable changes. The population of the capitals, of large railway junctions, and of almost all more or less important towns, was rapidly growing. At first this was due to the arrival of large contingents of men for the formation of new military units, subsequently it was due to the influx of wounded and sick from the front and of refugees. The development of businesses working for national defense created a fresh demand for labor and attracted large numbers of workmen.

At the outbreak of the War the population of Petrograd, including the suburbs, was 2,103,000. On 1st November 1915, it was estimated at 2,347,850; by the middle of 1916 it had risen to 2,415,700. The highest point was reached at the time of the Revolution of February 1917, when Petrograd had 2,465,000 inhabitants. After that date the population began to decrease; in the middle of 1917 it was only a little greater than in 1916, numbering 2,420,000; in the autumn of the same year it was 2,300,000. The decline during the following period became very rapid. It stood at 1,468,845 in June 1918, and by August 1920 had fallen to 722,229.[7]

[7] Z. G. Frenkel, *Petrograd vo vremya voini i revolutsii (Petrograd during the War and the Revolution)*, Petrograd, 1923, p. 13.

The increase of the population of Moscow was 2.84 per cent in 1902-1907, 3.53 per cent in 1907-1912, and 5.66 per cent in 1912-1915. Numbering 1,617,700 in 1912, it rose to 1,949,500 on 27th November 1915, and reached 2,043,594 on 1st February 1917 (including suburbs which were afterwards comprised within the territory of the city). But the census of 17th September 1917 shows that only 1,854,426 inhabitants were then left in Moscow, and that of 28th August 1920 registers a further reduction of the population to 1,028,000.[8]

The growth of the population of other towns during the War was no less rapid. We shall quote a few instances, using the data of the Union of Towns. The pre-war population was increased during the War as follows: Ryazan—from 49,600 (1912) to 56,000 (1916); Kursk—from 89,800 (1913) to 125,000 (1916); Nicholaev—from 106,279 to 150,000; Simbirsk—from 70,500 to 136,000; Sizran—from 75,000 to 125,000; Samara—from 150,000 to 300,000; Voronezh—from 94,800 to 122,894; Irkutsk—from 129,700 to 145,000; Kiev—from 594,000 to 650,000; Kharkov—from 258,360 to 400,000, etc. The population of small towns was also growing; for instance, Bryansk grew from 35,000 to 90,000; and Chita from 20,000 to 80,000.

The total urban population of Russia before the War was estimated at some 22 millions; in 1916 the records of the registration of urban population, and the statistics relating to its demand for the necessaries of life show that this figure had risen to 28 millions.[9] After the Revolution it fell to 21 millions, as shown by the census of 1920.

In 1911 the urban population of Russia was only 13.9 per cent of her total population; in the same year the proportion of urban to total population was 78 per cent in England and Wales; it was 57 per cent in Germany in 1905; 46.3 per cent in the United States in 1910, and 42 per cent in France in 1906.

Faced with new economic conditions and a greatly increased urban population, the municipalities which now had the task of supplying this population with food were helpless; and they were denied free-

[8] *Krasnaya Moskwa 1917-1920 (Red Moscow, 1917-1920)*, Moscow, 1920, p. 51.

[9] *Izvestya Soyuza Gorodov (Bulletin of the Union of Towns)*, 1916, No. 36, p. 238.

dom in the choice of measures for the prevention of the rise in the cost of living. The creation of organizations for the feeding of the civilian population led to a kind of unintentional competition between the municipalities and the Army Supply Service, in which the latter had, of course, the upper hand.

The single market which provided commodities for both civilians and army was divided by the policy of the Government, to protect the interests of the troops. By a decree of 17th February 1915 the officers commanding military areas (*voenni okrug*) were given the power to prohibit the export of commodities from the territory under their control. The extensive use of this power, which prevented the removal of goods from one province to another, prevented the normal workings of private trade, and created great technical difficulties in the administration of the municipalities. Intercourse between producers and consumers was prevented; the whole country was covered with barriers between provinces, and brought to an end the free exchange of goods. The north of Russia, with the two capitals, was particularly affected by this policy. Under these conditions the independent attempts of municipalities to control and organize the food supply bore little fruit. They were obliged to have recourse to fixed prices, which, in their turn, had small effect, and to attempts to organize wholesale purchasing and distribution among the people. Lack of money, however, frustrated any organization of supply on an adequate scale; though even the little that was done by the municipalities in this respect proved a valuable help.

The Central Committee of the Union of Towns made a number of investigations into the actual conditions governing the supply of food for the towns. In the spring of 1915, 250 towns sent their replies; in November of the same year 94 of the largest provided information, and 101 replied in August 1916. These answers give a complete picture of the far-reaching economic disorganization of the country. They show how the municipalities understood the new situation with which they were confronted, and what measures they took to safeguard their interests.

At the end of 1915 the main complaint of the towns was the shortage of sugar, flour, firewood, salt, coal, and groats. Next came the general rise in the prices of foodstuffs and fuel, which in certain cases was alarmingly rapid. The municipalities gave the disorganization of transport and profiteering as the main causes which had led to the economic crisis. The measures for the relief of the situation were framed accordingly. The municipalities pointed out the necessity of a definite policy of State control over the railways and of an elimination of their shortcomings, the desirability of requisitions, of the control of prices on an imperial or, at least, regional, scale, of the limitation of profits, etc. The general nature of these suggestions clearly showed, in spite of the narrowness of the municipal franchise, that the municipalities were in favor of the intervention of the State in commercial and industrial life. In their replies to the Central Committee the municipalities insisted on the necessity of an immediate revision of the existing legislation controlling local government, in the direction of a broadened municipal franchise and the removal of the heavy-handed control of the central Government. In the opinion of many municipalities, no efficient measures for the prevention of the rise in the cost of living could be taken unless these demands were complied with. But the ardent desire for municipal reforms did not prevent the municipalities from devoting all their energies to the promotion of social welfare. Indeed, even under the most unfavorable conditions, they did not give up their fight against the rise in the cost of living, and the result of their struggle was, in many cases, substantial.

Special committees were appointed to organize the supply of foodstuffs and fuel, in 49 towns. In other towns the fight against the high cost of living was concentrated in the hands of the Executive of the Municipal Council. Representatives of coöperative and consumers' societies, and sometimes of labor organizations and of the zemstvos, were invited to participate in the work of the committees. In the majority of towns the committees consisted of representatives of government departments and of public bodies.

Almost immediately after the declaration of war the Ministry of the Interior instructed the governors of provinces to issue regulations establishing fixed prices for the necessaries of life. The municipalities always looked with suspicion on the introduction of local price control, and did not share the view of the government departments, which saw in it "a powerful weapon for the prevention of the rise in the cost of living." But under the pressure of the Government fixed prices were introduced by 86 municipal Dumas in July 1914, by 56 in August, and by 54 in September of the same year. Many municipalities established fixed prices for a number of commodities not enumerated in the Municipal Act. The control of the price of meat was especially popular. It was adopted by 321 towns out of 353; the regulation of the price of wheat bread and rye bread followed. More than one-half of the towns mentioned above fixed the price of petroleum, sugar, flour, salt, groats, grain, and hay. From 40 per cent to 50 per cent of the towns controlled the price of vegetable oils, butter, vegetables, and firewood; from 30 per cent to 40 per cent, eggs, candles, matches, and peas; from 20 per cent to 30 per cent, milk, dairy products, soap, cereals, and sausages; less than 20 per cent, fresh and salt fish, tea, and coal. The market price of a commodity at the time was usually taken as a basis when establishing its fixed price. Only in very rare instances was the introduction of fixed prices preceded by an inquiry into the available stocks of the commodities in question. In general the fixing of prices was strongly opposed by the town's wholesale and retail tradesmen, and the refusal to raise prices occasionally led to the closing of shops, as in Chelyabinsk, Kazan, Novgorod, Yaroslavl, Tashkent, Tiflis, Vladikavkaz, Kerch, etc. Towns that established a low scale of fixed prices found themselves with a failing supply of goods; and the commodities they particularly needed did not reach them. Municipalities had no real means of enforcing the acceptance of fixed prices. Merchants found various ways of evading the regulations; they reduced the weight, and lowered the quality of goods. As a result of this situation fixed prices followed the general movement of prices, but usually did not fall when market prices fell.

The experience of the majority of towns soon led them to the conclusion that local control of prices was not only useless, but often harmful. In Samara and in Moscow conferences held to consider economic problems decided "that under existing conditions local control of prices cannot prevent their rise, but delays their reduction." The rise in prices depended in the majority of cases on general, and not on local, economic conditions. This naturally led to a plan for the control of prices on a regional or even country-wide scale. But such attempts proved failures. The economic conference, called by the Union of Towns on 11th-15th July 1915, condemned this system and declared that "the introduction of fixed prices for regions or for the whole Empire—which can be considered only in connection with the control of production and distribution, and a strict registration of available stocks of goods—is absolutely out of the question under existing conditions."

In the meantime profiteering by private merchants, which was a consequence of the decay and disruption of the economic system, led to a further increase in the cost of living. All hopes of the establishment of salutary State control had vanished, and the municipalities had to take the organization of supply and distribution into their own hands. They followed an energetic and successful policy of wholesale purchases, and brought about a number of new forms of coöperation with private trade. At first the municipalities conducted their operations on a small scale; and they pointed out that the development of their policy of wholesale purchases could not be achieved unless the Government was prepared to help them with a liberal system of credit. Credit for this purpose was obtained only in November 1915, with the publication of regulations governing municipal subsidies, and guarantees for loans in order to provide the funds required for municipal purchases of foodstuffs and fuel. But the amount of these credits was utterly inadequate. The applications of municipalities for subsidies and guarantees were usually met only in part, and the sum granted was sometimes as little as one-fifth of what was asked for. The municipalities, therefore, could not undertake to meet the whole demand of the population, for any commodity. Municipal purchases were made a means of regulating prices and, in certain cases, a method of obtaining goods otherwise lacking. The municipal purchasing organizations took no account of obtaining a profit; they often abandoned the fundamental principles of private commerce, and sold their goods below cost price, for example, in Vladikavkaz, Kostroma, and Nizhni-Novgorod.

Up to 1st December 1915, the subsidies granted by the Government to 89 towns for the purchase of foodstuffs amounted to 11,634,-915 rubles, and advances on loans guaranteed by the Government to 690,000 rubles. On 1st April 1916, the subsidies made to 149 towns had risen to 13,463,915 rubles, advances to 1,820,000 rubles, and guarantees for municipal loans, 2,630,000 rubles.[10] The Government allowed 75 towns the sum of 7,354,625 rubles for the purchase of firewood. The data quoted above are by no means complete, and they represent neither all the towns that undertook the organization

[10] *Vestnik Finansov, Promishlennosti i Torgovli,* No. 34, 21st August 1916.

of supply nor all the capital involved in these transactions. In 1916 and 1917 almost all the more or less important towns set up organizations for wholesale buying, in spite of the difficulties put in the way of obtaining goods by the dislocation of transport; and they carried on this work until the very end. Purchases were financed from municipal funds, from "special" capital, and by means of loans. Occasionally, as in Tomsk, the municipalities applied to wealthy citizens and asked them to advance free of interest the funds required for the buying of foodstuffs. The principal goods purchased were cereals, sugar, salt, meat, cattle, firewood, fuel oil, etc. The field covered by municipal buying expanded proportionately with the rise in the cost of living.

Coming to methods of distribution, some towns distributed through local merchants. Written agreements were often entered into by the municipality and the representatives of commerce, to guarantee the main purpose of the operation, that is, the lowering of prices on the local market. These agreements usually determined the price at which merchants undertook to sell the goods supplied to them by the municipalities; sometimes they also contained provisions defining the class of customers, the district where the sale should be conducted, and, lastly, the amount to which one customer was entitled. The fulfilment of the agreements was controlled through the local police, through district relief committees (*popechitelstva*), by the examination of books, and, at a later period, by a rationing system. The distribution of municipal stocks on these lines was adopted by Penza, Peterhof, Kozlov, Novgorod, Pskov, Rzhev, Ryazan, Smolensk, Tambov, Tver, etc.

In course of time the municipalities were compelled to adopt the system of rationing the chief commodities. Rationing systems in Russia were varied greatly, and some were by no means perfect. Then, the Union of Towns helped the municipalities by supplying them with technical information, and by keeping them informed as to the results obtained in other places. On 1st July 1916, the rationing system was adopted by 54 towns, of which 25 were provincial, and 29 district towns. Rationing, as a rule, was introduced in the larger cities. Fifty-one towns rationed sugar, 21 flour, 12 meat, 10 salt; in the remaining cases there was a rationing of coal, dairy products, etc. The rationing of flour was introduced in the very heart of the wheat country (in the town of Pokrovsk in the province of Samara).[11]

A number of municipalities arranged to sell their stocks of goods at retail, from municipal warehouses and from regular shops. Other towns established municipal bakeries and the like. And it was very hard to arrange a wide network of such shops at short notice; some towns—Kherson, Krasnoyarsk, Ostrogozhsk, Ryazan, Nezhin, Minsk, Petrograd, Moscow, Kiev, Tiflis, Perm, Kharkov, Saratov, etc.—sought the assistance of coöperative societies.

In their replies to the questionnaire of the Union of Towns most municipalities stressed the need of State and public control over private commerce; but there was less agreement as to the extent to which State interference with the freedom of trade should be permitted. Municipalities thought it desirable in certain case to substitute municipal shops in part for those conducted by private trade. But they denied the possibility of any complete municipalization of the food supply. Private initiative, in their opinion, should continue to be its principal source; and the municipality, therefore, ought to support private trading as long as it was carried on in the public interest. At any rate the municipality should avail itself of such resources and experience. Some municipalities pointed out the unsoundness of an economic policy which aimed at replacing the "powerful machinery of private trading by such utterly inadequate substitutes as municipal buying, and subsidies to coöperative societies." Other municipalities rejected as entirely impracticable any plan for coöperation between the municipality and private tradings, for in private trading they saw one of the factors which stimulated the rise of prices. In certain towns the whole merchant class seemed to be under great suspicion. It was accused of profiteering. In others the merchants coöperated with the authorities and with various public bodies in their endeavor to organize the service of supply.

Experience resulted in different forms of coöperation and agreements between municipalities and private trade. We have quoted above a few instances dealing with the distribution of goods. Sometimes the municipality undertook both to produce the goods and to settle the wholesale price, the necessary funds being supplied by private traders, upon whom there also rested the responsibility of doing

[11] Data of the inquiry of the Union of Towns.

the selling. This particular form of municipal trading was adopted in Tver, Tyumen, and a number of other towns. Kharkov, Saratov, Tver, etc., followed a practice in accordance with which the municipality purchased large quantities of flour from the warehouses, and distributed it among the bakers and consumers on the understanding that the price of the bread supplied by them to the local market should be kept down to a specified level.

A popular form of agreement between municipalities and private traders consisted in allowing the latter to have their goods consigned to the municipalities. Many municipal executive councils conceded to private traders their right to priority in the delivery of goods by rail, and permitted them to ship their goods in the name of the municipality. Of the 94 towns which answered the questionnaire above mentioned, 49 followed this plan for ensuring the delivery by rail of goods actually intended for the use of private firms. In these cases mutual advantages were derived by making full but joint use of the resources and the rights both of the private firm and of the municipality. By putting at the disposal of private trade the special privileges they themselves enjoyed, municipalities took advantage of the adaptability and enterprising spirit of private trade, and reserved for themselves the right of disposing of the goods in question.

Most municipalities agreed in recommending municipal buying as one method of mitigating the economic crisis. Public organizations which made special investigations of the problem of the high cost of living came to similar conclusions. Under the conditions then prevailing, when prices were rising not only in the centers of consumption but also in the centers of production, when profiteering on the one hand, and the corruption of railroad officials on the other were becoming commoner than ever, when quantities of goods bought were not delivered, when large purchases for the army entirely upset the normal balance of supply and demand, when the export of commodities from certain regions was prohibited,—under these conditions municipal buying was recognized as the fundamental and almost the only effective policy left to municipalities. For as a general rule it led to the reduction of prices or to their stabilization.

Although the municipalities were in favor of wholesale purchases, they believed that this policy could be successful only if the following conditions were observed: (1) municipal buyers must command sums large enough to allow them to buy in quantities sufficient to control market prices; (2) the coördination of the municipal buying of one municipality with that of others and that of other public bodies; (3) a systematic distribution of purchases over the whole Empire, and the arrangement of some general system of delivery by rail; (4) the representation on the municipal purchasing committees of the large masses of consumers, and the extension of the powers of these committees; (5) the reorganization of railroads which had fallen into chaos.

But it was too late. The rise in the cost of living could not be stopped by anything that could now be devised. The process of general disintegration was proceeding too rapidly. And every month of the War brought new complications. The scope in which municipal buying could be done was becoming narrower and narrower; and distribution was beset by difficulties that became always greater. The experience of the great centers of consumption, indeed, of Petrograd and Moscow, may serve as illustrations of the conditions that prevailed.

In Petrograd the rise in prices had become alarming within six months after the outbreak of war, the chief reason lying in the capital's unfavorable geographical position. For it was separated by enormous distances from the centers of production. Another reason lay in the disorganization of the commercial service of the railroads. The situation was further complicated by the fact that in 1914 the provinces of northern Russia, which provided Petrograd to a certain extent with meat, butter, milk, oats, and hay, had an exceedingly poor harvest. The supplies of coal and firewood were the first to be affected. Before the War Petrograd obtained a large part of its coal supply from abroad, mainly from England *via* the Baltic Sea; in 1913, 125,000,000 puds[12] were so imported. In 1914, some of it could still come in. But in 1915 such imports were entirely suspended. Everything had to come from the mines of the Donetz Valley. (The Dombrovsky mining district was occupied by the enemy.) The transport of coal from the Donetz Valley, however, met with enormous difficulties. Of the 11,625 coal cars required, only 5,185 were actually supplied.[13] Under the system as planned, the municipality of Petrograd was to receive 250 carloads a month. But as a matter of fact,

[12] One ton = 62 puds.

[13] Report of the chairman of the financial committee of the municipality of Petrograd, 1916.

in September it received only 41 carloads; in October, eight; in November, none; in December, 50. Of the 140,000 cubic sachines[14] of firewood for which contracts were entered into by the executive board of the municipality, only about 60,000 cubic sachines were actually delivered. The firewood bought by the municipality—and it had paid 70 per cent of the price in advance—was requisitioned by the railways. The rise in the cost of the necessaries of life was utterly out of proportion to what the poorer working-men could pay. Declarations made by the representatives of labor in the Central War Industries Committee show that the working class was hard hit, and that the position of unskilled labor and that of women had become particularly difficult.

In 1915 the organization of all supplies for the capital was entrusted to the governor of the city.[15] The municipality was without any power to deal with the problem as a whole, its share being limited to certain sections. One of the measures employed by the municipality in its struggle against the rise in the cost of living was price control, which had been strongly advocated both by public opinion and by departments of the Government. But the introduction of fixed prices did not give the results anticipated; for, because of the dislocation of rail transport, there was no certainty of the delivery of needed goods which had been purchased in other parts of the country. To provide for municipal institutions and for the poorest peoples, the municipality had to adopt the system of wholesale purchases of meat, bread and flour, butter, eggs, sugar, firewood, and coal. After six months' experience in struggling with both railroad disorganization and the contradictory orders of those authorities which controlled the districts where purchases had been made, the buying officials came to the conclusion that the problem of supplying the capital was linked so closely with the general economic condition of the country that no measures in Petrograd for the prevention of the exhaustion of stock of goods and ensuing price increases would be effective unless the Government itself took up the problem, and merged all the municipal and administrative organizations into one country-wide organization for the control of supply. And such an organization must be given full powers to deal with every aspect of the food problem, including the supply of the army and the civilian population alike, and the control of railroads. In January 1915, the

[14] One cubic sachine = 343 cubic feet.   [15] *Gradonachalnik.*

municipality of Petrograd submitted to the Government a memorandum embodying these views. It described the actual conditions of supply in the capital and pointed out the obstacles put in the way by certain government departments, which ignored the needs of the city and of the population. In the meantime Petrograd continued to engage in municipal buying, and distributed the goods thus obtained among the poor and the institutions of the city. Foodstuffs to the value of 17,000,000 rubles were purchased in 1916; a total of 14,-021,000 rubles was spent during the same period on the purchase of fuel.

Soon after the outbreak of war the municipality of Moscow was also forced to conclude that its ordinary means were utterly inadequate for dealing with the rise in the cost of living and the organization of supply. In February 1915 its municipal Duma petitioned the Government for an inquiry into the amount of the stocks of foodstuffs in Moscow and adjoining districts, for the repeal of the orders made by the governors of the central provinces prohibiting the removal of foodstuffs and hay, and for the adequate organization of the delivery by rail of the foodstuffs, hay, and fuel required for the city. A scheme for a food campaign was approved by the Duma of Moscow on 18th March of the same year, and the executive council was empowered to organize local purchases of foodstuffs and other necessaries of life; a grant of 5,000,000 rubles was voted for this purpose. The goods were sold to the people at cost price. Fully conscious of the importance of one unified plan for the organization of supply for the urban and rural population, and for the army as well, the municipality of Moscow pointed out the necessity of setting up a special and central committee for the whole country, on which committee the departments concerned, the capitals, the larger towns, and municipal organizations should be represented.

This plan, like so many others, was ignored by the Government, and the conditions upon which Moscow depended for its supplies were no better than those of other cities. The work of supplying all foodstuffs was entrusted to the governor of the city, and that of supplying fuel to a commissioner representing the Ministry of Commerce and Industry. The activities of the municipality in the organization of supply had to be coördinated with the policy and views of governor and deputies; and both were constantly being changed. The interference of the central Government in the problem of supplies made the task of the municipality no easier. In its endeavors to supply its citizens Moscow continued to encounter insurmountable obstacles. The regulations prohibiting export from one part of the country to another were still in force, and occasionally whole trains of goods purchased by the municipality were requisitioned while *en route* for the capital. In 1915 the normal delivery of Donetz coal was cut down by some 50 per cent. During the last four months of the same year, of 8,500 carloads of goods to which the municipality was entitled, only 247 were actually received. The demand for coal for heating purposes was met to the extent of 60 per cent for hospitals, and otherwise to the extent of only 30 per cent. From the point of view of the supply of foodstuffs and fuel the position of Moscow was exceedingly bad.

To safeguard the interests of the population and to organize the distribution of foodstuffs and fuel, the municipality took a number of measures. The output of municipal bakeries was increased to 6,800 puds (110 tons) a day; and a further increase to 20,000 puds (320 tons) a day was expected in 1917. The municipality of Moscow possessed 60 food stores and 20 butchers' shops. In 30 yards the municipality sold fuel at retail. A plan, adopted by the municipal Duma on 12th July 1916, provided for meeting 25 per cent to 35 per cent of the total demand of the population for the twelve months from July 1916 to July 1917. The entire demand for coal for domestic purposes was to be met, and from 34 to 40 per cent of the demand for firewood.

From 1st April 1915 to 1st August 1916, the executive council of the municipality purchased foodstuffs to the value of 14,928,592 rubles; and stocks on hand were valued at 10,786,285 rubles. The expenditure on fuel during the same period amounted to 5,795,933 rubles. The value of goods supplied to the hospitals, to municipal institutions, and to the people may be seen in the following data: grain, 4,316,507 rubles; foodstuffs other than grain and meat, 9,236,105 rubles; meat, 4,799,886 rubles; fuel, 6,576,720 rubles; total, 24,929,219 rubles. The plan for 1916-1917 provided for supplying the population with bread to the value of 20,000,000 rubles; meat to the value of 15,000,000 rubles; fuel, 30,000,000 rubles; the total contemplated expenditure being some 65,000,000 rubles.

The experiences of other towns and cities in the organization of supply were similar to those of Petrograd and Moscow. They differ rather in scale than in means. We give herewith a few examples.

The municipality of Ufa directed its energy to the organization of municipal buying on a large scale by means of special agents, and to the establishment of a number of municipal enterprises; for example, eight food stores, two bakeries, three restaurants supplying cheap meals, and seven depots of firewood. It successfully applied the rationing system first to sugar, and later to flour, groats, firewood, etc. The representatives of large sections of the population, including labor, were invited to take part in the work of committees. The turnover of the municipal supply service for the year ending on 1st October 1916 was 1,035,664 rubles. In 1917 the turnover of municipal shops and bakeries reached 3,060,000 rubles, and the whole estimate for 1917 amounted to 5,100,000 rubles. The total sum required for the purchase of firewood in 1917-1918 was put at 1,800,000 rubles. The capital needed for these transactions was generally obtained by loans.

The municipality of Chelyabinsk organized the purchase and distribution of necessaries of life such as bread and flour, sugar, tea, butter, matches, firewood, petroleum, coal. Up to October 1916, 1,374,779 rubles had been spent on the buying of foodstuffs and hay. Commodities were distributed among the people by ration cards. The sums required for municipal buying were obtained by means of loans from local merchants, on which no interest was charged, or by advances on stocks on hand. The general conditions of supply were utterly inadequate. For instance, of 5,217 carloads of firewood which in October 1916 were awaiting dispatch at various railway stations, only 20 reached their destination, though Chelyabinsk really required 1,000 carloads per month.

The municipality of Ryazan made an energetic beginning, in its plan to prevent profiteering and a rise in the cost of living. Its Duma set aside 25,000 rubles in June, and 250,000 rubles in October 1915, for the purchase of flour, groats, and corn. The sale of municipal stocks was entrusted in part to the local coöperative society and in part to private firms. The development of municipal operations worked notably to lower local market prices. When the price of meat began to rise the executive council of the municipality bought a drove of cattle, opened a municipal butcher's shop; and the price of meat immediately went down again. A stop was also put to speculation in salt.

The shortage of all the necessaries of life in Kiev at the beginning of 1916 became so acute that the Commander-in-Chief on the South-western Front directed the officer in charge of the Army Supply Service to issue an order to the local administration to take "decisive measures for the reëstablishment of normal conditions, for the prevention of the high cost of living, and for providing the population with foodstuffs." The work of the municipality in organizing the supply of foodstuffs and fuel was put under the control of government departments. On the suggestion of the latter a special supply committee was formed; it included representatives of the departments concerned, of the municipality, of commerce, industry, and coöperative societies. But no drastic measures could remedy the general economic depression and Kiev did not return to normal conditions. Acute economic crises followed one after another. In February 1916 sugar disappeared from the market; and when the city called upon its sugar refineries to supply it with 25,000 puds (c. 400 tons) at fixed prices, they refused. An inquiry and registration of available stocks disclosed great quantities of hoarded sugar. In the case of other supplies the railroad station was blocked with goods; but it was impossible to remove them because of the absence of any means of transport within the city. The executive council of the municipality purchased goods of various kinds, and distributed them among the people through private stores and coöperative societies. In September 1916 three municipal bakeries produced bread to the extent of 3,700 puds (c. 510 tons). Meals at low prices or free of charge were distributed to some 20,000 homeless men and women of the working class, and to the poorest section of the intellectual classes.

In Minsk profiteering was rampant. The municipality and the central authorities were equally unable to deal with it. The governor appealed to the population, asking for the support of every citizen in the struggle to stop it. Meat prices were particularly affected.

The municipality of Samara devised and carried out an extensive plan for supplying the city up to the middle of 1917; a total of 4,500,000 rubles was spent on the purchase of foodstuffs, forage, and fuel. Municipal stocks were sold to the population at cost price through municipal shops and by other methods. The capital required for these operations was obtained by means of a loan.

Similar conditions prevailed in other towns, and by like methods they were met. The towns of Russia, without distinction as to their energy, resources, and means, were all forced into the same position, and all were confronted with insuperable difficulties. By energetic measures they obtained a temporary relief. But it was followed by conditions that were worse. The efforts of municipalities to provide the population of their towns with foodstuffs were hopelessly overwhelmed by the collapse of the whole economic system of the country.

To check the approaching economic breakdown the Government provided no comprehensive system of measures which could be efficiently employed. Frequent changes among the leaders responsible for the economic policy of the country increased the element of uncertainty and instability, and led to sharp transitions from one system to some other entirely opposed to it. Measures of this kind did not relieve the economic difficulties; on the contrary, they contributed to its disorganization and helped to bring about the final collapse.

During the first months of the War purchases for the army and the execution of orders for the War Office were effected through the commissioners of the Ministry of Agriculture, while the organization of civilian supplies was controlled by the Ministry of the Interior. Large quantities of bread intended for the army were often destroyed or seized by the enemy. In February 1915 the final decision as to question of supply was made by the military authorities of the districts in question, who had been given extensive powers allowing them to prohibit the removal of commodities required for the army, to control prices, and to requisition stocks at a reduced price if the owner refused to sell them. This policy resulted in the creation of numerous local authorities though there was no general scheme of supply and no central authority. Prohibitive measures were not supported by a constructive policy. The unsystematic and often contradictory activities of local authorities contributed to the confusion, paralyzed the normal functioning of the machinery of commerce, and fostered profiteering. In May 1915 the organization of supply was transferred to the Central Supply Committee of the Ministry of Commerce and Industry, which was given the power to conduct inquiries as to the available stocks and to requisition them; the local organization of supply was entrusted to Provincial Supply Committees.[16] The Central Committee, however, was soon abolished

[16] See Zagorsky, op. cit., Chapter IV.

and its place was taken by the Special Councils created under the Act of 17th August 1915; these took charge of the organization of various branches of supply. Instead of a united central organization, the necessity of which had been urged by the municipalities, the Act created Special Councils as follows: for national defense, under the chairmanship of the Minister for War; for food supply, under the Minister of Agriculture; for fuel, under the Minister of Commerce and Industry; and the transport, under the Minister of Transport.

Thus all essential unity of plan for supplying the country with foodstuffs and fuel was ended; and the organization of various branches of supply was entrusted to separate committees independent of one another, each pursuing its own policy. Instead of there being one general scheme, various and sometimes contradictory decisions were taken on the same subject. The creation of Special Councils brought no appreciable improvement in the question of food supply. The process of disintegration went on. Mutually nullifying instructions, sent from headquarters, clashed when attempts were made to apply them to the settlement of practical problems. At the same time, the country was giving new signs of disquieting anxiety and disturbance. The Government tried to find a remedy by conferring dictatorial powers, first on the President of the Council of Ministers, and then on the last Minister of the Interior, and also by issuing decrees which did not pass through the normal channels of legislative procedure.

The municipalities were aware from the very outbreak of hostilities that the War would surely lead to a food shortage, and that it would inevitably be felt in all its severity in the cities, the centers of consumption. Accordingly, as early as the first Conference of Mayors, held in Moscow in August 1914, it was pointed out that the control of food supplies for urban populations should be included within the powers of the Union. The Government vetoed this proposal. But by the very force of events the Union soon became involved in the economic struggle; and in February 1915 the Central and Regional Committees of the Union appointed economic subcommittees to consider what measures were best adapted for the prevention of a rise in the cost of living. An economic department was attached to the Central Committee of the Union, and counted among its members the greatest authorities on economic questions.

The Union of Towns believed that one essential condition of victory lay in organizing the country for war, and that the coöperation of all the organized forces of the nation could alone make it possible to carry on the War on the scale it had assumed. The Union, therefore, endeavored to obtain the support of the masses in a coöperation that would join with the Government in its measures for the conduct of the War, and at the same time take part in all other and general measures for the defense of the country. The Union's whole economic policy during the War may be explained by the following summary. On the one hand its economic department made a scientific and searching inquiry into every economic possibility. It called conferences where economic problems were discussed by the representatives of all sections of the community; and it made itself an effective bond to link together municipalities engaged in a struggle against economic disorganization. On the other hand, it continued to collaborate with the Government, endeavoring, through its representatives on the special committees, to induce it to adopt a plan of supply based on sound and well-established principles.

The Union of Towns was convinced that Russia did not suffer from an actual lack of the principal foodstuffs, and that the real problem lay in the methods of securing and distributing the products of agriculture, that is, in the domain of economic policy. Accordingly, for the prevention of the rise in the cost of living, it was necessary to devise a general plan, and to bring into common application those measures which were suggested by practical experience, and which had already been advocated by the public men of Russia at different times and on different occasions.

In order to obtain the necessary information the Union of Towns undertook a number of inquiries into the economic position of the urban population, and called in July 1915 a great economic conference, at which the municipalities, the zemstvos, trade, industry, coöperative societies, learned societies, and labor organizations were represented. This conference laid down the main outlines of a scheme of supply. The root idea was the necessity of State control of prices, of railways, of the distribution of commodities among the people and, in certain cases, State control of production. While the conference supported the principle of the intervention of the State in the freedom of private trade and commercial intercourse, it pointed out that no system of State control would lead to an adequate organization of supply and remedy the shortcomings under the régime of commercial and industrial freedom unless it followed strictly the lines of a comprehensive scheme of supply covering the whole of the Empire. The conference was of opinion that the control of the economic life of the country should be entrusted to a central government committee with far-reaching powers; that municipal organizations should be liberally represented on the committee, and that its work should be carried on through an extensive network of local institutions of a similar type. The work of the new economic machinery should be guided by a uniform system of registration of stocks of foodstuffs and fuel and of their geographical distribution, and by an estimate of the requirements of the civilian population and the army. The registration of food stocks and the estimates of the quantities required should be used for preparing a scheme of railway transport of the necessaries of life; this should guarantee the conveyance of goods by way of the shortest routes, and should be based on the actual state of the railways and on information as to the respective food stocks and requirements of the different towns and districts. The purchase, transport, and distribution of goods could not be effected without making an extensive use of private enterprise, but this should be submitted to a definite government control. The chief instrument employed for enforcing State control should be a system of special permits for the conveyance of goods from producers to consumers. Private trade should be supplemented by a wide development of municipal and coöperative activities; and these should be supported and financed by the State.

The Union of Towns and the leaders of social and economic thought were of the opinion that free competition, and the free play of interests, should be replaced by State control as a measure necessary for national defense and for the safeguarding of national interests. They did not advocate State control as an equitable principle, nor did they aim at the destruction of the machinery of private trading; they merely endeavored to regulate it, and to adapt it to the new demands caused by the War under conditions of exceptional difficulty. In this respect economic and social ideas in Russia were simply moving in the same direction as in other belligerent countries, where the necessity of effective State control of the exchange of goods had been fully recognized, and the system was energetically being put into practice.

The Special Council for Supply, which had been assigned the task of "coördinating all measures relating to the problems of the supply of the army and of the civilian population, and of all institutions concerned with the same," began its work by rejecting the one essential thing in the plan suggested by the Union. Instead, it adopted the method of settling minor problems and discussing private applications, and proceeded from one isolated case to another. The representatives of the Union of Towns endeavored to force through the Council certain portions of the Union's economic policy. For instance, they introduced schemes for the mass purchase of foodstuffs, for the general requisition of Donetz coal, for the supplying of the population with sugar, for the opening of credits for community buying, and for controlling the production, exchange, and distribution of various articles. In connection with the breakdown of the railroad service they suggested measures for remedying technical shortcomings and abuses, and emphasized the necessity of the immediate reorganization of railroad transportation when conditions had been bettered. The representatives of the Union always insisted that the drafting of some general scheme of supply, and its rigorous application, were above all essential.

After lengthy consideration the Special Council was at last driven to the conclusion that a general plan of supply was necessary. A draft scheme was produced in February 1916. Its leading ideas were a combination of price control with the control of rail transportation,[17] and, if necessary, the fixing of prices and the introduction of rationing cards. The first Russian agricultural census, which supplied important data for the further work of State control, was taken at the request of municipal bodies. Thus the Government was at last compelled to adopt the idea and the elements of the scheme prepared by the municipal organizations; but this was done when the process of deterioration had reached an advanced stage, and it was done too late.

The local organization of institutions in charge of the carrying out of the scheme of supply proved exceedingly unsatisfactory. Everywhere two sets of commissioners were at work; one was in charge of supply for the army, the other of that for the civil population. These commissioners, who numbered 220, acted independently, on their own responsibility, and often in opposition to one another. Some of them introduced fixed prices; others established a fixed percentage of

[17] *Razreshitelnaya systema planovikh perevozok.*

profit for retailers on each particular commodity; still others prohibited the increase of prices altogether, on pain of fines, arrest, and
deportation. The institutions in charge of supply competed with one
another and requisitioned the goods acquired by the municipalities.
The systematic transport of goods had little success; for example, in
the six provinces controlled by the Moscow Regional Committee in
June 1916, only 34.9 per cent of the scheme was carried out, and
33.9 per cent in July. Fixed prices were introduced without system,
and they were anything but "fixed." They were frequently altered
under the pressure of the parties concerned. Local prices were not coordinated and were usually most excessive. Hopes for a further rise
in the price of grain prevented the farmers from selling their stocks.
In spite of the excellent harvest of 1916 and the accumulation of
grain at railheads, inadequate use was made of rail transportation,
"as a result of the small amount of business done by the sellers and
buyers."[18] Some of the commissioners advised the farmers to postpone
the sale of the new harvest until the publication of a new scale of
fixed prices. In 1916 fixed prices of bread were increased by 30 per
cent over those of the previous year. This increase, which was made
under the pressure of the landlords, was protested against by zemstvos and municipal organizations. Their protest was supported by
the War Office, and prices were slightly reduced.

As a part of the general discontent, the relations between the producers and the consumers of agricultural products, that is, between
the rural community and the towns, became greatly strained. In
order to allay this feeling, and to conclude a "social contract" between organizations representing these differing interests and classes,
the Union of Towns proposed to summon a new conference on supply
at the end of 1916, in which the representatives of zemstvos, municipalities, peasants, trade, industry, and labor should be invited to
participate. The work preliminary to calling this conference was entered into on the assumption that the conference would succeed in
bridging the gulf between the towns and the rural community; this
was rapidly widening as a result of the failure of the policy of supply,
and the inefficiency of the control of industry. But a new change took
place at that time in the economic policy of the Government—a
change that plunged the whole problem of supply into a state of

[18] Report of the Minister of Transport presented to the President of the
Council of Ministers, August 1916.

hopeless confusion. The new Minister of the Interior—he was also the last (M. Protopopov)—declared himself in favor of freedom of trade; and, with the support of private banks, he began a struggle against the Ministry of Agriculture for the control of supply. The whole previous work of the Special Council for food supply was declared to be along wrong lines, and all attempts to bring about State control and maximum prices were pronounced harmful. As an alternative policy it was proposed that the whole organization of supply for the army and the civilian population should be entrusted to private banks and to the governors of the provinces. The conference projected by the Union of Towns was prohibited, and a meeting of the representatives of municipalities was dispersed by the police. The new policy of the Government further increased the confusion in the organization of supply, made the shortage of foodstuffs still more acute, and added to the excitement now spreading among the people. The levy of grain in kind for the needs of the army was an heroic measure, and, in accordance with an approved schedule, it was followed by a general grain tax.

The State Duma insisted on the necessity of a single scheme of supply for both army and people, the introduction of firmly established fixed prices, systematization of transport, and equitable principles in the distribution of the grain tax. It advocated the control of prices and control of production in the case of the most important manufactured articles. Hitherto State control had been applied mainly to foodstuffs, while industry had remained free; and, taking advantage of the economic breakdown of the country, it had realized enormous profits. The whole system of State control was, therefore, one-sided; and in rural districts promoted hostile feelings against the towns. Much more, the State Duma had now come to feel that for any comprehensive economic policy during the War, the necessary first step was the creation of a Government which would enjoy the confidence of the country and work in coöperation with the majority of the legislative institutions. The alteration of the existing system of government was, in the opinion of the Duma, an unavoidable preliminary to the settlement of all war problems.[19]

At the beginning of 1917 the confusion of the problem of supply was worse than ever. The grain tax, as assessed, put an unbearable burden upon certain provinces. In some provinces the towns were

[19] Reports of the State Duma, Session of 5th December 1916.

utterly deprived of bread. The rural communities refused to supply the towns with vegetables, dairy products, and meat, on the ground that they could not receive in exchange boots, textiles, petroleum, etc. Disquieting news was arriving from cities both large and small. Municipalities were informing the Central Committee of the Union that the "population is in a state of anxiety," that "the general discontent threatens to lead to dangerous outbursts," that "demonstrations of workmen are to be expected." "The situation is alarming"— other municipalities reported—"and the people are desperate."

The patience of the nation was at an end. Tsardom fell on 3rd March 1917. The Provisional Government which took its place was quite willing to meet the demands of public bodies with which it was closely united, and to which its members belonged; but its policy proved as inefficient as those of the old Government. The new Government was confronted not only with the complete and hopeless collapse of the organization of supply, and of the whole life of the country, but also with the rapidly rising waves of the revolutionary storm.

In the meantime certain sections of the front had only a half day's ration of bread and flour in reserve. The supply of foodstuffs for other millions of men in the army was in a most precarious position. And the Government had almost completely exhausted its stocks.[20] It was idle to make schemes for the restoration of freedom in trade in a country which no longer enjoyed the freedom either of railroad transportation or of trade competition. Only one course was left open to the Government—to undertake the control of all stocks of grain, that is, to introduce a grain monopoly. On 30th March 1917, the Provisional Government published a Decree by which all grain on hand as well as that of the forthcoming harvest of 1917 was declared preempted for the Government; those possessing it were allowed to keep what they needed for their families, their cattle, and for sowing purposes. At the same time provincial, district, and *volost*[21] committees of supply were established throughout the country. In order to induce the peasants to part with their stocks, maximum prices were doubled and the help of coöperative societies was secured. The powers of the Minister of Agriculture were enlarged. It was decided to extend the control of civilian supply to necessaries of life other than

[20] From a speech by M. Shingarev, Minister of Agriculture, delivered at a conference of the Union of Towns on 9th April 1917.
[21] *See* p. 14, n. 19.

foodstuffs; and the question was raised of general and country-wide food-rationing. The daily ration of bread was, in Petrograd, put at one pound per head. Workmen were allowed 1½ pounds.

These measures did not give the results anticipated. Large cities, and particularly the capitals, were threatened with famine. With the spring thaw and the resulting bad roads in country districts, the delivery of grain to railhead by horse-drawn carts fell off greatly. The quantity of grain supplied to the towns was steadily growing less. Instead of the 70,000 puds (c. 11,300 tons) a day to which Moscow was entitled according to schedule, only about 25,000-30,000 puds were delivered.[22] Of the 2,100 carloads of grain and flour allotted to Moscow, only 868 were received in March 1917, and only 679 in April, that is, 22½ carloads a day, or half a pound per head. In the following months the conditions of supply improved: 2,019 loads were received in May, and 1,052 in June; but the number fell steadily thereafter, and dropped to 883 in July, and 785 in August. The daily ration of bread was again reduced to half a pound. The grain-growing provinces did not carry out the part assigned to them by the arrangement above. Only one-third or one-half of the quantity of bread required for the needs of the army and of the urban population was actually delivered in August 1917. Railway lines were crowded with so-called "sack-pedlars" (*meshochniki*),[23] who brought in enormous quantities of wheat from the wheat districts, and sold it on the open market. The people, excited by their newly acquired freedom, were little inclined to comply with the Provisional Government's decree which expropriated grain; and the Government itself was powerless to enforce it.

The last conference of the Union of Towns, held on 14th-17th October 1917, took the view that a wheat monopoly, under State control, was the only policy that could possibly relieve the economic tension. It considered, however, that the government machinery for the control of supply should be further strengthened, not only by the collaboration of coöperative societies, but also by the assistance of private trade and its capital, the same to be utilized in accord-

---

[22] *Opit Moskwi v prodovolstvennom dele* (*Experiment of Moscow in Organizing Food Supply*); Report presented to the conference of the Union of Towns in October 1917.

[23] Soldiers and others engaged in illegal dealings in grain, which they brought in sacks from agricultural districts to the towns.

ance with the directions and under the supervision of the Government. The conference recognized that the whole population must be provided with the necessaries of life at fixed prices; that all demands should be met by a proportional and equitable distribution of the commodities available; and that it was, therefore, essential to systematize production and put it under the control of the community. The conference further held that the purchase and distribution of foodstuffs should be entrusted to the municipalities and to zemstvos newly elected under universal franchise. And it called upon them to undertake these duties, not merely in order to meet local needs, but a part of a policy for the nation.

This was the final expression of the views of the conference of the Union of Towns, after its reëlection. The Government was expected to undertake the utterly impossible task of supplying the population not only with foodstuffs, but with all the necessaries of life. The views of the Union chanced to coincide with the decision of the Government; but external conditions were too unfavorable to allow of these plans being carried out.

The conditions of other branches of supply were by no means better. The shortage of fuel during the Revolution remained as bad as before, the old factors that caused it had even been reinforced by new ones. It led to the closing down of gas-works in many towns for an indefinite period, and to a considerable reduction of the supply of electric power. In many towns it was no longer possible to carry on even the street railway service. And the whole urban population had to live in houses no longer heated. The plans of the municipalities were also frustrated by the scarcity of labor and by the decline in the man-power output of the coal mines. A report of this decline may be found, in fact, in the "Bulletin" of the Soviet of Workmen's and Soldiers' Deputies, which states that the output per head in the second half of 1917 was 33 per cent less than that for the same period in 1914, and 10 per cent less than for the same six months in 1916.

The decline in the efficiency of labor was largely due to the acute conflicts between the administration and the miners which began soon after the Revolution. Month by month the number of locomotives and the amount of rolling stock in need of repair was steadily growing. For instance, on the Ekaterinsky Railroad, 283 locomotives were wholly unfit for service on 1st April 1917. Ten weeks later 323 were out of repair. On the same line the number of cars requiring repair was 2,861 on 1st April; on 15th June, 4,195. On the Donetz Railway, 29 per cent of all locomotives were in need of repair on 15th June, the normal percentage being fifteen. In the first six months of 1917 the railroads moved 700,000 fewer cars of freight than they did in the same period in 1916. In other words, consumers were deprived of some 700,000,000 puds (c. 11,600,000 tons) of needed commodities, including more than 100,000,000 puds (c. 1,600,000 tons) of coal.[24]

The same reasons prevented any increase in firewood transport. The peasants opposed the cutting of timber in the forests, whether they belonged to the Government or to private owners; and they objected to the removal of wood already cut. And this ended such supplies in the case of Orel, Mtsensk, Ryazan, Ekaterinoslav, Moscow, Tambov, Pokrov, and of many other towns. Certain districts levied special duties on all firewood which they allowed buyers to take away. The district committee of Kassimovsk requisitioned the wood purchased by the municipality of Moscow; the Committee of Ryazan seized a consignment of timber which was intended for Moscow and was being sent down the river Oka. The district Soviets of Workmen's Deputies seized trains loaded with wood and *en route* to Moscow. Similar occurrences took place everywhere. And even when municipalities succeeded in getting their firewood supplies safely over all the obstacles set up by the peasants, there was no certainty that the consignments would not be appropriated by the railways for their own use.

In these circumstances it is not surprising that from all parts of Russia came the same voice of distress, and it told the same story of complete breakdown of normal conditions, of impoverishment and anarchy. The municipality of Moscow appealed to the Provisional Government, and made it clear that the scarcity of fuel due to the collapse of railways was endangering every kind of work, both for the national defense and for the good of the people; and that it might lead to the closing of schools and hospitals. Indeed, fifteen provinces arranged to save fuel by suspending the normal heating of all school buildings. It was proposed that schools should be closed from 10th December to 28th February, and that when they were in use, 38 degrees Fahrenheit should be held to be an adequate temperature.

[24] *Izvestya Soyuza Gorodov,* Nos. 47-48, August-September 1917, p. 114.

Like conditions prevailed in Petrograd. The scarcity of fuel endangered the work of shops and factories. The municipality of Kiev reported that it had had to close its power station, its waterworks, and all enterprises working for the national defense. It asked for fuel to enable such enterprises, and its schools and hospitals to carry on. Similar petitions were sent by the municipalities of Odessa, Kazan, Ekaterinoslav, Novocherkask, Kremenchug, Kharkov, Poltava, Rostov-on-Don, Tula, Mogilev, and Samara. And the story was the same in the towns of Transcaucasia and Siberia. Apparently, economic disintegration had reached its climax. And, sweeping the country, the storm of revolution was throwing down all that was left of a system already undermined by the War.

All economic measures, whether those of Tsardom or of the Provisional Government, had proved to be inadequate. In their endeavor to provide for the needs of the army the organizations responsible had swept the country bare. The food crisis in Russia's towns and cities helped to bring Revolution in the midst of war, and paved the way for Bolshevism.

CHAPTER XIV

THE UNION OF TOWNS AND THE MUNICIPALITIES DURING THE REVOLUTION

THE ceaseless financial difficulties experienced by Russian municipalities in peace-time were further aggravated during the War. The break-up of the economic system of the country, much more rapid after the Revolution, led in the end to a complete collapse of municipal finances. The estimates of municipal revenues and expenditure had long been regarded as a mere formality. During the last years of the War such estimates no longer gave any true picture of the situation. And the disparity between income and outgo was growing at a speed which made all attempts to anticipate it utterly futile.

Public utilities had, only a short time before, been a source of municipal prosperity. Now they were not merely absorbing the entire revenue, they even required subsidies from municipal funds to meet their working expenses. The increased charges they made for their services could not keep pace with the increase of their expenses, and proved to be no remedy. Towns and cities were without any means whatever wherewith to meet these difficulties. The enormous increase in the price of labor, with the cost of office maintenance and the like undertakings, absorbed all revenues, irrespective of the purposes for which moneys had been voted; and at the same time they demanded always more and more.

Far-reaching changes were also taking place in municipal offices and enterprises employing large staffs. Here the enthusiasm of the opening days of the Revolution was soon followed first by a decline in the efficiency of labor noted above, and then by the disorganization of the administrative services. These changes were accompanied by a general demand for higher wages. Such demands were growing and multiplying out of all proportion to the actual revenues and financial resources of municipalities. Their pay offices were simply besieged. Municipal funds were no longer spent in accordance with prearranged financial plans, but under the pressure of new and unforeseen demands. Revolutionary aspirations and the revolutionary storm still raged about the old municipal administrations; they invaded them and tore to pieces their former projects for public work. After the Revolution of February 1917, the composition of the majority of municipal Dumas was entirely altered by the introduction of representatives of new revolutionary organizations, who had no constitutional right to any place in them. These "democratized" Dumas introduced new principles for the conduct of local government, and willingly accepted the demands of freshly created labor organizations. In consequence, as we have already said, the normal balance between revenue and expenditure was utterly destroyed. Budget deficits and cash shortages became an alarming feature of municipal finance. Municipalities passing through the process of "democratization," and also those which preserved their prerevolutionary character, simply lived from one payment to the next; and the next payment was always many times larger than the one before it. The committees of workmen and of junior employees which sprang up after the Revolution completely disorganized the routine of municipal offices and enterprises and ceaselessly presented fresh demands for increases of salary and wages.

Public utilities and private businesses both had to endure the same violent crises. As in the case of industry, in general, public utilities, with their great repair shops and their extensive staffs of workmen and minor employees, were seriously affected by the decrease in the quality and purchasing power of labor, the abolition of piecework, and the introduction of an eight-hour day, accompanied by large wage increases. Workmen insisted that the municipalities should show an example, and create "normal" conditions for labor in the offices and enterprises of the town. The revolutionary excitement which had entirely overwhelmed labor *en masse* made any resistance useless and impossible. Wages rose even more rapidly than prices.[1] This is made plain by the following percentage ratios, as between prices and wages, prepared by S. N. Prokopovich.

	Prices	Wages of an adult man
1st July 1914	100	102
1st July 1915	131	119
1st July 1916	185	215
1st January 1917	...	256
1st July 1917	248	512

[1] For a detailed treatment of the problem of wages *see* Miss Anna G. Eisenstadt: *Wages in War-time,* in this series of the *Economic and Social History of the World War.*

"After the revolution," says M. Prokopovich, "and as a result of the political strength of the proletariat, which paved the way for its dictatorship, wages, in the determination of prices, were in a class alone."[2]

Town and city administrations had to devote all their energies to seeking resources from which they could meet the expenditures of each successive month. But even here they were handicapped by the absorption of all available credit by mere current public expenses. It became more and more difficult to obtain capital. Municipal finances were moving toward certain bankruptcy.

A striking and typical picture of the effects of the War and the Revolution upon the municipal finances may be seen in the history of those of Moscow, which had always enjoyed the well-deserved reputation of being entirely sound. They had seemed, indeed, as a model for the governance of other Russian cities.

The ordinary expenditures of Moscow were 57,800,000 rubles in 1915, 70,037,000 rubles in 1916, and 99,240,000 rubles in 1917, whereas in 1914 such expenditures had been only slightly more than 53,000,000 rubles. This increase of expenditures was by no means the result of a normal and healthy development of the activities of the municipality. It was an unhealthy process due to the economic confusion caused by the War. The increase of expenditure under almost every estimates heading had for its purpose not the expansion of municipal work, but the mere desire to maintain it at its pre-war level. For instance, during the War the amount expended by Moscow on public health, sanitary engineering, and medical aid grew rapidly. It was 13,684,000 rubles in 1914, 15,501,000 rubles in 1915, and 17,763,000 rubles in 1916. This increase of expenditure, however, was not accompanied by the creation of any more or less important new service, or by any great betterment of the existing ones. The money was absorbed by the rise in the cost of living, increased wages, and the higher cost of maintaining the existing services. As a result of the rise in the prices of the necessaries of life, the estimates for the carrying on of the public utilities for 1916 were increased by 1,400,000 rubles; in the estimates for 1917 the increase under the same heading was 6,400,000 rubles.[3] The wages of the personnel of

[2] Prokopovich, op. cit., p. 263.

[3] Memorandum (Zapiska) of the Municipality of Moscow on the estimates for 1917.

Moscow's municipal services and city departments amounted to 4,750,000 rubles in 1904, to 7,750,000 rubles in 1907, to 12,750,000 rubles in 1911, and to 24,250,000 rubles in 1915. The second supplementary estimate for 1917 brings the wages of civic employees and municipal staff up to 54,000,000 rubles. (In 1917, 15,000 clerks and 70,000 other employees were on the pay rolls of the city.) A total of more than 9,500,000 rubles was spent in 1916, in accordance with the estimates and in special grants, for increases in salaries for minor employees and workmen alone, and on bonus and allowances to the mobilized members of the staff. A sum of 13,000,000 rubles was included for this purpose in the estimate for 1917, but the amount actually paid was many times as great.

An estimated deficit for 1916 was covered by raising the taxes on real property up to the legal limit; and a general revaluation of property had taken place in 1915. The estimates for 1917 show a deficit of 19,371,000 rubles, which was met by increasing the water rates from 6 to 12 copecks per 100 buckets (*vedro*),[4] and by increasing street-car fares. But these measures only met the estimates; they did not meet the actual needs of the municipality, nor get rid of its hidden deficit. The financial committee, when submitting the estimates for 1916 to the municipal Duma, stated in its memorandum that various extraordinary items of expenditure and unforeseen causes of outlay, which were a heavy burden on the budget of the municipality, could not be met by local taxation and should be taken over by the State Treasury. "Local government institutions cannot be called upon to provide for expenditure of a national character. All the outlay due to the War should therefore be met by the Treasury." In the meantime, of the total expenditure on purposes not connected with normal municipal work, but due to the War (such as the relief of wounded and refugees, the organization of supply, etc.), which in 1916 amounted to 172,508,000 rubles, the sum of 22,127,000 rubles was provided by the municipality. An additional sum of approximately 44,000,000 rubles was required in the same year for the organization of the supply of the population with the necessaries of life, and of the army with munitions, equipment, and foodstuffs. The deficit of the ordinary and "war" budget on 1st January 1916 reached 27,238,000 rubles. It was only partly covered

---

[4] One *vedro* = 2.7 gallons.

by short-term loans, government subsidies, and the issue of debentures which had been intended for a very different purpose. In the middle of 1917 the deficit rose to over 85,000,000 rubles, and in September of the same year to 98,000,000 rubles. After the Revolution of 1917 the municipality had to bear the enormous expense of the maintenance of the civic guard, which replaced the police of the old régime.

The growth of the budget of Petrograd was on the same scale. In 1914 it was 52,000,000 rubles; and by 1917 it had become substantially 100,000,000 rubles. Far from improving the conditions of municipal work, this only just prevented it from collapsing. The war expenditure of the municipality of Petrograd on 1st January 1916 amounted to 15,995,440 rubles. Of this sum 10,062,576 rubles was provided from the municipal funds, 300,000 rubles was to be refunded by the Treasury, and 5,632,863 rubles was invested in stocks, etc. The war expenses borne by the municipality were as follows: sundry expenditure due to the War, 1,461,173 rubles; equipment and upkeep of hospital beds for wounded and sick, 1,186,379 rubles; winter underwear and boots, 199,996 rubles; salaries of employees who were substituted for mobilized men, 1,486,316; subsidies to the families of mobilized members of the staff, 447,250 rubles; bonus to the staff due to the rise in the cost of living, 902,842 rubles; distributed to the families of the mobilized members of the reserve force through the district relief committees, 2,564,375 rubles. In 1917 the war expenditure of the municipalities rose enormously, for the reasons stated above, and produced in the finances of Petrograd a deficit which amounted to 90,000,000 rubles.

Such was the financial position of the two capitals in 1917. That of other towns was very similar. Municipalities were no longer in a position to face the deficits of their budgets. The lack of funds could be remedied neither by the increase of revenue, nor by the straining of all resources to the utmost, nor by the raising of water rates and the like. The claims of labor, expenditures for the maintenance of public utilities and the city's various departments, and payments on loans absorbed the entire revenue. By 1916 the deficits of some municipalities had reached large amounts. They were greatly increased in 1917 and, not being covered by any assets, completely disorganized municipal finances. Here are a few examples of the deficits of a number of communities, both large and small. Those of the capitals are given above.

1916.

	Budget	Deficit
	(in rubles)	
Riga	7,872,500	2,774,600
Samara	6,788,900	1,930,200
Nizhni-Novgorod	6,000,000	785,000
Minsk	2,010,000	483,000
Yaroslavl	1,917,700	328,000
Kremenchug	1,157,400	130,000
Barnaul	1,079,500	343,700
Ivanovo-Voznesensk	723,300	73,500
Elabuga	300,000	55,900

1917.

	Budget	Deficit
	(in rubles)	
Odessa	32,660,000	10,000,000[5]
Tiflis	12,458,700	3,000,000
Kiev	8,657,200	31,000,000
Tambov	1,780,000	127,000
Novgorod	641,100	122,000

1917.

	Deficit
	(in rubles)
Baku	5,000,000
Ekaterinoslav	4,000,000
Nizhni-Novgorod	3,000,000
Yaroslavl	1,500,000
Tula	1,000,000
Archangel	508,000
Simferopol	471,200
Smolensk	301,000
Poltava	230,000
Ivanovo-Voznesensk	163,200

At the same time the financial resources of the municipalities had been strained to the very limit. The returns made by fifty-six towns (among which the capitals are not included) for 1917 show that municipal budgets increased by an average of 45.7 per cent, the rate

[5] In 1918 the deficit of Odessa rose to 22,000,000 rubles.

of increase varying from 1 per cent to 415 per cent. Both appeals for rigorous economy, and discussions of the necessity of a revision of a new Act dealing with the improvement of municipal finance (suggested in a resolution passed by the last conference of the Union of Towns) were equally superfluous; neither could prevent the impending collapse. The municipalities were face to face with a catastrophe.

The reform of local government brought little relief to the situation. Even at the beginning of the War it had been obvious that the municipalities could not deal adequately with the new problems now confronting them unless fundamental changes were introduced in the existing law, for time and again they were compelled by the force of events to go beyond the narrow limits of their powers. In July 1915 the Union of Towns passed a resolution demanding an immediate reform of local government on a wide democratic basis, accompanied by an extension of its own powers, and a guarantee of its immunity from government interference. In the Ministry of the Interior and in the Committee of the State Duma, however, discussion of the Municipal Government Bill proceeded very slowly and was delayed by frequent divergences of belief and opinion between the Government and the State Duma. The Union of Towns and the municipalities were forbidden to discuss any questions connected with the reform of local government or to express their views on the matter. The draft of the new Municipal Act prepared by the Union of Towns could not, therefore, be laid before a conference of representatives of municipalities specially called for this purpose. It was only after the downfall of the old régime that the Provisional Government could take immediate steps for the introduction of the new Municipal Act, which was drafted with the help of the representatives of the municipalities. The Act was sanctioned on 9th June 1917, and was immediately put into operation.

It is an act strongly impregnated with the spirit and conditions of the moment when it was made law. The influence of war and revolution can easily be traced in the regulations concerning the elections to the municipal Dumas. The right of municipal suffrage was extended to all citizens of either sex, without distinction of race or religion, who had reached the age of twenty on the day when the register was completed, provided that they were residents of the town when the electoral lists were prepared, or had their domicile, employment or any definite work which required their presence, in the town. The abolition of almost all bars that might render citizens ineligible for the suffrage was accompanied by the extension of municipal franchise to men serving in the army.

The powers bestowed on the new municipalities included the administration of their own local affairs and the supervision of municipal property. Municipalities were granted the right to call conferences and to enter into agreements and unions with zemstvos, with other municipalities, and with village communities. They were made responsible for the defense of private security, for the maintenance of public order, and for the control of the civic guard. The central Government, through the Commissary for the province, preserved the right of ruling upon the activities of the municipalities only when there arose considerations of their constitutional validity; and the central Government lost its former power to set aside the decisions of the municipalities on the ground that they were "undesirable" or contrary to public policy.

The new Municipal Act was in operation for five months. As stated above,[6] the Act for the improvement of municipal finance was published only a few weeks before the Bolshevik *coup d'état*. This Act provided for an increase of the income tax, a portion of which was to be handed over to municipalities, and for the levy of a tax on dwelling houses; it raised the tax on real property to 20 per cent of the revenue therefrom, or to 2 per cent of the gross value, and gave the municipalities the right to levy a number of minor taxes, relieving them at the same time of some of the financial burdens imposed upon them by the former Act. New sources of revenue were expected to bring in some 100,000,000 rubles. The State was unable to afford any further relief, as it was itself passing through a severe financial crisis.

By October 1917 the new municipal Dumas were elected in 643 towns. In accordance with the new Act granting universal suffrage, the elections had begun in July 1917, and they resulted in an entire change in the composition of the Dumas. In fifty provincial towns the representatives included 65.7 per cent socialists, 34.3 per cent other parties. In 413 district towns 36.7 per cent were socialists, and 63.3 per cent belonged to other parties. The presiding committees of

[6] Chapter III.

the Dumas included almost everywhere a large representation of the socialist majority. Party quarrels and electioneering propaganda were carried into the new Dumas. All the problems which the country had at heart, such as the question of war and peace, the causes of the War and its responsibilities, the breakdown of the national economic system—were now introduced into the debates of the municipal Dumas, which could not concentrate for any time on purely local problems. The appeals to develop the work of the Revolution and to defend its "conquests" found a hearty response among the mass of the newly elected members of the municipalities. The declarations made by the Socialist-Revolutionaries, Socialist-Democrats, and other Socialist groups—now for the first time admitted to a share in local government—committed the municipalities to new activities in all directions, paying no attention to the dilapidated condition of municipal finances. Hopes of obtaining new revenues by a rigorous assessment of "capitalistic classes," and by a progressive capital levy on real estate, were put forward as a remedy for deficits, a means for the repayment of short-term loans, and for the satisfaction of all the demands of the working classes. But such hopes had no relation whatever to the real state of affairs. Funds were required immediately, and legislation by the Government could not keep pace with the demands of the "revolutionary democracy." The shadow of class warfare was already hanging over the meetings of the municipal Dumas, and appeals to maintain the unity of the local government bodies, in their endeavor to provide for the needs of all classes of the population, were doomed to failure.

The new municipalities, however, were soon compelled to take up purely practical business. A number of towns were menaced by the immediate suspension of the supply of electric power because of strikes and lack of fuel. New difficulties were created by the question of housing and of the possibility of having to requisition premises in the event of the evacuation of Petrograd and the arrival of a new wave of refugees. With the disbanding of the old police and the organization of the civic guard, the municipalities undertook a heavy responsibility, the defense of the lives and property of their citizens, and the prevention of theft, robbery, murders, and other offenses, the number of which was rapidly growing. The civic guard, brought into existence at a moment's notice, proved inadequate to its task both in numbers and in efficiency. Much zeal and initiative were called for by the problems of supply of foodstuffs. The municipalities had to give proofs of great energy and organizing capacity. They needed large funds. At the same time it was clear that their economic development was closely connected with the future of the country as a whole, and that their financial and economic life could be put on a sound foundation only by the relief of the general economic tension.

The far-reaching changes brought about by the Revolution, and the economic breakdown of the municipalities affected the nature and character of the Union of Towns. Its position as the natural center of municipal Russia was a strong one; all municipalities looked to it for support, advice, and help. During the revolutionary year the Central and local committees of the Union became gradually aware that the real center of its work had been removed from the war front to the country itself. The war work had to be carried on; it had to be maintained as far as possible at its former standard, but the disorganization of the front and the deterioration of the army, which had already begun, frustrated all efforts in this direction. Any further extension of its war activities was out of the question. It was necessary to adapt the whole organization to the new conditions in the army and in the country. The attention of the Union was more and more diverted to the organization of purely municipal work, to the raising of its standard to the requirements created by new political conditions, to assistance in the rebuilding of the economic life of the municipalities, and to the discovery of new measures for the restoration of their finances. The main lines of this work were laid down as early as April 1916, when the purpose of the Union after the termination of the War was put into four words: "All for municipal Russia."[7] The work of the Union of Towns was to be organized on the following lines: (1) the winding up of war institutions, the relief of disabled men and convalescents, their training in various crafts, the care of orphans and widows, the defense of motherhood and infants, and the restoration of municipal life in the devastated areas; (2) the improvement of municipal sanitation and measures for the promotion of public health; (3) measures for improving the economic and financial position of municipalities. "The Union should be the principal adviser of municipalities on all questions of municipal economy, and should assist them in meeting their needs and requirements."

[7] Minutes of the meeting of the Central Committee of the Union of Towns, 17th April 1916.

The program outlined in 1916 was eventually developed into a vast plan of future work of the Union. Purely municipal problems were brought to the fore, together with questions connected with the imminent end of the War, its consequences, the problems of demobilization in the wide sense of the term, the reconstruction of towns ruined during the War, and the systematic adaptation of war industry to the requirements of post-war conditions. The Union prepared an elaborate scheme for the creation of a municipal bank, and extended the activities of the Central Department of Municipal Affairs, which was already one of the institutions attached to the Central Committee. The purpose of this Department was to assist municipalities on the largest scale, both in their financial policy and in other matters of municipal economy. It supplied municipalities with information, advised them on questions of credit and on methods of procuring the needed authority for the issue of municipal debentures, and assisted them in obtaining short- and long-term credit. On the demand of the municipalities, the Central Department undertook the coördination of municipal wholesale purchases of various materials and goods, among which medical goods and stationery for schools occupied important places. It also dealt with the publication of text-books. The establishment of a special institute for the training of officers in all branches of municipal work, and the organization of exhibitions, of a municipal museum, and of experimental institutions, and so on, were other proposals. The Union of Towns had to prepare plans and estimates for various municipal institutions, public utilities, etc. The last conference of the Union of Towns, held on 14th-17th October 1917, drafted and approved an extensive scheme of the work of the Union in peace-time, which embodies the principles stated above. Such were the main outlines of the future work of the "Union of the Free Towns of Russia" after the suspension of hostilities.

The events of February 1917 were followed by the *coup d'état* of 25th October. The Communist Party which came into power, proclaiming the dictatorship of the proletariat and the advent of the new "commonwealth of workers," began its work by smashing to pieces not only all the machinery of the Government but its very foundations. Throughout the country municipal dumas and their executive councils were dispersed by force. The recently promulgated Municipal Act introducing the democratic organization of local government was annulled, together with the other legislation of the Provisional Government. Soviets of Workmen and Soldiers were set up everywhere. Local government was abolished, and its place was taken by representatives of the central Government acting under its strict supervision. The authority of local Soviets was wide.

The Union of Towns as a democratic and public organization could not carry on under the conditions of the new régime. Only reluctantly tolerated by the Tsarist Government, it was abolished by the dictatorship of the proletariat; it continued to exist for two months after the advent of the Bolsheviks, and a decree of the Soviet Government, dated 9th January 1918, brought its life to an end. By this decree the property and capital of the Russian Red Cross as also that of the All-Russian Union of Towns were nationalized. During the last two months the central and local institutions of the Unions at the front and in the rear had been slowly disappearing. In some places they had been dispersed by the Soviets of Soldiers and Workmen; in others, they had continued to exist without being able, however, to work. They were merely awaiting their dissolution. Their labors were not concluded. They were simply broken off; and the records of what was accomplished are not complete. The new dictators cared little for these records. Some of the books of the Union, their accounts, and archives, were destroyed or stolen; some were transferred to the institutions of the new administration. Some of the members of the staff of the Unions agreed to work under the Soviets, and joined the personnel of the new institutions. The majority of the old leaders of the Unions, its founders, dispersed to the remotest parts of the Empire, and used their administrative experience for the creation of Red Cross organizations; these worked under the flag of the Union of Towns in the parts of the country which were still struggling against the dictatorship of the Bolsheviks. When this struggle was brought to an end large numbers of Russians were compelled to withdraw from their country, and some of the old leaders of the Union of Towns have resumed their work for the relief of Russian refugees in other countries. This work is almost exclusively confined to the care and education of children.

The War, unexampled in its scope and the way in which it was carried on, made plain the disorganization and backwardness of Russian municipalities. The old régime, which prevented the free development of national resources, could not deal adequately with the new problems confronting it. Under the conditions of this régime the country was unable to remodel its economic organization in accordance with the requirements of the War. The failure of its efforts to cope with the situation resulted in its utter breakdown, and this eventually led to revolution during the War. The general collapse naturally swept away the municipalities, still weak enough, in spite of their recent progress. It was impossible to save them amidst the general ruin. And their fate was shared by the All-Russian Union of Towns.

The old Russian municipalities and their Union are dead. A whole era of historical development has been brought to its close. Nevertheless, the great cultural work of the municipalities has left behind a deep and indelible mark. In the new period of Russian history which has now begun the cultural traditions accumulated by the old municipalities are bound to play a part; the rising generation will use them as a precious inheritance of the past as soon as political conditions make this possible.

APPENDICES

APPENDIX I

MUNICIPAL BUDGETS IN 1910, 1914, AND 1915 SHOWING INCREASE IN 1915 AS COMPARED WITH 1914

Towns	1910	1914 (in rubles)	1915	
Petrograd	36,472,500	53,162,000	59,300,000	In 1916—68,545,000
Moscow	34,244,340	52,600,000	57,800,000	In 1916—70,037,000
Odessa	8,564,200	10,000,000		
Riga	6,149,000	8,113,110	9,483,932	In 1916— 7,872,500 Special conditions due to the alteration of the front.
Saratov	3,914,600	7,161,200		
Kharkov	3,297,500	7,252,000	9,500,000	
Rostov-on-Don	1,852,300	2,639,100	8,113,110	
Ekatrinodar	1,748,092	2,461,100	2,611,213	
Irkutsk	1,625,514	2,447,700	2,717,954	
Vilna	1,279,700	2,081,586	2,090,775	
Kazan	1,200,300	2,288,500	2,831,066	
Nicholaev (Province of Kherson)	1,172,400	2,205,031	2,336,724	
Blagoveshchensk	1,058,400	1,970,143	2,202,297	
Tula	913,400	1,517,600	1,734,500	
Revel	844,200	1,830,500	1,862,867	
Ufa	794,100	1,210,773	1,554,150	
Perm	689,000	1,062,000	2,953,300	
Minsk	597,100	1,176,512	1,630,124	
Yaroslavl	614,900	1,105,156	1,299,311	
Vitebsk	592,400	648,050	657,622	
Penza	567,500	808,385	891,660	
Nakhichevan	537,600	828,669	849,372	
Orel	483,300	692,586	727,878	
Tambov	457,000	1,005,100	1,139,440	
Nicholaev-on-Amur	450,300	502,369	587,409	
Simferopol	454,000	796,980	831,451	
Stavropol	442,700	676,484	690,971	
Kerch-Yenikale	433,100	562,807	750,620	
Kutais	417,000	486,035	521,455	
Khabarovsk	405,000	839,094	935,932	
Smolensk	402,180	602,400	832,098	
Taganrog	394,500	741,858	779,141	

Towns	1910	1914	1915
		(in rubles)	
Vyatka	389,700	649,549	724,015
Ribinsk	375,500	574,918	721,097
Chernigov	371,900	485,369	540,033
Kamishin	354,700	595,432	629,795
Ivanov-Voznesensk	352,600	618,474	669,781
Yesk	328,300	478,450	528,248
Pskov	300,100	542,459	641,284
Pyatigorsk	298,000	447,072	558,120
Erivan	264,800	212,387	397,314
Sumy	223,100	383,112	400,930
Tobolsk	223,100	241,200	273,236
Petropavlovsk	218,900	313,778	374,143
Vladimir	204,200	281,853	283,601
Troitsk	189,300	235,473	368,577
Pavlograd	163,100	90,684	100,930
Novgorod	152,100	216,534	250,073
Azov	151,700	279,812	323,875
Kungur	145,600	127,177	130,136
Oranienbaum	128,200	65,000	89,000
Semipalatinsk	142,200	217,990	229,671
Sterlitomak	127,300	271,041	278,676
Novouzensk	123,400	157,407	162,276
Verny	120,100	220,000	285,000
Vinnitsa	116,900	482,363	506,723
Uman	116,700	142,144	172,337
Buguruslan	115,100	167,676	341,895
Pavlovsk	112,900	172,136	180,321
Karachev	86,400	128,019	136,051
Vyazma	81,100	123,248	127,848
Izyum	80,000	226,670	275,728
Rylsk	76,800	92,857	93,787
Melenky	75,800	87,174	90,147
Orekhov	75,300	75,011	83,732
Novokhopersk	69,400	123,531	157,740
Pishlek	63,200	87,234	100,917
Berezovka	62,900	68,864	80,200
Kamyshlov	59,300	107,892	119,496
Kupyansk	56,300	79,824	109,933
Pereslavl	55,100	57,865	83,029
Kasimov	54,100	118,695	123,402
Oboyan	49,900	32,026	36,620
Michailov	43,600	62,100	66,175
Ishim	35,900	67,698	86,840
Bogorodsk	33,800	48,936	52,943

Towns	1910	1914	1915
		(in rubles)	
Belozersk	32,100	44,007	57,559
Krasnoufimsk	29,000	37,527	38,691
Volmar	28,600	53,777	60,036
Danilov	28,100	32,481	38,782
Mayaky	27,900	48,604	49,514
Aleshky	24,400	28,379	28,729
Letichev	22,900	56,530	85,507
Krasnoslobodsk	22,800	31,007	34,444
Alexin	22,800	28,760	30,586
Zenkov	22,200	69,175	101,223
Weisenshtein	16,600	19,784	21,329
Ustsysolsk	16,200	22,782	23,322
Gorbatov	16,500	17,948	21,244
Totma	14,800	18,679	20,363
Velsk	13,300	14,001	19,798
Papushoy	11,900	15,676	17,652
Okhansk	11,500	15,800	18,130
Varnavin	11,200	20,700	22,471
Kopaly	9,000	14,580	16,043
Kem	7,300	6,346	9,398

APPENDIX II

MUNICIPAL BUDGETS IN 1910, 1914, AND 1915 SHOWING A DECREASE IN 1915 AS COMPARED WITH 1914

Towns	1910	1914 (in rubles)	1915
Baku	6,718,300	14,950,199	13,454,229
Samara	2,702,500	7,161,232	6,788,900
Tiflis	2,138,300	3,925,864	3,649,651
Astrakhan	1,701,500	4,728,244	3,735,342
Tomsk	1,299,500	1,977,381	1,972,267
Ekaterinburg	731,000	1,473,376	1,325,227
Kherson	625,400	1,068,836	969,419
Barnaul	587,400	515,991	
Simbirsk	548,400	1,372,095	1,166,451
Yalta	531,400	1,020,084	758,000
Batum	475,000	794,549	506,778
Alexandrovsk (Province of Eka-terinoslav)	295,800	467,514	438,267
Archangel	293,400	502,460	497,222
Maykop	253,400	336,744	311,968
Lugansk	238,200	490,274	406,408
Belgorod	230,300	330,968	308,129
Shuya	195,400	284,840	263,633
Ismail	194,300	318,694	282,504
Biysk	187,500	231,972	230,242
Pavlograd	163,100	262,016	253,958
Nezhin	157,900	220,157	159,970
Bendery	150,500	356,872	323,076
Alexandrya	145,400	172,209	159,998
Shadrinsk	143,700	182,258	180,963
Kansk	137,600	234,027	148,234
Chistopol	118,300	171,533	171,484
Irbit	117,600	138,443	129,920
Murom	105,500	221,607	214,464
Radomysl	102,100	225,591	81,418
Novo-Moskovsk	99,100	118,375	115,420
Pavlovsk (possad)	90,600	148,771	133,043
Ostrogozhsk	88,400	262,838	200,756
Georgievsk	87,400	210,840	174,362
Verkhnednieprovsk	85,000	117,617	91,355
Rovno	81,200	278,868	265,615

Towns	1910	1914 (in rubles)	1915
Klintsy	77,500	148,800	125,345
Novozybkov	75,600	91,414	90,181
Kustanay	74,800	118,325	111,253
Achinsk	62,300	118,768	109,310
Grozny	59,800	651,902	632,346
Soroky	57,400	82,206	81,288
Olinopol	53,800	91,185	73,926
Korocha	48,900	75,486	68,235
Bugulma	44,900	93,327	86,401
Volchansk	44,700	163,236	162,270
Osa	47,600	61,872	59,543
Kotelnich	43,100	79,266	75,096
Arensburg	42,300	52,664	36,979
Akhtyrka	39,400	106,749	91,028
Staro-Krym	31,400	62,378	62,102
Yamburg	27,100	19,200	18,682
Urzhum	24,000	47,823	43,661
Vasilsursk	23,700	31,836	30,662
Mamadysh	17,900	24,875	23,250
Sapozhok	16,400	35,227	27,431
Tsarevosanchursk	12,300	22,394	17,239
Pronsk	8,200	11,970	10,750
Bolshya Soly	5,200	8,142	8,008

APPENDIX III

EXPENDITURE ON EDUCATION, PUBLIC UTILITIES (EXCLUDING MUNICIPAL ENTERPRISES), AND PUBLIC HEALTH IN THE MUNICIPAL ESTIMATES FOR 1914

Towns	Education	Public utilities (in rubles)	Public health
Archangel	58,446	39,115	33,708
Astrakhan	332,607	162,621	862,267
Batum	76,688	128,902	77,092
Blagoveshchensk	388,772	82,806	261,092
Vilna	90,763	243,790	100,080
Vitebsk	31,670	29,571	39,824
Valdikavkaz	115,485	98,781	120,760
Vladimir	46,218	27,614	7,456
Vologda	71,810	31,396	26,995
Voronezh	193,684	123,027	54,659
Vyatka	90,134	31,907	32,056
Grodno	17,336	29,890	13,586
Elisavetpol	22,205	23,910	27,911
Ekaterinoslav	381,455	263,903	375,345
Zhitomir	46,861	14,251	5,525
Irkutsk	279,068	102,424	209,695
Kamenets-Podolsk	36,762	30,677	34,031
Kazan	266,837	259,855	201,632
Kiev	930,464	690,407	791,657
Kovno	14,796	24,308	12,355
Kostroma	79,784	33,573	58,660
Krasnoyarsk	165,009	40,289	66,592
Kursk	140,776	26,141	50,291
Kutais	34,469	55,360	75,364
Minsk	76,121	133,284	67,678
Nizhni-Novgorod	276,313	98,604	194,420
Novgorod	30,756	18,469	10,280
Novorossysk	107,633	36,144	77,067
Omsk	222,268	176,723	132,834
Orenburg	234,213	576,653	129,412
Penza	130,016	49,127	52,910
Perm	167,200	39,270	51,560
Petrozavodsk	4,092	4,469	2,652
Poltava	129,162	112,601	74,265

Towns	Education	Public utilities (in rubles)	Public health
Pskov	29,338	33,715	7,298
Revel	341,638	26,002	72,842
Riga	824,310	1,049,126	1,286,850
Rostov-on-Don	833,947	199,776	1,099,008
Ryazan	79,748	489,443	11,871
Samara	740,779	284,941	1,003,134
Saratov	1,694,818	419,822	745,218
Simbirsk	117,475	31,738	70,348
Simferopol	83,331	37,602	61,404
Smolensk	71,019	24,100	23,500
Stavropol	110,215	64,167	47,384
Tambov	199,419	151,701	93,142
Tver	126,333	54,362	66,286
Temir-Khan-Shura	9,742	5,843	5,966
Tiflis	434,455	466,295	418,825
Tula	147,038	168,533	138,908
Ufa	299,816	83,200	112,572
Khabarovsk	140,374	55,701	124,100
Kharkov	292,109	108,434	121,946
Chernigov	68,349	60,972	23,372
Erivan	24,879	36,720	41,345
Yaroslavl	122,204	97,940	145,660

BIBLIOGRAPHY

Gorodovoe Polozhenie 1892 goda (*The Municipal Act of 1892*).

Zakon Vremennago Pravitelstva ob izmenenii Gorodovogo Polozhenya 1892 goda.

Slovar yuridicheskikh i gosudarstvennikh nauk, St. Petersburg, 1903, Vol. II, Part VI.

Gr. Dzhanchiev, *Epokha velikikh reform*, St. Petersburg, 1905.

A. A. Kizevetter, *Mestnoe samoupravlenie v Rossii IX-XIX st.*, Moscow, 1910.

Sir Paul Vinogradoff, *Self-Government in Russia*, London, 1915.

A. J. Elistratov, *Osnovnya nachala administrativnago prava*, Moscow, 1917.

V. Tverdokhlebov, *Mestnie finansi*, Odessa, 1919.

S. N. Prokopovich, *Voina i narodnoe khozyaistvo*, Moscow, 1918.

S. Chvitau, *Revolutsya i narodnoe khozyaistvo v Rossii 1917-1921*, Leipzig, 1922.

Voronoff et Belevsky, *Organisations publiques russes pendant la guerre*, Paris, 1917.

Rudolf Claus, *Die Kreigswirtschaft Russlands bis zur Bolschewistischer Revolution*, 1922, Vol. I.

Lydia Bach, *Le droit et les institutions de la Russie Sovietique*, Paris, 1923.

S. S. Demosthenov, *Obshchya soobrazhenya o prichinakh sovremennoi dorogovizni*, Petrograd, 1916.

Z. G. Frenkel, *Petrograd vo vremya voini i revolutsii*, Petrograd, 1923.

Kalendari-spravochniki gorodskogo deyatelya for 1914-1917, published by *Gorodskoe Delo* and *Zemskoe Delo*, Petrograd.

Trudi komissii po izuchenyu sovremennoi dorogovisni, published by *Obshchestvo imeni A. I. Chuprova*, Moscow, 1915 and 1916, Vols. I-IV.

Izvestya Osobago Soveshchanya po prodovolstvennomu delu, Petrograd, 1915 and 1916.

Sovremennoe polozhenie taksirovki predmetov prodovolstva v Rossii i meri k ego uporyadochenyu, published by *Upravlenie Osobago Soveshchanya po prodovolstvennomu delu*, Petrograd, 1915.

Statisticheski ezhegodnik Rossii na 1914 god, published by *Tsentralni Statisticheski Komitet*, Petrograd, 1915.

Statisticheski sbornik za 1913-1917 godi, in *Trudi Tsentralnago Statisticheskago Upravlenya*, Petrograd, Vol. VII, Part II.

Trudi komissii po izsledovanyu sanitarnikh posledstvi mirovoi voini 1914-1920 gg., officially published, Moscow-Petrograd, 1923.

Sbornik voprosov mirovoi voini, edited by M. J. Tugan-Baranovsky, Moscow, 1915.

Chego zhdet Rossya ot voini?, collection of essays, Petrograd, 1915.

Spravochnaya knizhka dlya derzhateley obligatsi russkikh gorodskikh zaimov, published by *Kassi Gorodskogo i Zemskago Kredita*, St. Petersburg, 1913.

Ocherk deyatelnosti Vserossiskago Soyuza Gorodov za 1914-1915 godi, Moscow, 1916.

Statisticheski ezhegodnik goroda Moskwi, for 1911-1913, Moscow, 1916, Vol. IV.

Statisticheskya dannya otnosyashchyasya k Petrogradu i k petrogradskomu gorodskomu khozyaistvu, Petrograd, 1916.

Sovremennoe khozyaistvo goroda Moskwi, Moscow, 1913.

Moskowskaya gorodskaya duma 1913-1916, published by *Komitet Grupi Progressivnikh Glasnikh*, Moscow, 1916.

Krasnaya Moskwa 1917-1920, published by *Moskowski Soviet Rabochikh i Krestyanskikh Deputatov*, Moscow, 1920.

Voina i finansi goroda Petrograda, Report of the Chairman of the Financial Committee of the municipal Duma of Petrograd, Petrograd, 1916.

Sbornik "Rech," Petrograd, 1915 and 1916.

Newspapers: *Russkya Vedomosti, Rech, Russkoe Slovo.*

Periodicals:

Gorodskoe Delo, especially article by M. P. Avsarkisov, *Finansovaya i kreditnaya konsultatsya pri Soyuze Gorodov*, 1916, No. 23.

Gorod, published by the All-Russian Union of Towns, Moscow, 1917.

Izvestya Vserossiskago Soyuza Gorodov, Moscow, 1916-1917; among the articles which appeared in *Izvestya Vserossiskago Soyuza Gorodov* the following should be specially mentioned:

A. D. Alferov, *Deyatelnost Vserossiskago Soyuza Gorodov na fronte*, No. 25/26.

J. H. Ananov, *Soyuz Gorodov*, No. 50/51.

N. J. Astrov, *Organizatsya tila*, No. 27/28.

S. V. Bakhrushin, *Soyuz Gorodov*, No. 35.

P. A. Burishkin, *Glavneishya osnovanya dlya razvitya kontrolnoi deyatelnosti v mestnikh komitetakh*, No. 36.

M. V. Vishnyak, *Yuridicheskaya priroda Vserossiskago Zemskago Soyuza i Soyuza Gorodov*, No. 33.

V. G. Groman, *Prodovolstvenni vopros i organizatsya narodnago khozyaistva*, No. 37.

N. M. Kishkin, *Materyali po voprosam of zadachakh Soyuza Gorodov posle voini i v oblastnikh organizatsyakh*, No. 31/32.

L. L. *Prodovolstvenni vopros*, No. 38.

M. V. Sabashnikov, *Ocherednya zadachi Soyuza Gorodov na yugo-zapadnom fronte*, No. 34.

A. A. Sokolov, *Tsentralnoe bureau po gorodskim delam*, No. 36.

A. N. Sysin, *Sanitarnya meropryatya Vserossiskago Soyuza Gorodov s nachala voini do 1 marta 1916 goda*, No. 29/30.

L. G. Shlezinger, *Borba s dorogoviznoi i gorodskya upravlenya*, No. 27/28.

N. N. Shchepkin, *Bezhintsi i organizatsya pomoshchi im v svyazi s rabotoi Osobago Soveshchanya*, No. 27/28.

INDEX

Academy of Sciences, 17, 18.
Acts: 17th October *1905*, 57; 3rd June *1907*, 12, 15, 16, 57; *1908*, 156; 22nd November *1911*, 216; 25th June *1912*, 210, 253; 5th December *1912*, 146; *1913*, 156;
  1915: 31st March, 32; 17th and 20th August, 184; 30th August, 234;
  1917: 3rd March, 54; 1st September, 97, 98.
Adzhemov, M. S., 61.
Agrarian reform, 78.
Agriculture, census, 291; control of, 32.
Alexander II, 132.
Alexander III, 136.
Alexandra, Empress, 30.
Alexeev, General M. V., 50, 60.
Alexis, Tsarevich, 50, 52.
Amnesty of political offenders, 49, 58.
Army and navy, administration of, 6; councils of the, 11; legislation, 11.
Army, medical department, 262; sanitary service, 250; supply, shortage of, 41; Supply Service, 225, 226, 274, 286; production of supplies, 33.
Association of Disabled Men, 219.
Austria-Hungary, 26, 28.
Avksentev, N. D., 84.

Bernatzky, Professor M. W., 84.
Bolsheviks, 79, 81, 102, 104, 111, 125.
Bread and flour, shortage of, 270, 294.
Brusilov, General A. A., 50.
Budget, 28; of *1906*, 22.
Budget Committee, 28.
Budgets, municipal, *1910-1915*, 315, 318.

Canteens, 200, 221.
Capital and labor, regulations concerning, 72.
Catherine II, 132.
Central Committee of the Unions of Zemstvos and Towns (*Zemgor*), 175, 188-192.
Central Committee on Plague, 248, 250.
Central Financial Committee, 83.
Central Labor Exchange, 237.
Central Land Committee, 78, 82.
Central Powers, 68.
Central Supply Committee of the Ministry of Commerce and Industry, 287.
Central War Industries Committee, 35, 46.

Centroflot, 113.
Chamber of Agriculture, 75.
Chambers of Commerce, 75.
Charter "for the defense of the rights and interests of towns," 132.
Chernov, V. M., 71, 79.
Chicherin, B. N., 136.
Children, care of refugee, 237, 254, 266.
Chkheidze, N. S., 45-48, 64, 69, 81, 84.
Civil Service Disciplinary Courts, 135.
Clergy, 14, 16, 17.
Coalition government, first, 79, 124; second, 85; third, 87, 104.
Coinage, right of, 9.
Committee of the Empress, 258.
Committee of the Grand Duchess Tatiana Nicholaevna for the temporary relief of war sufferers, 30, 31, 236.
Committee on National Defense, 28.
Committee on Sanitary Engineering, 251.
Committee on Trade and Industry, 19.
Committees of the Front, 191.
Communist Party, 309.
Conference of the Representatives of Trade and Commerce, 174.
Conference of Stockholm, 258.
Conferences of Mayors, 181, 288.
Congress of Statisticians, 75.
Conscription, Law of, 27.
Constituent Assembly, 49, 50, 53, 58, 59, 66, 68-70, 76, 107, 123-125, 180; statutes on the elections, 60, 72, 76, 77, 82, 87, 89, 92, 126; Juridical Committee on statutes, 60, 61, 76, 106.
Constitutional-Democratic Party, 70, 71, 79, 81, 83-85, 96, 104, 124; congress, 85.
Constitutional reform, 4.
Contact Committee of the Petrograd Soviet, 64-66, 71, 123.
Coöperative associations, 75, 77, 86, 100, 106.
Cotton Committee, 73.
Council of Elders, 17, 45, 54, 122.
Council of Five (the Directory), 95.
Council of Ministers, 8, 10, 12, 22, 24-27, 40, 56, 57, 66, 99, 119, 183, 234, 288; Resolutions: 1st September *1914*, 31; 19th May *1915*, 32; 7th June *1915*, 33.
Council of People's Commissaries, 117, 118, 127.
Curiae, 13.
Customs duties, 27.